OTTO PERRY'S
RAILROAD PILGRIMAGE

The 4% grade on Cerro Summit is graphically shown as 361, 454 and 456 pound up the hill in 1949. The 361, an outside-frame 2-8-0 had come from the Crystal River railroad in 1916.

ELMORE FREDERICK COLLECTION

OTTO PERRY'S
RAILROAD PILGRIMAGE

Featuring Photo Postcards From Private Collectors: David S. Digerness, Richard A. Ronzio, Elmore Frederick, Morris W. Abbott - Wm. R. Jones, and Dell A. McCoy.

OTTO PERRY'S
RAILROAD PILGRIMAGE

SUNDANCE PUBLICATIONS *Limited*
P. O. BOX 597 • SILVERTON, COLORADO 81433

Graphical presentation-
   Sundance Publications, Ltd. Silverton, Colorado
Photolithography-
   Sundance Publications, Ltd., Silverton, Colorado
Binding-
   Schaffer Bindery, Magna, Utah
Typesetting-
   The Silverton Standard and The Miner, Silverton, Colorado

Editorial Staff - Dell A. McCoy, Wm. R. Jones, John H. Coker
Assistant Editor - Robert A. LeMassena
Production Manager - Dell A. McCoy
Index - Allen Nossaman
Director of Photography - John Shufelt
Copyright information:

© 1981 by SUNDANCE Publications, Limited, Silverton, Colorado 81433, Printed in U.S.A. All rights reserved. This book, or parts thereof, may not be reproduced in any form without written permission of the publisher.

ISBN O-913582-25-5
First Printing - April, 1981

   FRONT COVER: Late fall of October 1940 has enveloped the San Miguel Range as a Rio Grande Southern stock train dropped down grade, from Dallas Divide. The double deck stock cars carry loads of sheep from Placerville to be delivered to the D&RGW at Ridgway in the Uncompaghre Valley.
                                                  RICHARD A. RONZIO COLLECTION

   BACK COVER: Lonesome but beautiful—extra 40 east with caboose 402 descend Dallas Divide after helping a freight over the top.
                                                  RICHARD A. RONZIO COLLECTION

PREFACE AND ACKNOWLEDGEMENTS

   The idea of pictorial books is not a new one for Sundance. During the very beginnings of Sundance the idea evolved into two pictorial books, THE RIO GRANDE PICTORIAL and THE CRYSTAL RIVER PICTORIAL. Both titles still make sales over a long period since 1970. The pictorial idea came to a halt once other authors discovered Sundance's emphasis on quality in printing of its books. Ever since, the idea has always been in mind, but the authors produced a considerable quantity of worthwhile text to accompany their remarkably extensive photo collections. As the economy drastically slowed down the publishing field in late 1979, Sundance decided to return to its original concept. Nothing helps bring joy to a person more than a really fine, well done, photo album of fond old visual memories, complimented with informative captions. And naturally the fabulous works of Otto Perry came first to mind.

   Many of my associates had collected photo postcards that Otto Perry had, himself, created by contact printing the negative on photo paper. This method produces the sharpest image possible. The clarity shows up graphically in the pages to follow with a great many photos enlarged three times. I feel this choice of original photo postcards adds a very personal touch to the album, just as Otto may have wished.

   Much constructive writing and ideas came from Wm. R. Jones, next door to Sundance where he runs an assay office in the old Silverton Northern ticket office. His associate John H. Coker added great depth of railroad language to many of the captions. David S. Digerness provided large quantities of photo postcards from his extensive collection. Richard A. Ronzio, without doubt an extremely generous person, contributed immeasurably to the Colorado section. Robert A. LeMassena, railroad author and photographer took on the task of writing captions for the photos unfamiliar to the Sundance staff. Elmore Frederick, a personal longtime friend of Otto Perry, acquired many photo postcards as the two rode trains together, Elmore Frederick is also my next door neighbor in Denver. The late Morris W. Abbott, Wm. R. Jones' grandfather was author of "The Pikes Peak Cog Road." As time and money permit, we at Sundance intend to bring about a series of these dramatic photo albums for your personal enjoyment.

                                                        Dell A. McCoy 1981

Note from the Publisher:

   Articulated locomotive types and wheel arrangements are referred to as - 2-6+6-4, or 2-8+8-0. The + symbol illustrates where the locomotive hinges or articulates. This additional symbol was devised by the author - Robert A. LeMassena in his book - ARTICULATED STEAM LOCOMOTIVES OF NORTH AMERICA. It is hopeful that you may find this addition useful.

This Northern Pacific photograph illustrates—full size, the negative size of Otto Perry's camera. Prints were made contact size on photo postcard paper.

This Union Pacific photo illustrates a smaller format camera used in 1949 by Otto Perry.

The Burlington Route passenger diesel photo represents yet another size camera used by Otto Perry.

INTRODUCTION

Otto Perry was one of that rare breed of individuals who would prefer to chase trains and photograph them, rather than eat, sleep or work. Otto never married, having found satisfactory home-life with his parents and family as they took care of his daily needs. For nearly 25 years, Otto lived within shouting distance of the Denver & Rio Grande Western mainline, his house located at No. 3 Fox Street in Denver, Colorado.

Otto's love life with trains probably began in earnest once his parents, Frank and Clara moved to Denver in 1907, along with his younger brother and sisters, Elmer, Viola and Nellie. Otto started photographing with his father's box camera shortly after 1913, and in 1915 he purchased an Eastman 3A folding Kodak, that used postcard film. This size film produced excellent contact prints, making enlarging unneccessary, so common with today's 35mm cameras. Otto traveled sometimes 100 miles by bicycle, until 1920 when he purchased a Harley-Davidson motorcycle. For many long years Otto worked for the Post Office taking advantage of government holidays for lengthy excursions, and using his vacation time to advantage, traveling to all corners of the United States to record on film, the railroads of that day. One of Otto's outstanding achievements was his 16mm movies that are often shown at Rocky Mountain Railroad Club meetings. A majority of photos were probably obtained under extremely difficult conditions due to the lack of paved roads and slow automobile travel of that day.

On occasional visits to Otto's home, he would tell me many of his experiences while out photographing trains. These visits were especially enjoyable, while we sat beside the fireplace amid the clutter of railroadiana that represented years of Otto's collecting. Otto's pride and joy was his attic where he housed a large collection of railroad lanterns from such bygone railroads as the Colorado Midland, Colorado Central, Denver South Park & Pacific and many more. Running about on the attic floor, Otto had a lengthy miniature railroad made up of American Flyer equipment. The locomotives were in what is referred to "S" scale today, and ran very well. Otto's house was probably built sometime at the turn-of-the-century, with the kitchen still sporting the old coal fed stove, a time consuming device, to say the least. It was here that Otto based his lifestyle as one of America's leading railroad photographers. Over a period of 57 years he made more than 20,000 negatives of railroading all over the U.S.A., as well as in Canada, Mexico and Europe, but scenes on Colorado's railroads predominated. It was always a great joy to have Otto ride up to Sundance on his bicycle to show off great handfulls of postcard photos. As one could imagine, one of my greatest desires was to bring out a book on Otto Perry.

This pictorial shows but a glimpse of the incredible variety of photos Otto had taken. And naturally the subject material should start off with the D&RGW narrow-gauge, one of Otto's favorites. The photos of this pictorial came mainly from the collections of David S. Digerness, Richard A. Ronzio, Elmore Frederick, Bill Jones [formerly Morris W. Abbott], and Dell McCoy, they having obtained them personally from Otto's own darkroom work. Otto Perry's negative collection now resides with the Denver Public Library Western History Collection.

Otto Conrad Perry was born in Kansas City, Missouri, on December 21, 1894 and died December 23, 1970. A great many railfans miss you—Otto Perry.

Dell A. McCoy 1981

On October 25, 1940, Otto Perry photographed his faithful steed which eventually carried him nearly 300,000 miles. This 1935 V-8 Ford always remained with Otto even though it became inoperable toward the end of his life. The endless Colorado sky overlooks Lizard Head pass, looking toward the south on the Rio Grande Southern as Goose Number 7 headed toward Telluride.

TABLE OF CONTENTS

I - D&RGW NARROW-GAUGE TRAVELS 9
II - AS THE EAGLE FLIES—RGS 43
III - THREE FOOT NARROW-GAUGE LINES OF COLORADO 75
IV - STANDARD-GAUGE RAILROADS OF THE ROCKY MOUNTAIN REGION 103
V - BEYOND THE ROCKY MOUNTAINS 129

Three days before the last Powderhorn roundup, 268 was doing her regular run on the Crested Butte branch, northbound at Almont, 10 miles from Gunnison.

The "Three-six-bits" as the locals called her, headed toward Silverton October 18, 1941 with supplies and empty concentrate cars for the Shenandoah-Dives Mine. This was known as the Silverton branch.

CHAPTER I
D&RGW Narrow-Gauge Travels

DAVID S. DIGERNESS COLLECTION

he D&RGW was noted for having traversed a large portion of the Rocky Mountain region of Colorado, Utah and New Mexico. As time would allow, Otto Perry would pack up his cameras and head for the high country. The contrast of the mountains, compared with Denver where Otto lived, gives a person a feeling of being re-born, traveling to great heights in crystal clear air. The D&RGW trackage gained these heights by traversing deep canyons and bridging wide rivers, finally reaching mountain passes, there to cross over in quest of ore, passengers, lumber, coal and livestock.

Until 1881 the D&RGW, then named the Denver & Rio Grande, was wholly narrow-gauge. The 3 foot gauge was chosen as the least expensive approach of purchasing equipment and grading of the line. Standard gauge track measures 4 feet 8½ inches between the rails which requires a much larger mass of steel and wood for rollingstock, and bridges. The D&RG found out very soon that narrow-gauge was most suitable for the narrow twisting canyons as graders cut expenses laying out much sharper curves, thus avoiding blasting away mountainsides, to permit construction of standard gauge track.

By 1880 the D&RG had penetrated the Royal Gorge and reached Salida, the point where this pictorial starts. The journey continues past Mears Junction, climbs over Marshall Pass, passes through Gunnison to the coalfields of Crested Butte. The pictorial picks up then at Alamosa, an important division point of the system and takes in the trackage to Santa Fe, New Mexico. Next, the Cumbres Pass trackage through Chama, Durango to Silverton, where construction ended in 1882, is shown.

SALIDA, WESTBOUND

The 488, in Salida, was equipped with a dual gauge coupler, shown under steam in Salida about 1930. This allowed the locomotive to be used as a switch engine in the dual gauge yards at this important division point. The locomotive now operates on the C&TS line in passenger service over Cumbres Pass, between Antonito, Colorado and Chama, New Mexico.

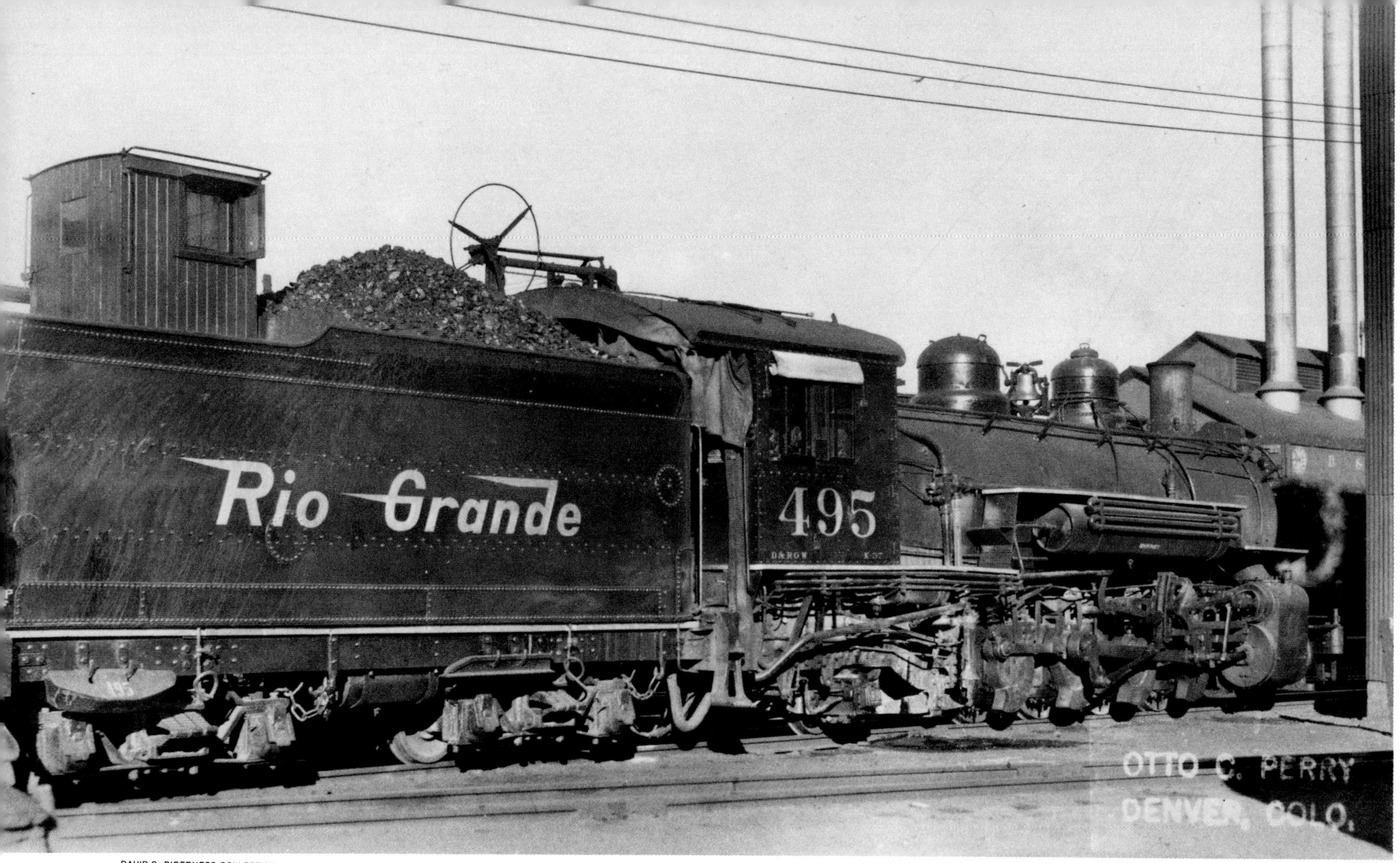

DAVID S. DIGERNESS COLLECTION

The outside-frame, counterbalances and side-rods, of the 495 make an excellent study of massive machinery, in good sunlight. This locomotive was originally a standard gauge compound, one of ten originally built in 1902 as a 2-8-0 wheel arrangement, and was converted in 1928. The setting was Salida, May 5, 1940.

The 300 was among the last six narrow-gauge 2-8-0's built for the Rio Grande. A spark arrestor sits atop her stack in Salida, during storage in 1929.

The 272 was near the end of its days when photographed at Salida in 1926. The old box headlight once contained a carbon-arc light system. A weighted board on top of the stack protected the smokebox from rust while in storage. The new round herald had not yet been applied.

RICHARD A. RONZIO COLLECTION

RICHARD A. RONZIO COLLECTION

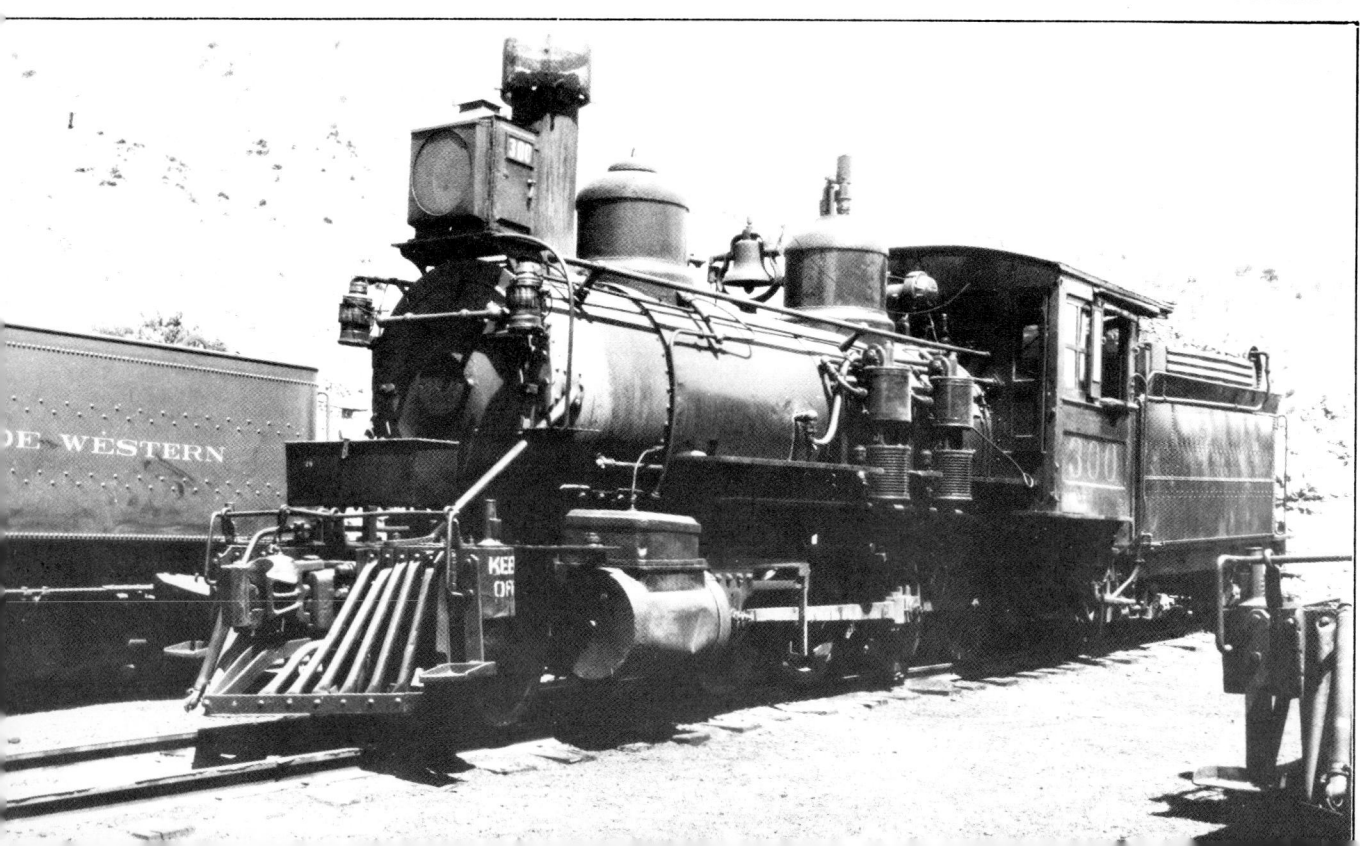

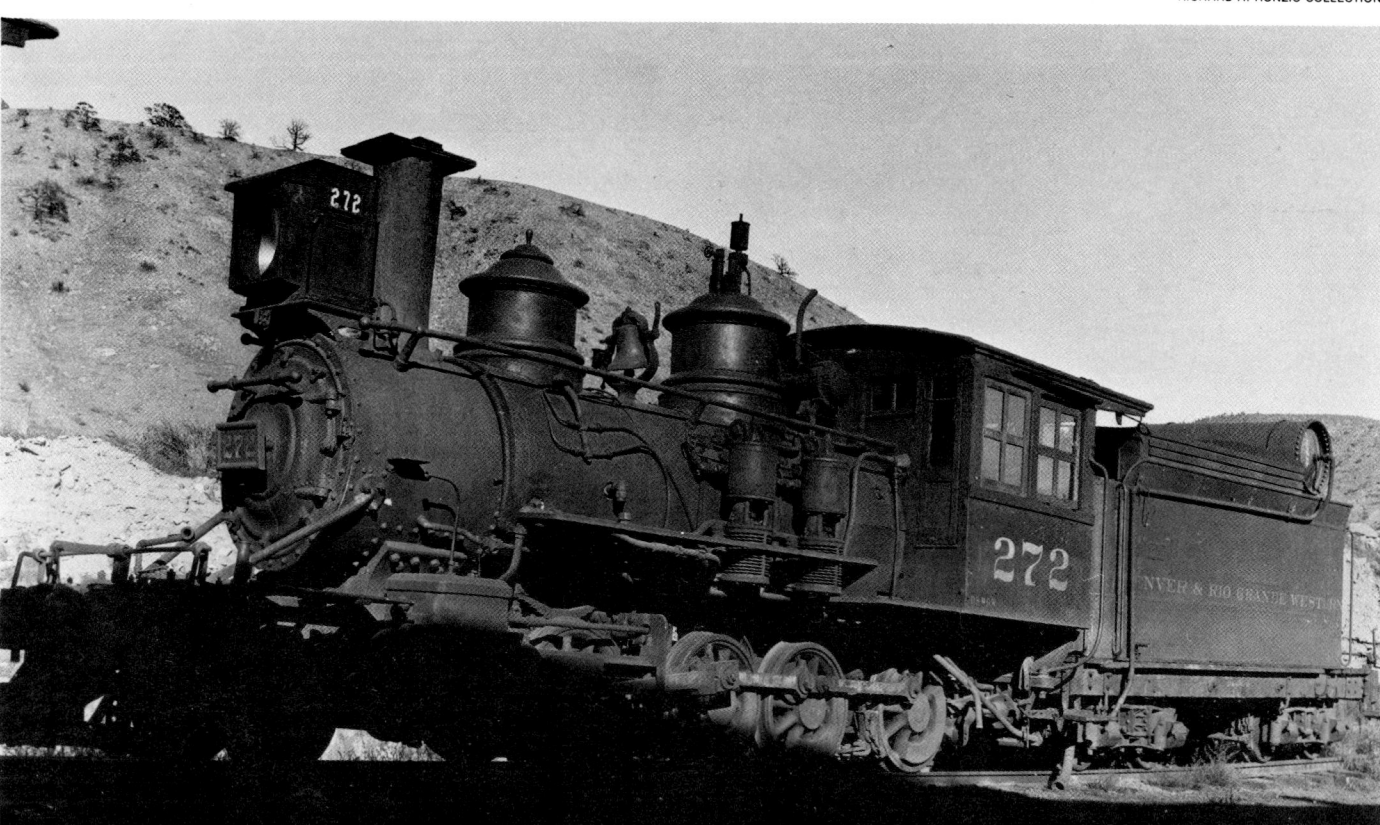

A heavy freight drag was ascending Poncha Pass from the San Luis Valley in the late 1930s. The impressive Sangre de Cristo range flanks this ancient lake bed.

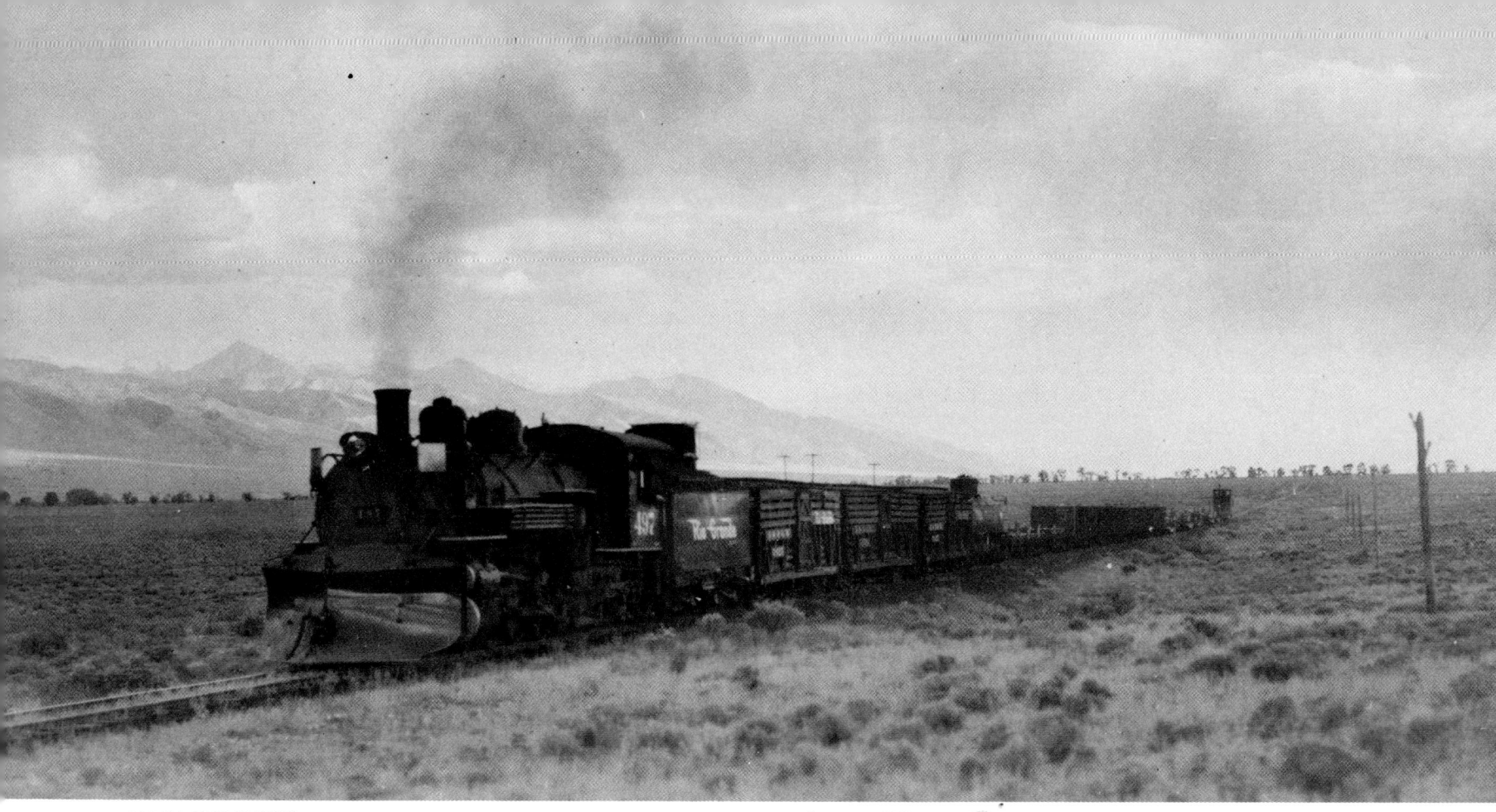

The 497, bearing flags of an extra, heads north near Villa Grove, Colorado, on the afternoon of October 7, 1945. She had been fitted recently with a snowplow. Shown pulling 22 cars upgrade, with the Sangre de Cristo range in the background.

RICHARD A. RONZIO COLLECTION

RICHARD A. RONZIO COLLECTION

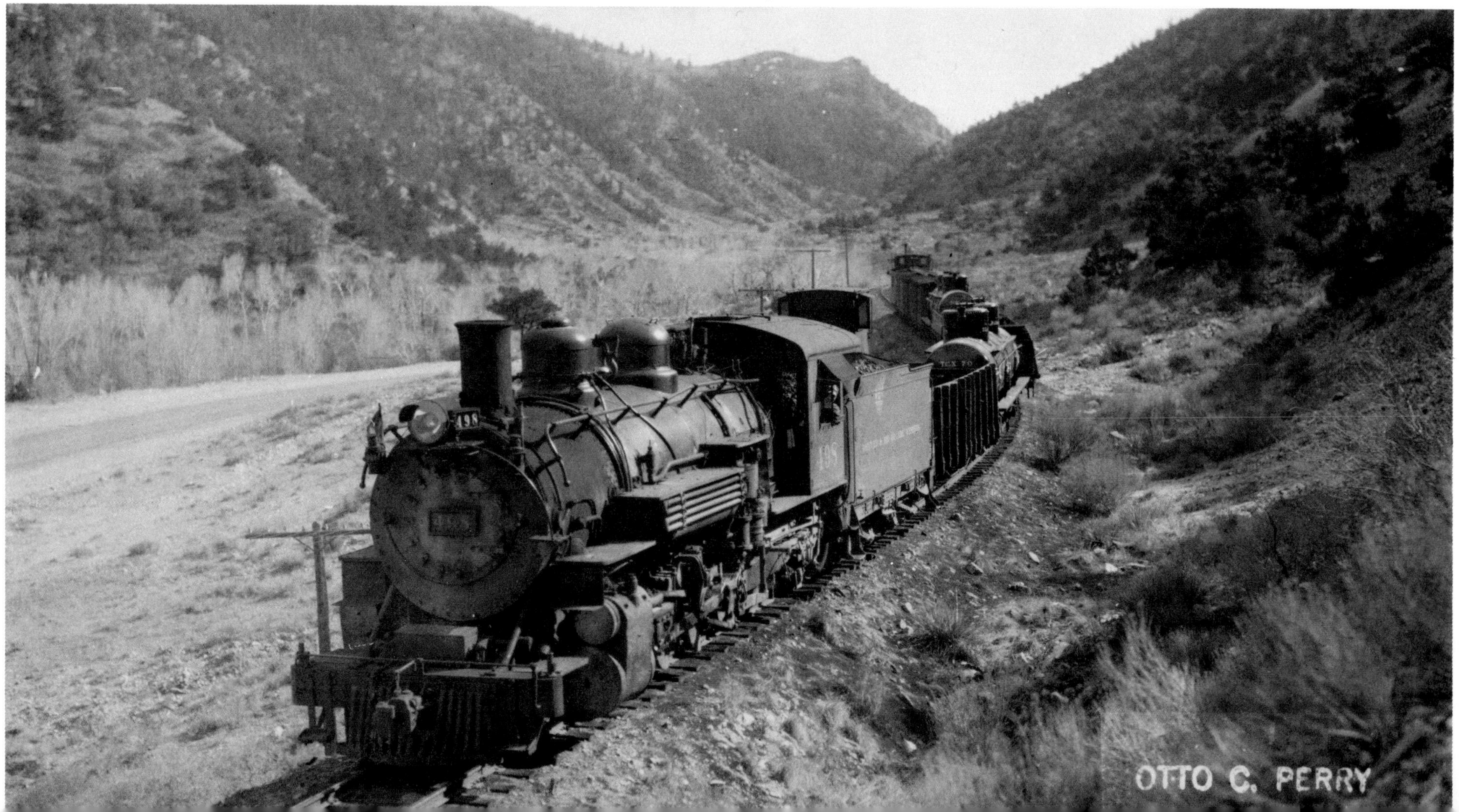

The 498 was cautiously descending the north slope of Poncha Pass on April 21, 1940. Note the unusual Texaco 2-dome tank cars in the consist.

No. 479 was heading west with train No. 315—the "Shavano" passenger mail and express train in this view on May 5, 1940. This location was the foot of the 4% grade climbing out of Poncha Junction on the route leading to Mear's Junction, Marshall Pass and Gunnison.

RICHARD A. RONZIO COLLECTION

MARSHALL PASS

Otto Perry managed to photograph an entire train of empties at Mears Junction. The freight train was headed west to the coal mines north of Crested Butte.

A long string of stock cars was in tow behind the 489 at Mear's Junction. Stock provided extra freight in the spring or fall because the animals were pastured in the high country.

On September 30, 1939, a stock extra had reached the top of Marshall Pass, headed for Salida. Motive power included Numbers 490, 491 and 498, all 1928 rebuilds from standard gauge 2-8-0's.

The crew of a stock extra turned up its retainers before leaving the top of Marshall Pass at elevation 10,856 feet above sea level. Taken October 9, 1953, this photo showed livestock being transported from the Gunnison area to lower pasturage during the fall.

RICHARD A. RONZIO COLLECTION

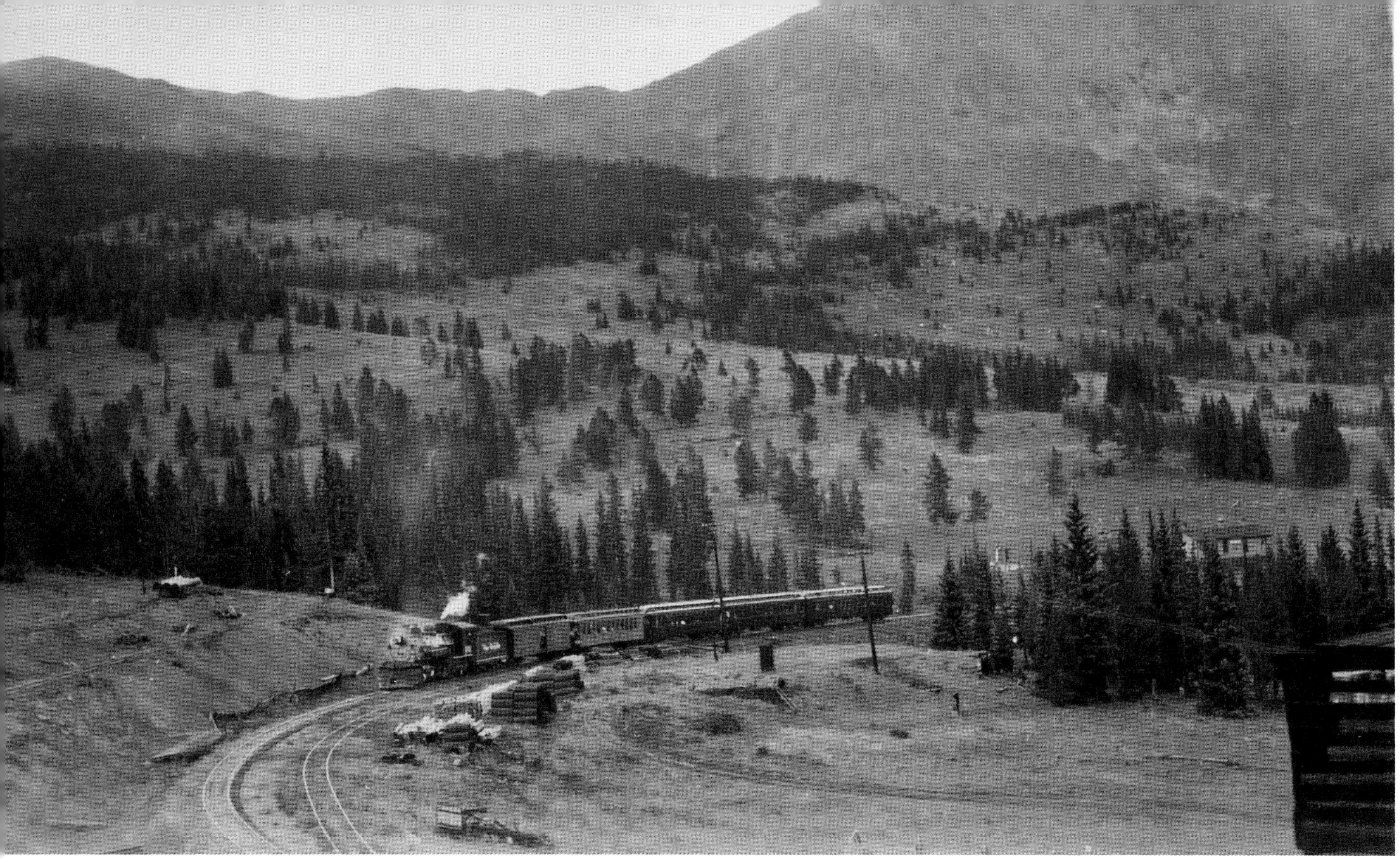

RICHARD A. RONZIO COLLECTION

A gathering of Rocky Mountain Railroad Club members found themselves at the crest of Marshall Pass on this "extra," September 6, 1947, headed for Gunnison behind Engine 499.

Returning from Gunnison, members of the Rocky Mountain Railroad Club looked over the interior of the snowsheds on top of Marshall Pass August 30, 1947.

The 499 had drifted out of the east portal of the snowshed on top of Marshall Pass for club members to take advantage of this striking view.

ELMORE FREDERICK COLLECTION

RICHARD A. RONZIO COLLECTION

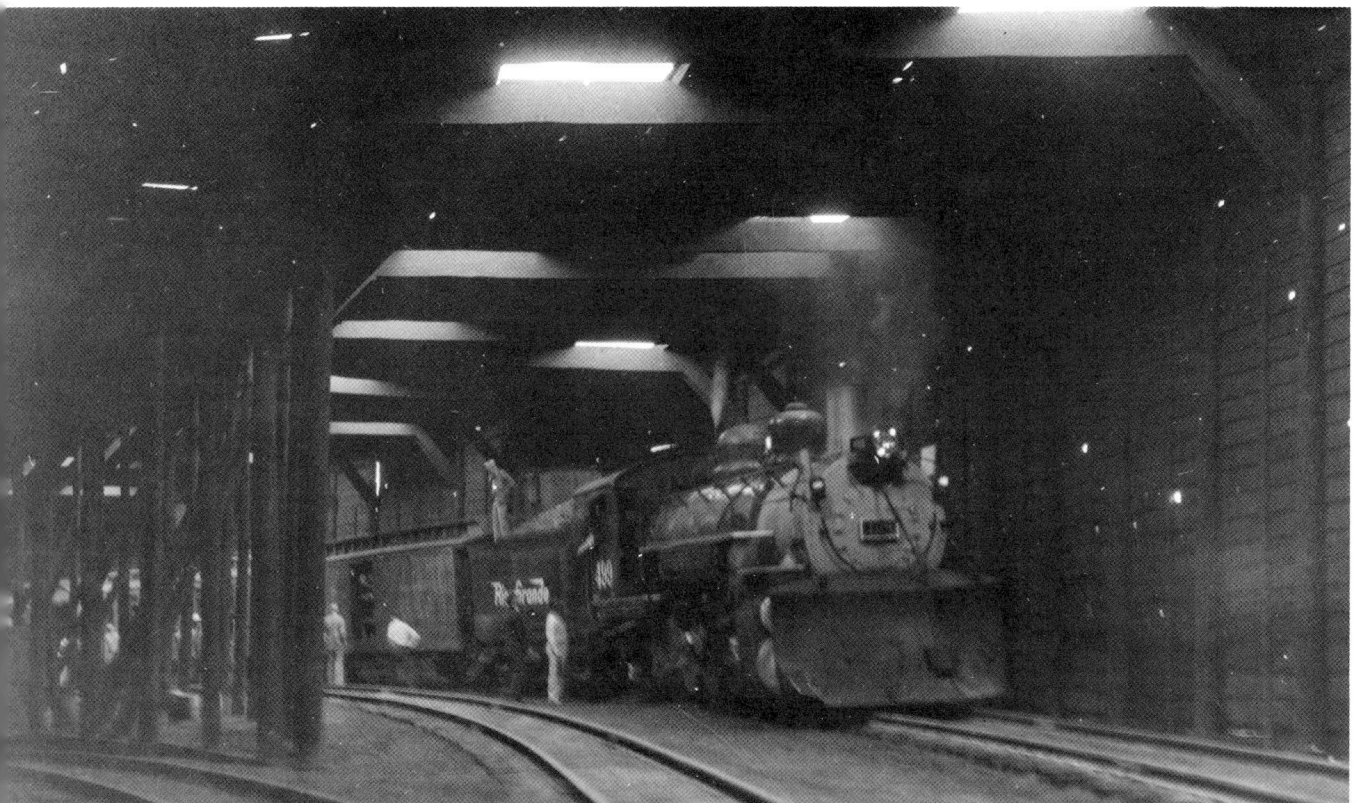

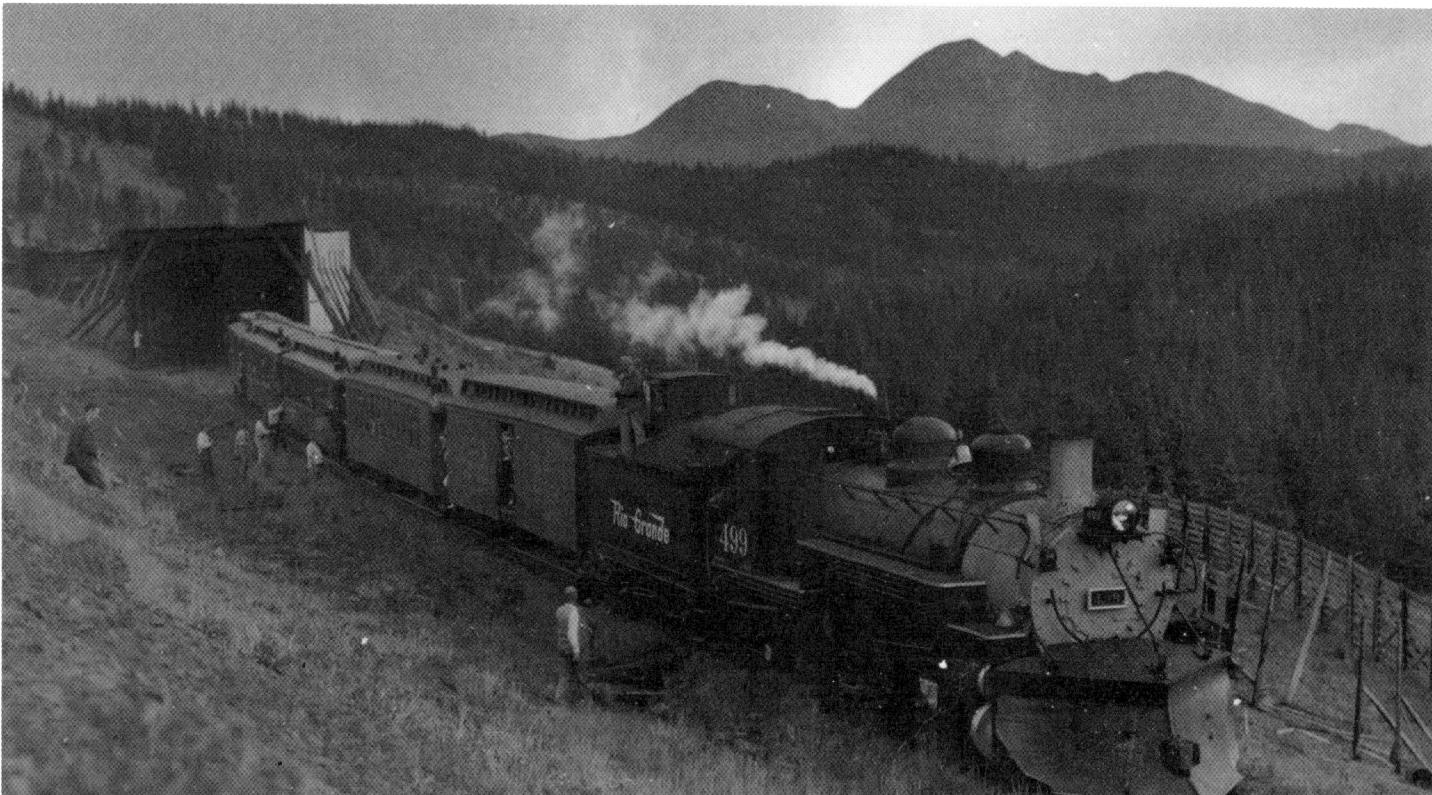

Locomotives Numbered 489, 483, 480 and 482 were hauling a stock extra eastbound by way of Marshall Pass on October 9, 1953. This was the last such movement using four locomotives—to eliminate a delay caused by doubling the west side of the pass by only two engines.

GUNNISON - CRESTED BUTTE

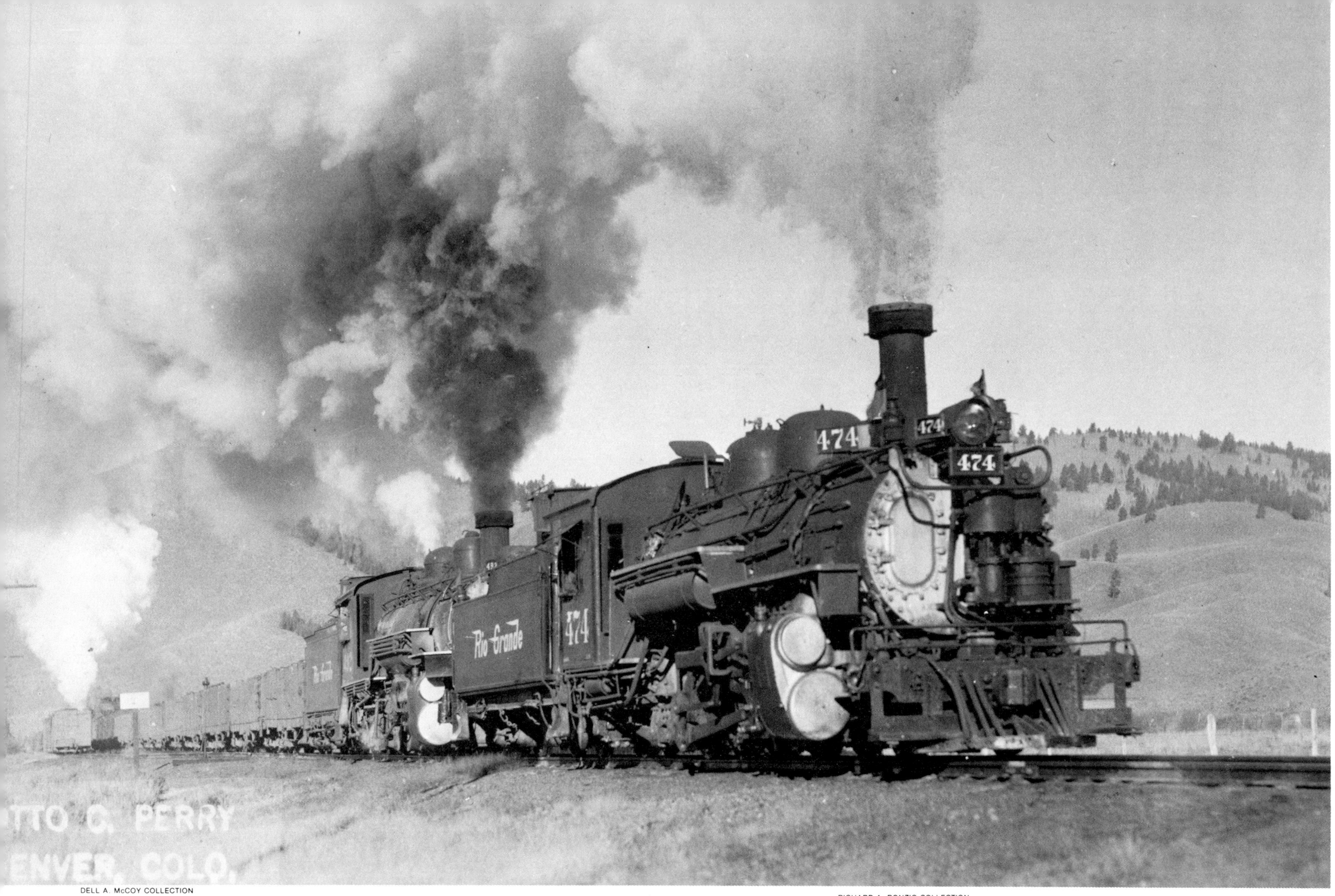

DELL A. McCOY COLLECTION

The 474 leads this 3 locomotive freight train leaving Sargents on October 16, 1941, for Marshall Pass.

RICHARD A. RONZIO COLLECTION

Another view of the final 4-engine. Stock movement was photographed east of Parlin, October 9, 1953.

RICHARD A. RONZIO COLLECTION

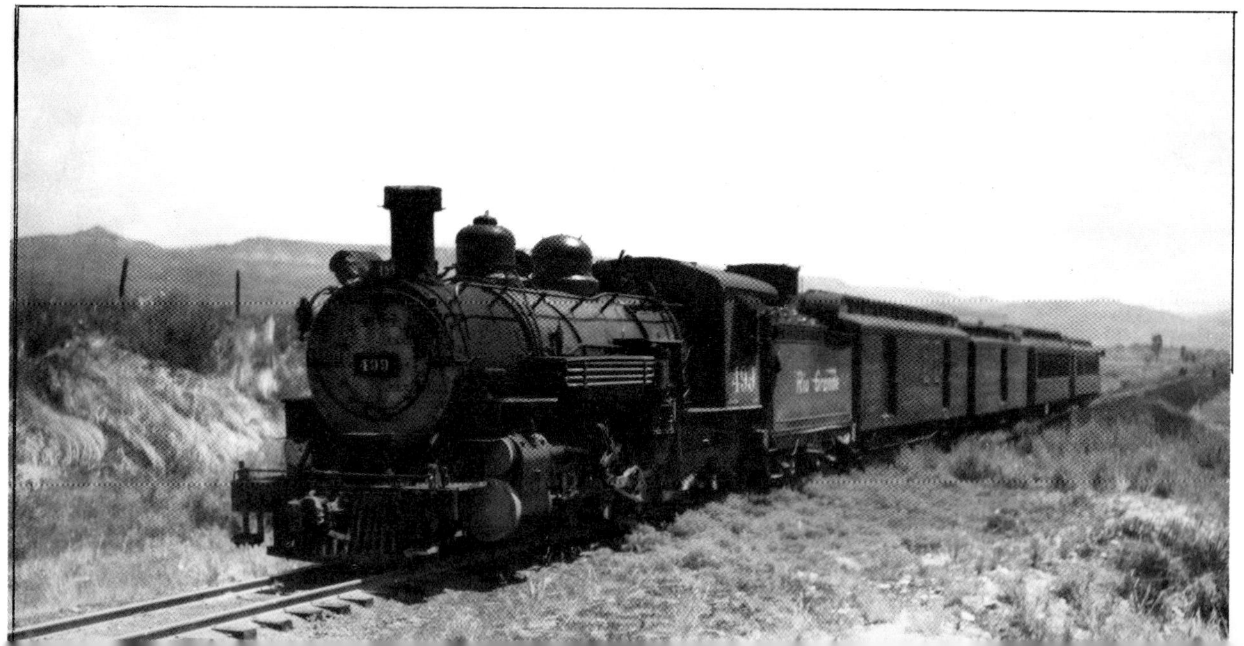

On a hot July 4, 1940, the westbound ''Shavano'' was rolling into Gunnison. Locomotive Number 499 was rarely seen on a passenger train. Usually the 470 or the 479 was assigned to this train.

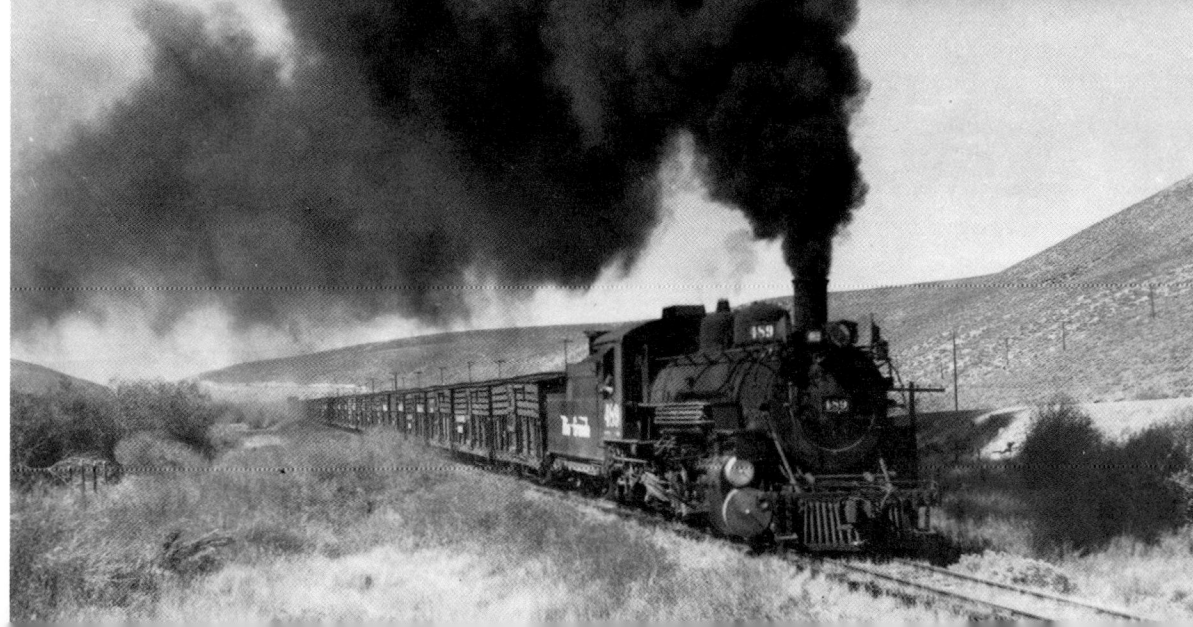

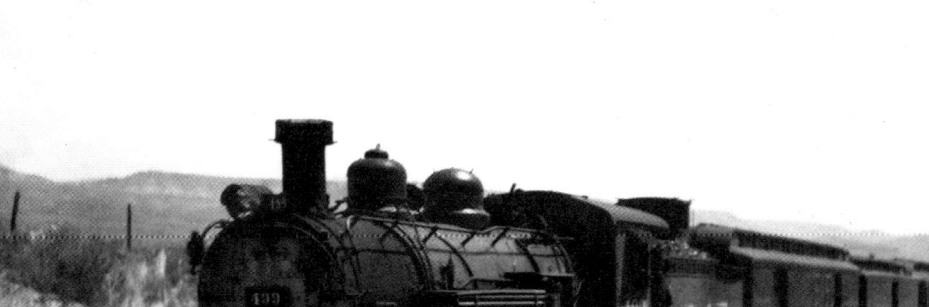

The hard working 268 was pulling empties about one-half mile outside Crested Butte, for loading with slack coal, in this view of October 3, 1953.

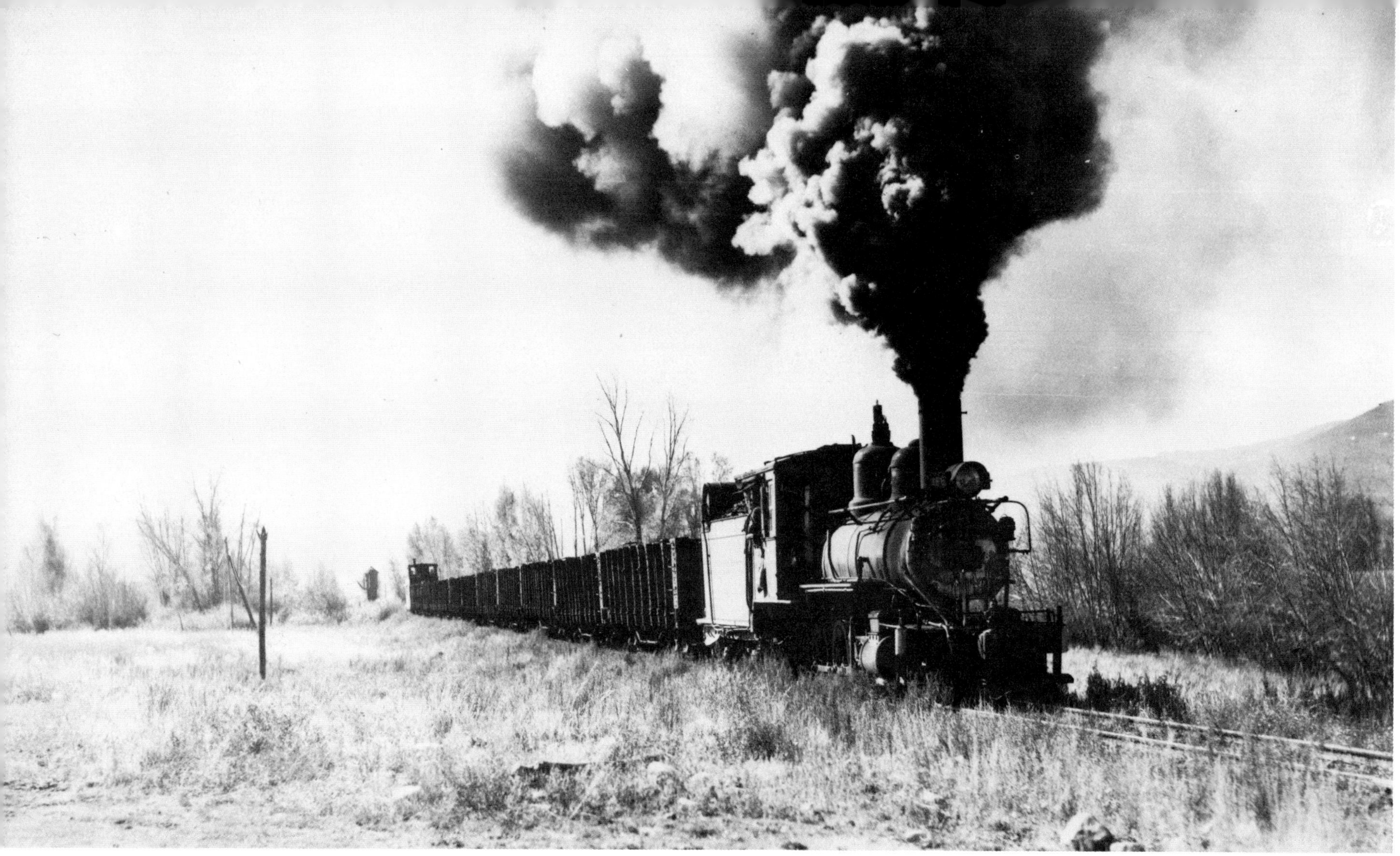

RICHARD A. RONZIO COLLECTION

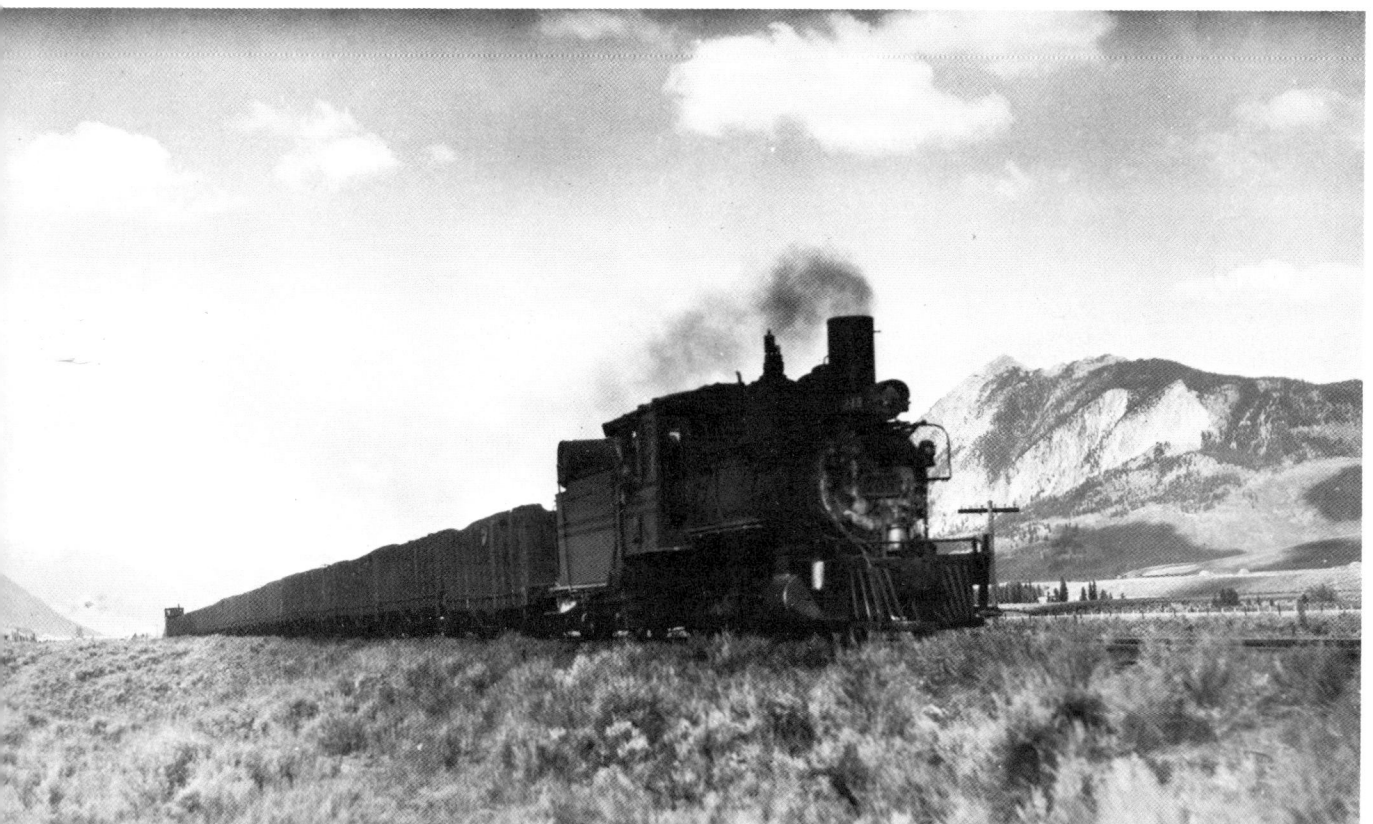

Leaving Jacks Cabin with empties for Crested Butte, the 268 works hard on the up-grade October 3, 1953. This was a stock loading point on the D&RGW. The small tank was built in the early 1940s and was not moved from Villa grove as some believe.

The town of Crested Butte was named after the peak to the right of the 268. Trainloads of slack coal from Smith Hill were some of the last freight from Crested Butte. Notice the homemade cinder catcher on the 268.

The last Powderhorn round up of October 9, 1953 was photographed coming out of Iola, headed eastbound toward Gunnison. This was the first section near Halls Siding, pulled by Engine 268.

RICHARD A. RONZIO COLLECTION

RICHARD A. RONZIO COLLECTION

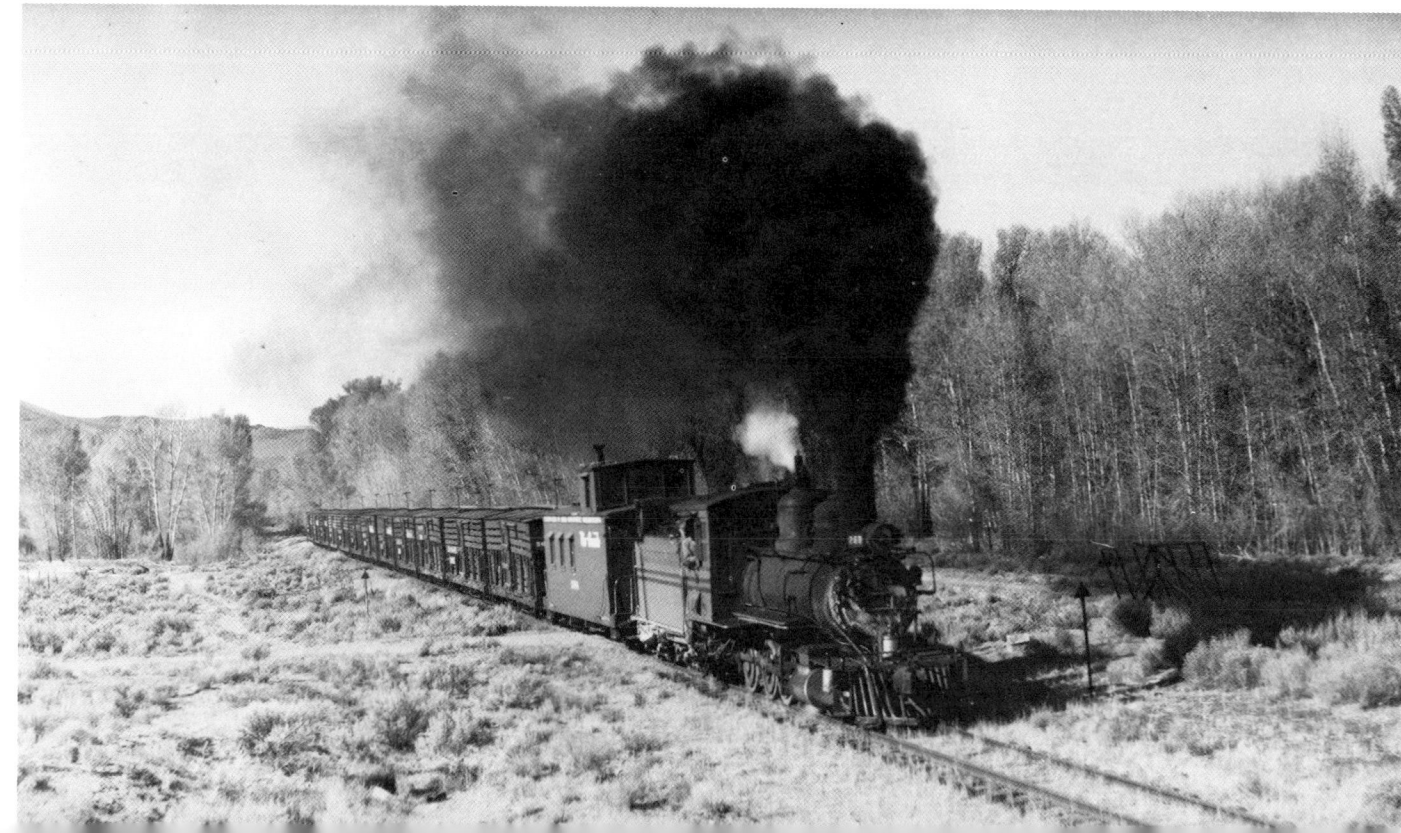

The last Rocky Mountain Railroad Club excursion to the Gunnison area took place May 30, 1949. The extra was eastbound below famous Sapinero Needles, now under the water of Blue Mesa Lake. The Silver Vista glassed-in car brings up the rear of the train pulled by Engine 361.

Here, the last excursion train, eastbound near Gunnison, passed the Chinery Ranch.

Trusty Locomotive Number 278 was northbound on the Baldwin branch, 1 hour and 13 minutes out of Gunnison, June 28, 1940. This was the former Colorado & Southern branch to the Baldwin coal fields. The light rail [45 lb.] restricted locomotive power to the light weight 30 ton class C-16's.

BALDWIN

Castleton on the Baldwin branch was where the line branched to the old and new Baldwin mines. It had a wye, an old C&S vintage water tank, and even Denver, South Park & Pacific switch stands. The conductor sported a panama hat that fine June day.

At Baldwin, the fireman and engineer are attempting to remove a large clinker from the grates. The tender tank was a cut down K-27 tender put on in 1935. The locomotive is now on loan to the National Park Service and is displayed in the Black Canyon, near Cimmaron.

RICHARD A. RONZIO COLLECTION

RICHARD A. RONZIO COLLECTION

This little Grant-built locomotive was entering the yards at Baldwin in 1940. The last of her kind, the 223 has now been placed on display by the Utah State Historical Society, on the platform of the D&RGW depot in Salt Lake City.

The 345 drifted down Cerro Summit May 8, 1949 with 13 stock cars and caboose. The eastbound freight would probably unload sheep somewhere up around Crested Butte for summer pasture.

For lack of foreground trees, Otto Perry chose boulders to frame the 361 in this classic view on May 27, 1949, upgrade on Cerro Summit.

ELMORE FREDERICK COLLECTION

RICHARD A. RONZIO COLLECTION

The 361 and 454 echo their exhaust while they worked up the 4% grades to Cerro Summit. The normally rare practice of pushing behind caboose Number 0577 proved hard on oak underframes.

ALAMOSA, WESTBOUND

The Burnham Shops in Denver transformed 10 2-8-0 standard-gauge locomotives to 2-8-2 narrow-gauge freight haulers. Resplendent in green boiler jacket, graphite grey smoke box, aluminium leaf lettering and black trim, the 497, "brand new" in 1930, sat in Alamosa on a standard-gauge flat car.

The 486 simmered at Alamosa in 1938. Lettering on the cab door reminded firemen to use flange oilers in order to prevent wear on sharp narrow-gauge curves. She is now on display at Royal Gorge.

The 481 sat dead in Alamosa in 1940, smokestack capped, awaiting routine maintenance. The locomotive sported the new Rio Grande emblem and 17"-high cab numbers instead of the former 12". She was the last engine shopped in Alamosa—in 1968—and now sits in Durango.

DAVID S. DIGERNESS COLLECTION

DAVID S. DIGERNESS COLLECTION

DAVID S. DIGERNESS COLLECTION

Embudo, New Mexico, was the meeting point for the north and south Chili line trains. Here locomotive Number 473 has an unusually long consist heading north to Colorado, with a newly painted short 30' reefer and other mixed cars, on March 22, 1941.

CHILI LINE

Only 4 months before the Chili Line closed, the 471 is shown with her regular consist of one freight car, U.S. Mail and express car and passenger car, crossing the Conejos river June 14, 1941, near Antonito, Colorado.

The southbound "Chile Line" train of the Santa Fe branch is shown at Milepost 307, near Palmilla siding, New Mexico on June 14, 1941. San Antonio Peak rises beyond locomotive Number 473.

Helper locomotive Number 283 was waiting at Embudo for a northbound Chili Line train. Ahead lay a 4% climb up Barranca Hill. Helper service was eliminated in the early 1930s with the advent of heavier rail and K-28 class locomotives. Number 283 was sold to California's Nevada County Narrow-Gauge Railroad in 1933, where she survived on a southern California industrial line until 1947.

RICHARD A. RONZIO COLLECTION

RICHARD A. RONZIO COLLECTION

RICHARD A. RONZIO COLLECTION

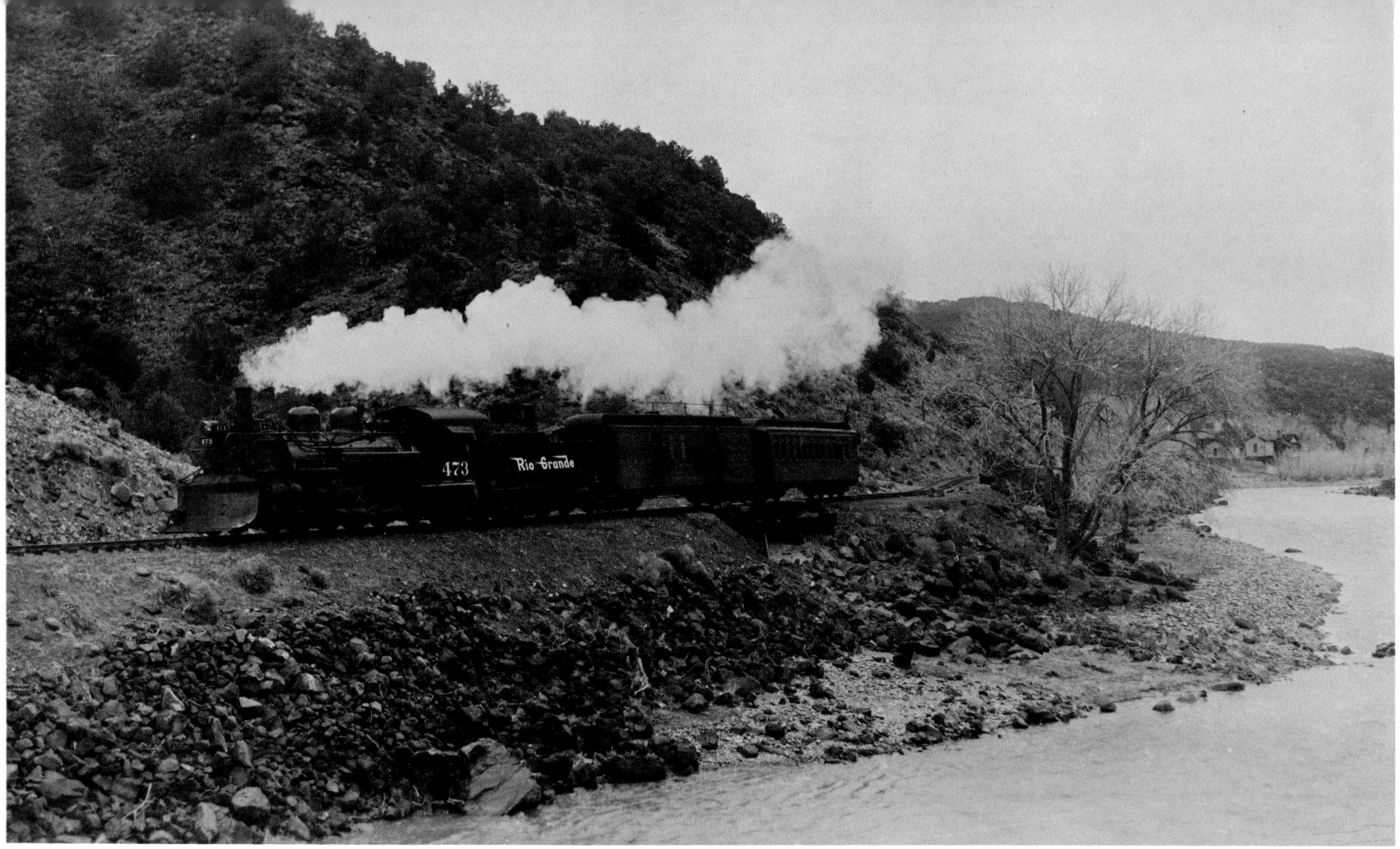

RICHARD A. RONZIO COLLECTION

RICHARD A. RONZIO COLLECTION

On March 1, 1941, ''Sport Model'' locomotive Number 473 hauled the short consist south, to Santa Fe, New Mexico. The helper station of Embudo, New Mexico, appears to the right.

The 475 was moving a bit fast for Otto Perry's lens in this snowbound view. The 3 car passenger train was southbound between Embudo and Alcalde, New Mexico, on a blustery January 13, 1940.

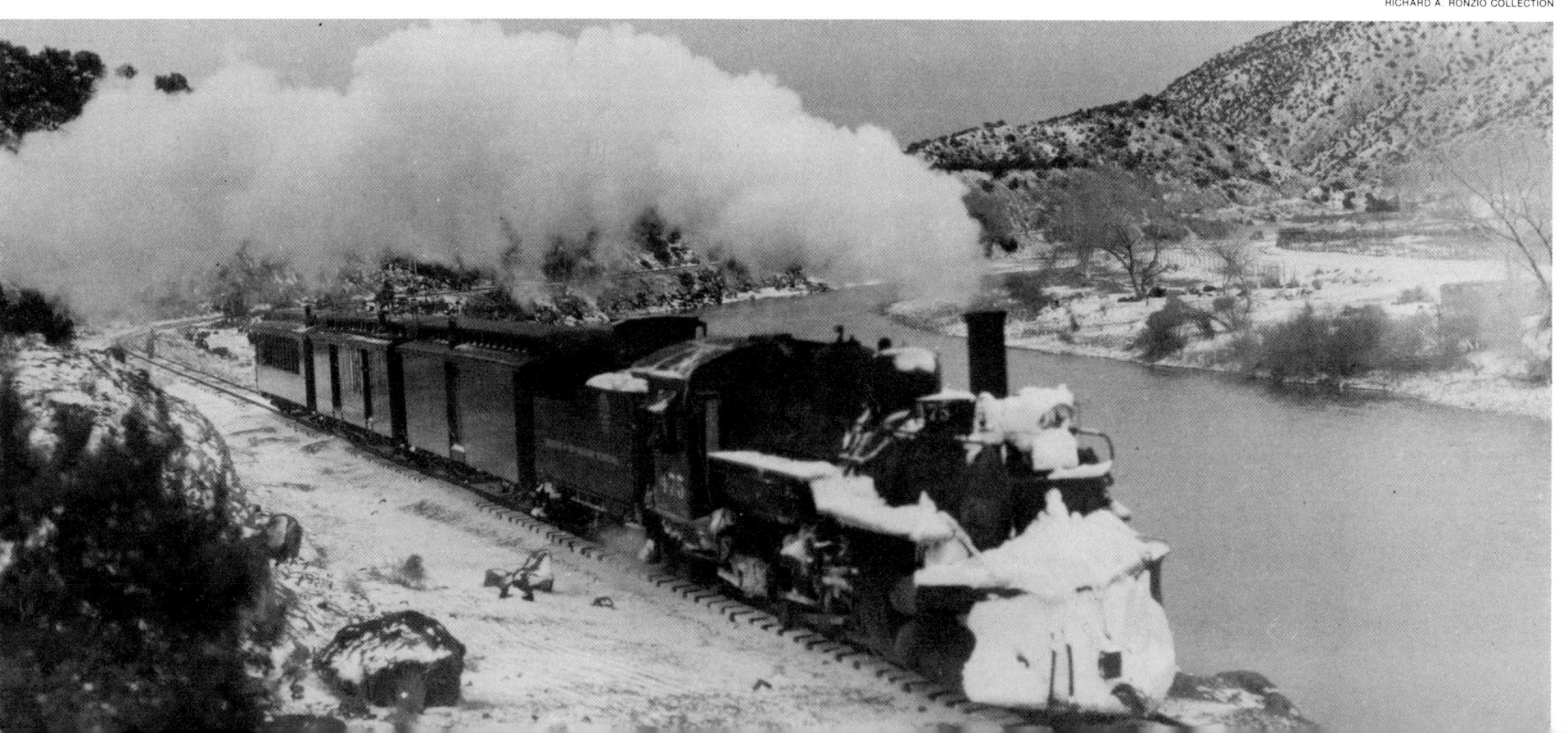

RICHARD A. RONZIO COLLECTION

RICHARD A. RONZIO COLLECTION

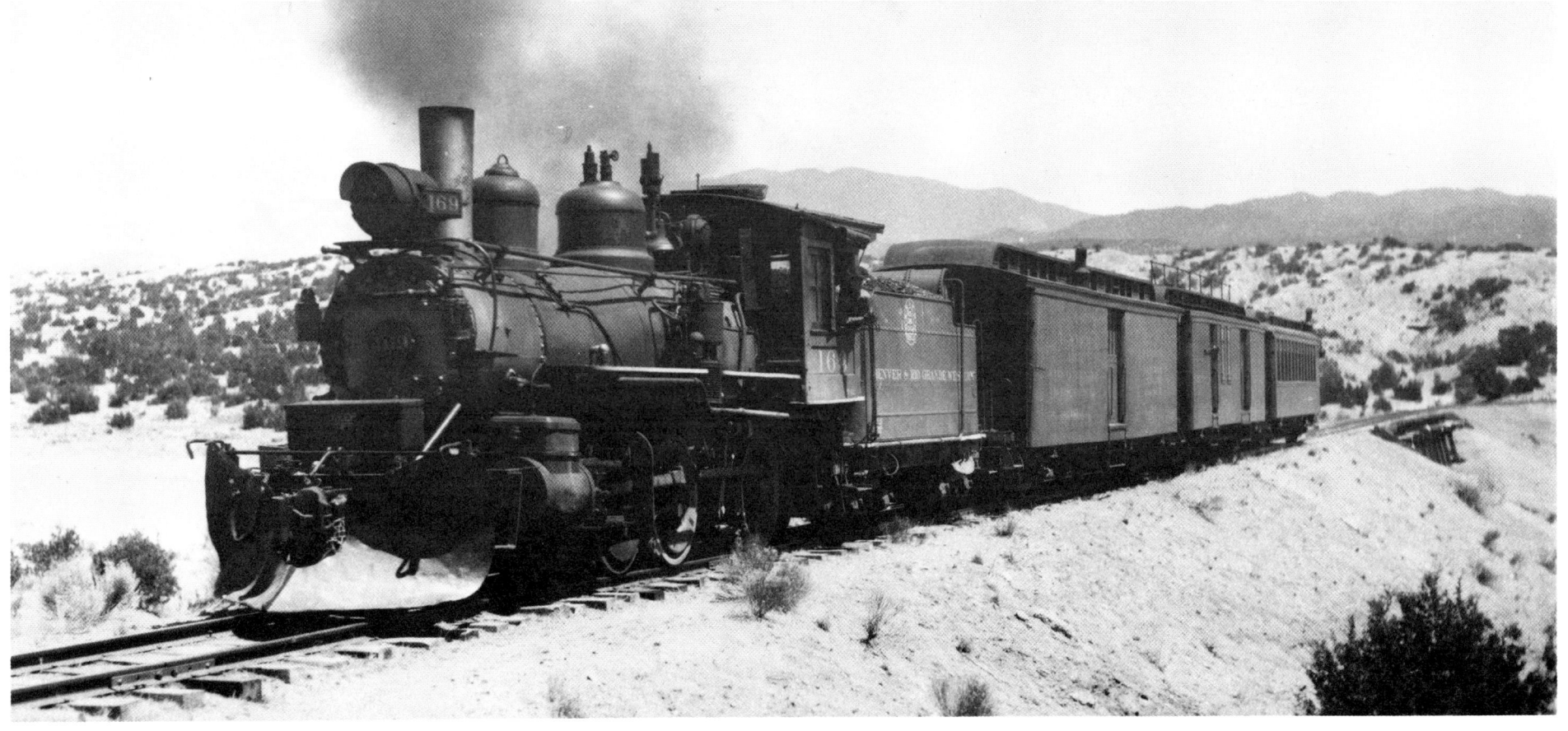

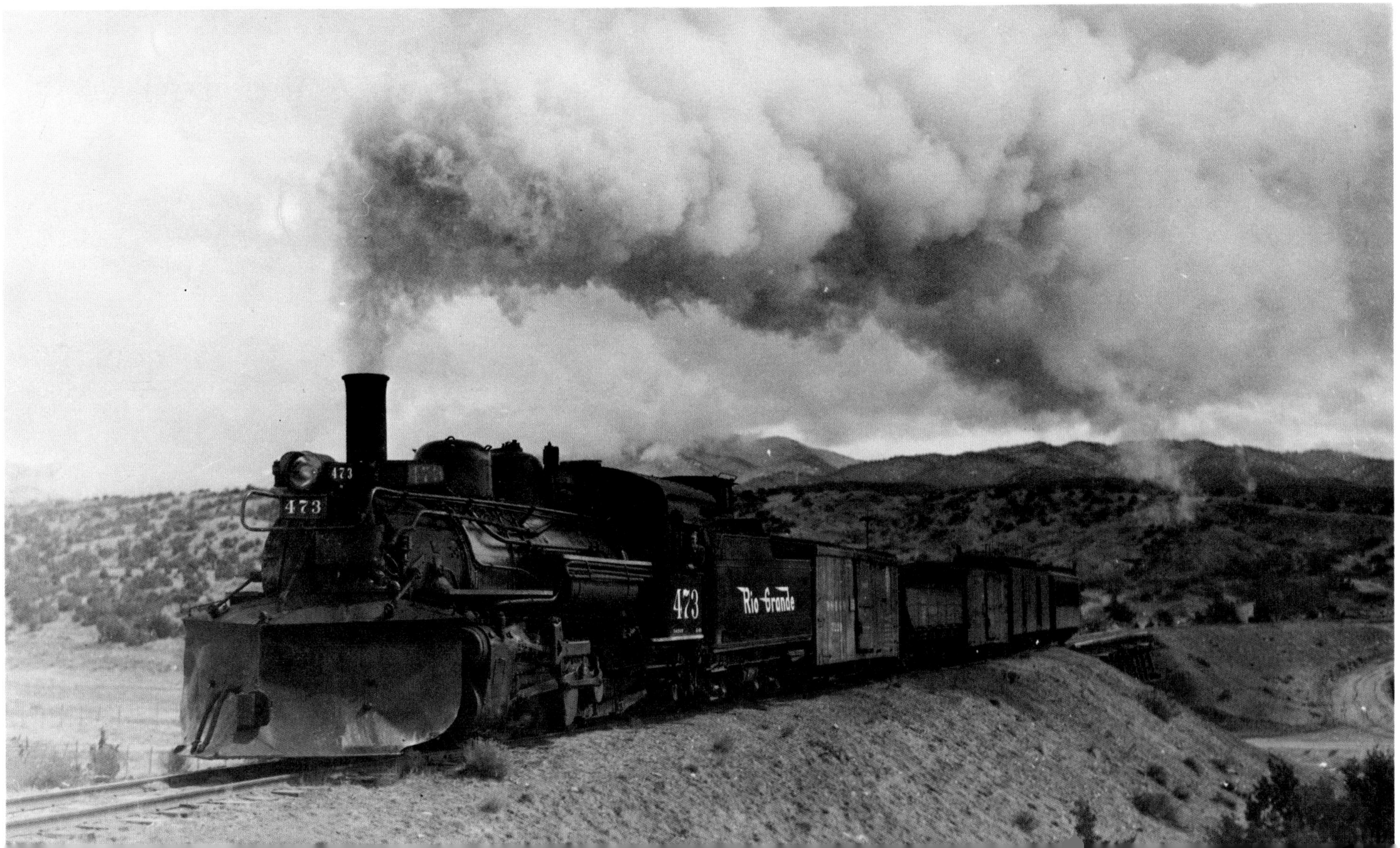

Prior to the use of Class K-28 locomotives, the 1880 vintage 4-6-0 class T-12's were used on the Chili Line. Here on April 17, 1933 the 169 was northbound just out of Santa Fe, at Buckman's Ranch.

Eight years later, only the motive power has changed as 473 headed past the Santa Fe hills, with the Sangre de Cristo mountains in the background.

RICHARD A. RONZIO COLLECTION

CUMBRES PASS

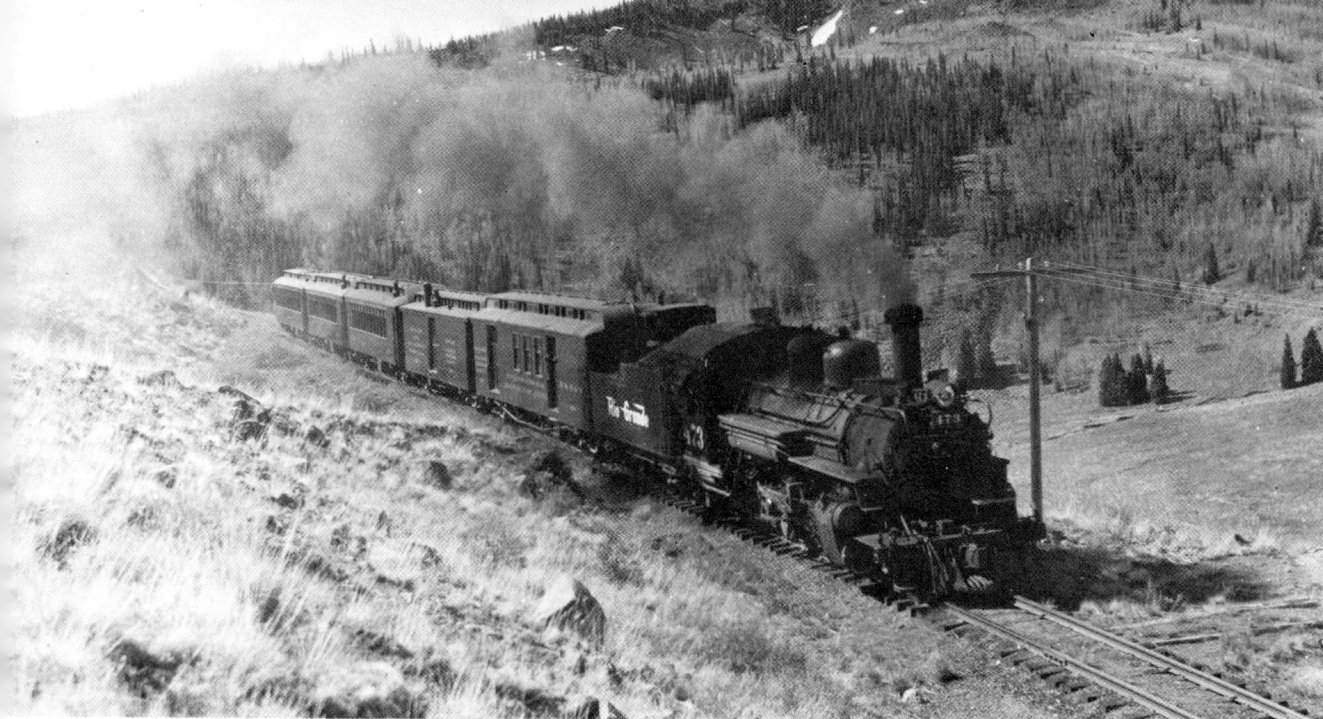

The "San Juan" was westbound near Osier, Colorado, in the late 1940s. This spectacular trip was just then becoming popular with the offbeat tourist and railfan.

The eastbound "San Juan", carrying passenger, mail, and express, was climbing Cumbres Pass on June 9, 1942 with train #116. Winter snow is still evident as the train pulls past the Coxo phone booth.

ELMORE FREDERICK COLLECTION

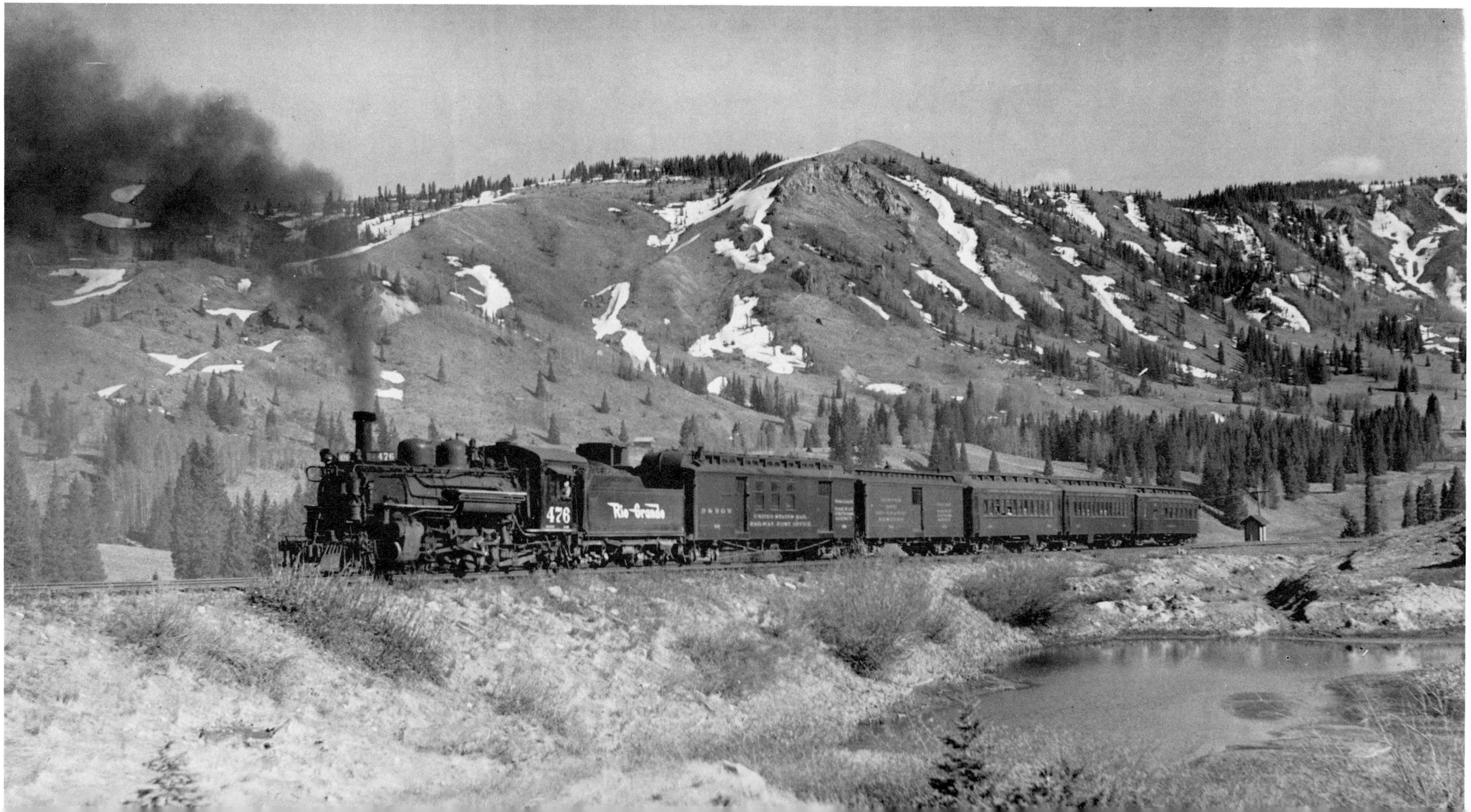

Coming down off Cumbres Pass June 23, 1943, the eastbound "San Juan" was painted in Pullman green with gold lettering. The Los Pinos loop was just ahead of train #116, while in the far background the line may be seen coming up the valley from Osier.

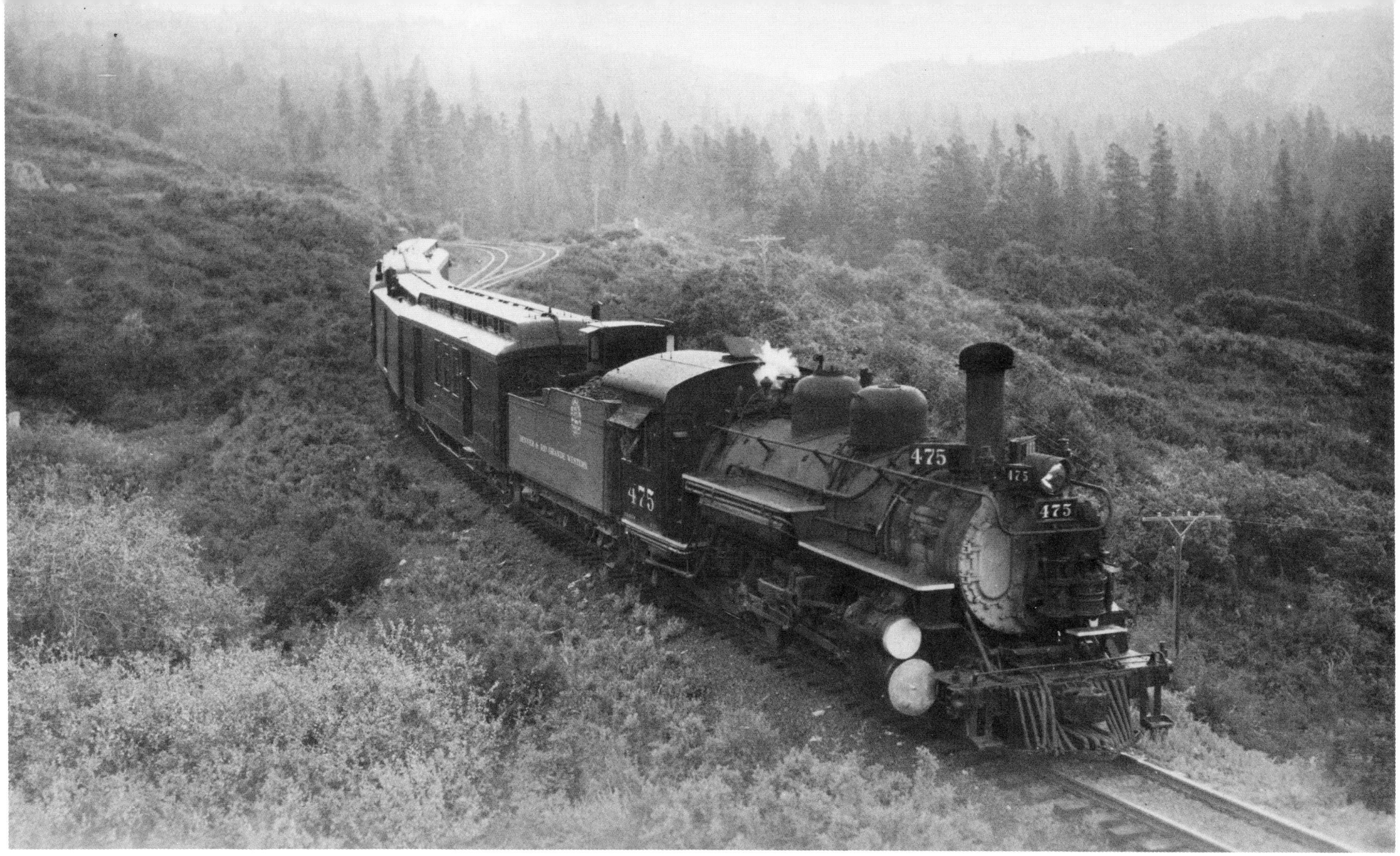

RICHARD A. RONZIO COLLECTION

Westbound, the "San Juan" was drifting off Cumbres Pass, and had just crossed the Colorado-New Mexico state line at the south end of the Cresco siding, June 16, 1940.

RICHARD A. RONZIO COLLECTION

The eastbound "San Juan" was traversing the high Lobato trestle on her climb up Cumbres Pass. Notice the absence of "cat walk," which was added in 1943 on the high steel structure.

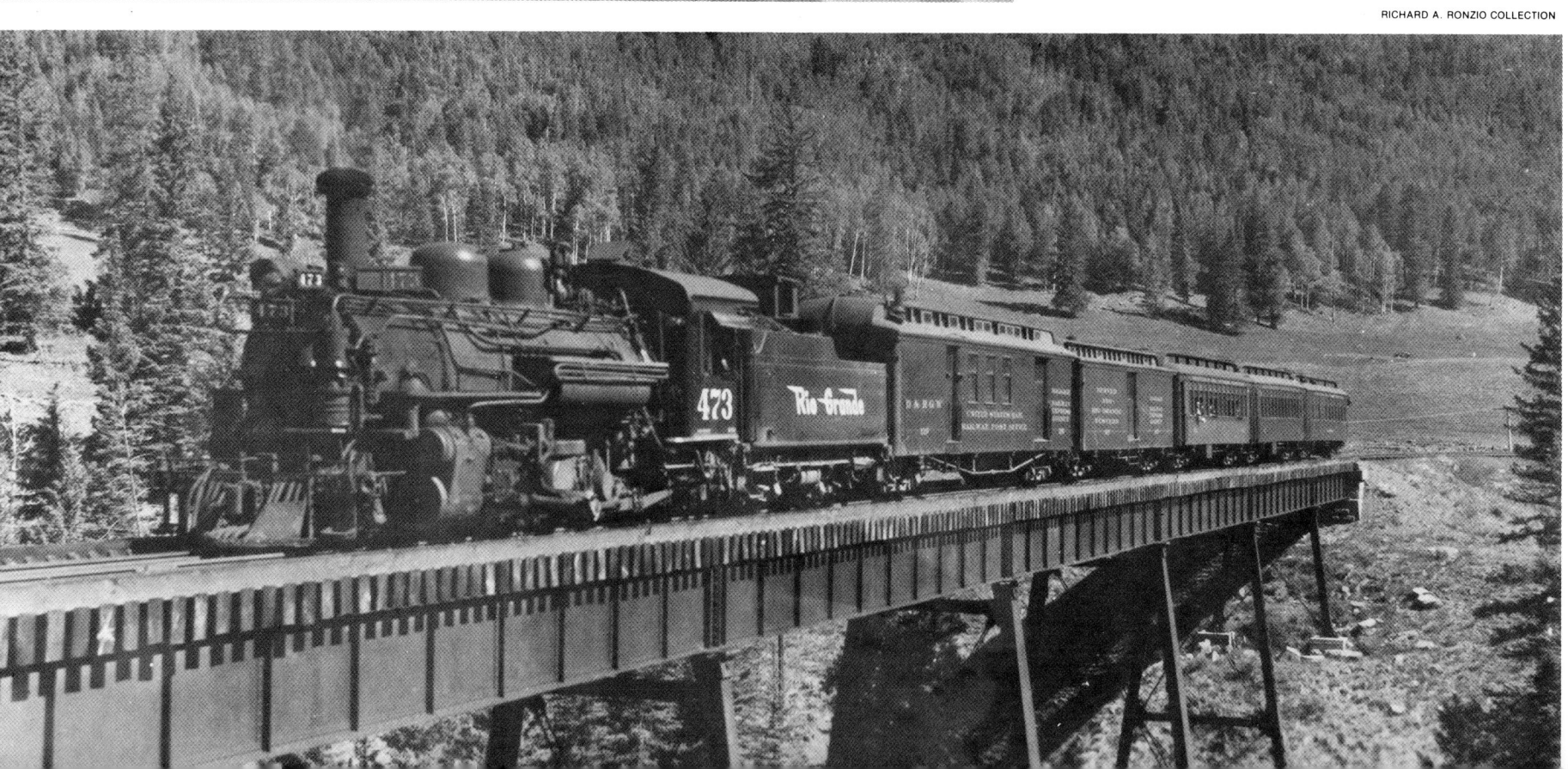

The westbound "San Juan" was 15 minutes out of Chama as it departed Lobato, New Mexico, June 16, 1940.

One of the 3 class K-36 2-8-2's equipped for passenger service, Number 488 handled an eastbound "San Juan" up Cumbres Pass August 12, 1950.

The 490 had "Silverton" rolling stock in tow for this Rocky Mountain Railroad Club excursion over Cumbres Pass June 2, 1956. The passenger equipment has been repainted "Rio Grande Gold" by this date, as the westbound train pulled into Chama, New Mexico.

The famous "Jukes" tree just north of Chama, New Mexico, formed the landscape for this unusual photograph taken March 24, 1951. The 473 still had her movie paint scheme as she and the 492, pushing, made their way up Cumbres Pass with a consist of crude oil. Gramps Hughes' oil was shipped by rail until 1962.

DAVID S. DIGERNESS COLLECTION

The ready track in Chama provided the setting for these 2 photos. Beyond the two class K-36 locomotives one may see the sheep pens.

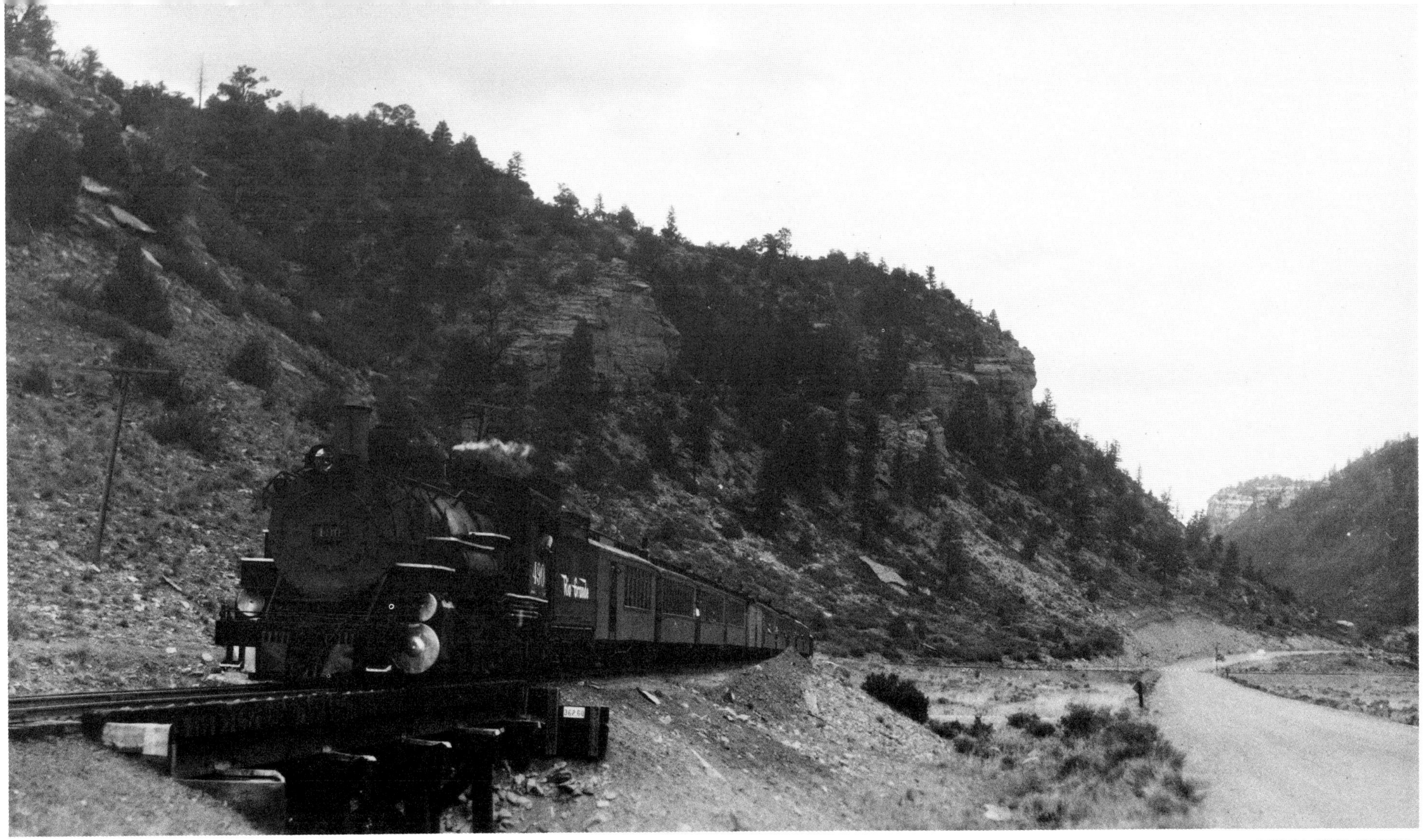

RICHARD A. RONZIO COLLECTION

DAVID S. DIGERNESS COLLECTION

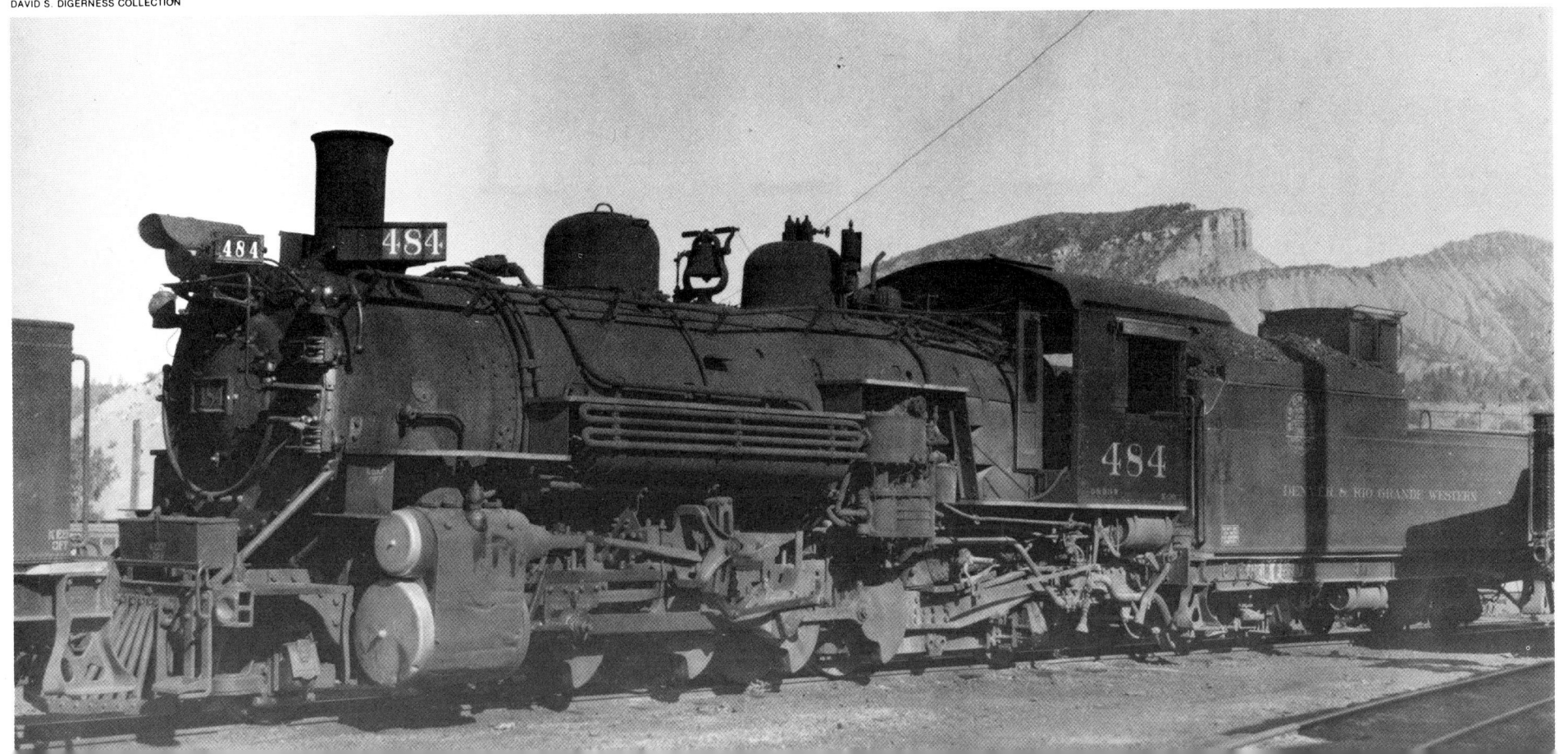

DURANGO

The Rocky Mountain Railroad club fan trip, headed west after crossing Highway 17 just west of Chama. The next stop, Monero, New Mexico, was on the mainline to Durango.

Ready for assignment, the 484 sat next to the Durango roundhouse during the summer of 1939. Years later she would pull tourist trains on the C&TS between Chama, New Mexico and Antonito, Colorado.

DAVID S. DIGERNESS COLLECTION

DAVID S. DIGERNESS COLLECTION

The 478 was switching the Durango yards in the summer of 1939.

Under steam, the 482 sat on the ready track in Durango.

The 473 was dolled up for her movie role during the summer of 1951, as she pulled the Silverton train out of Durango. Several coaches were still painted for the "San Juan" in Pullman green with gold lettering.

The glass enclosed "Silver Vista" car was coupled to the rear of the Silverton train August 13, 1950. Locomotive Number 473 was headed downgrade with the passenger train just below Silverton, along the Rio de Los Animas river.

Locomotive Number 42 leads a consist of oil from Farmington and new automobiles west out of the Durango yards. She was starting down the balloon loop to the RGS lead. The old smelter foot bridge shows to the right. Famous railroad photographer Richard Kindig rode the tender along with the front end brakeman.

As the Eagle Flies - RGS

CHAPTER II

he Rio Grande Southern started out as an independent narrow gauge railway to serve the silver mines and mills of the Telluride area. Otto Mears, founder and president, invested his own resources of money and design in the railroad. In 1890 construction began from Durango and Ridgway, connecting with the D&RG at both points. The entire railway was completed during 1891 and began operations by borrowing or leasing much of its equipment from the D&RG in order to meet business demands. The boom years were short lived, however, due to the repeal of the Sherman Act in 1892, which brought about falling silver prices. This in turn caused mines and mills to close down, severely effecting the economy of the San Juan area of Colorado. The D&RG attempted to step in and salvage its own investment in the RGS at that time. Attempts were made to attract passenger and tourist business, but they achieved little success in keeping the operation successful. During the 1930s homemade railbuses—called "Galloping Geese" were used in place of steam powered passenger trains, but even this was not enough to sustain operations. All operations were terminated in 1951.

Some of the most spectacular scenery in the U.S.A. may be viewed along the line of the RGS. The Telluride area, Lizard Head Pass, and Ophir remind one of Switzerland. Here the RGS built a great deal of 4% grade and constructed several tall, wood trestles.

Otto Perry managed a great many trips to the RGS as evidenced by the photo collection following. He was greatly saddened to witness the decay of this three foot gauge railway during the years he traveled to the San Juan region of Colorado.

RICHARD A. RONZIO COLLECTION

DURANGO

Three miles west of Durango, the Rio Grande Southern mainline crossed Lightner Creek. Locomotive Number 20, acting as a helper was photographed September 6, 1941.

The same train viewed on page 42 was again photographed near Porter, July 4, 1938. Richard Kindig, riding the boxcar, was shielding his camera equipment from the cinders blasting out of locomotive Number 42's stack.

Once again, the same RGS train was photographed July 4, 1938 surmounting Pine Ridge. Richard Kindig was not in view, probably riding in the cab by then. Highway 160 crossed the RGS right-of-way at this point.

A westbound stock train near Porter was pulled by the good looking locomotive Number 20, now housed at the Colorado Railroad Museum at Golden. October 13, 1951 dates this photo as the end of stock train operations during the fall.

An eastbound doubleheader was about a mile west of Hesperus during the first months of World War II. These locomotives were rarely seen on the RGS south end.

Locomotive Number 319 had been performing as the Durango switch engine during the period this photo was taken, September 21, 1943. Road engine Number 461 followed with the long freight near Hesperus.

A long mixed train had completed switching at a siding at Mayday June 28, 1946. The consist was eastbound with locomotive Number 20.

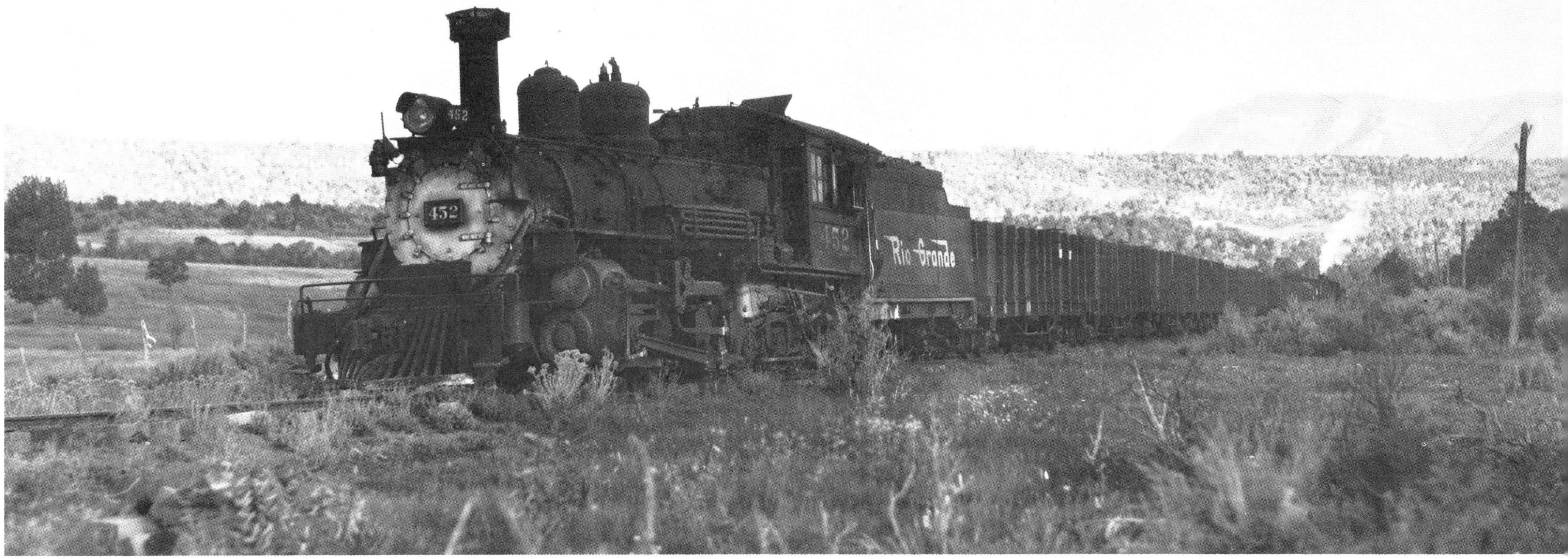

RICHARD A. RONZIO COLLECTION

RICHARD A. RONZIO COLLECTION

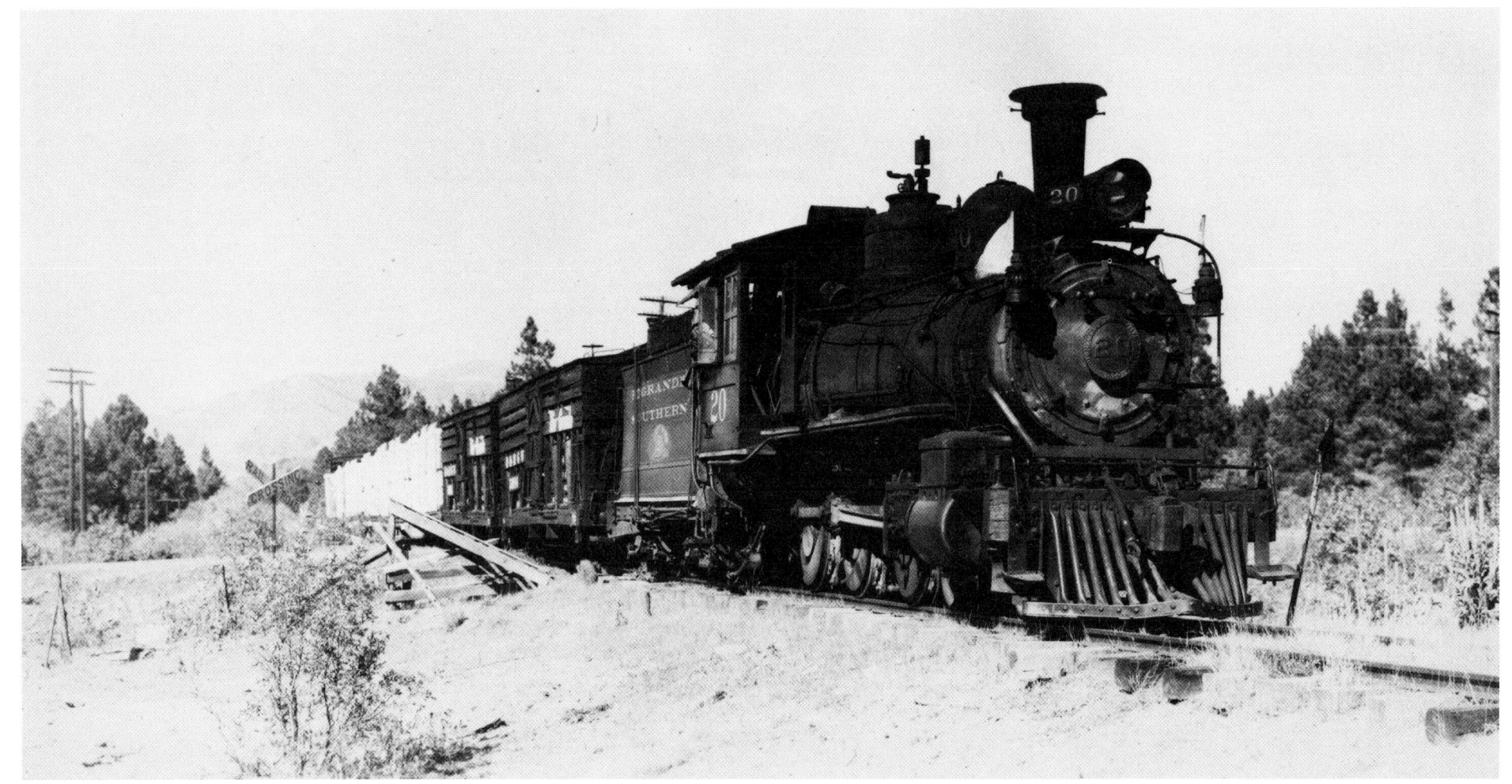

D&RGW locomotive Number 452, leased to the RGS, headed a long consist with Number 20 pushing. This was just above Mancos, with Mesa Verde in the background; October 2, 1947.

The Number 20 was southbound near Porter in this view taken October 8, 1951.

A smokey portrait of south-end locomotive Number 42 near Millwood
June 20, 1944.

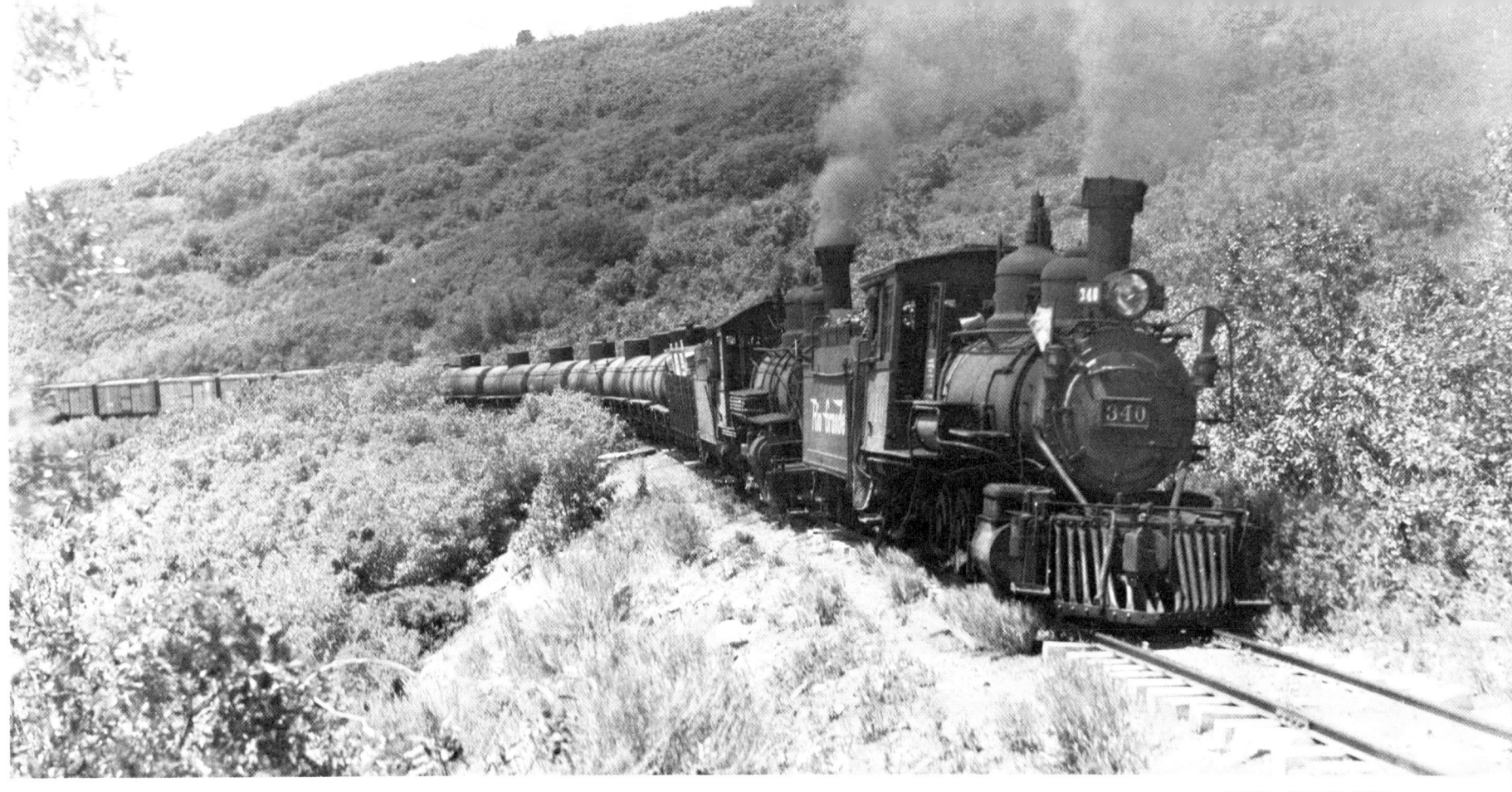

A heavy RGS train climbing Cima Summit must have scared the engine crews half to death as they hit a bad sag in the track. The 340 ended up at the Knotts Berry Farm in California.

RICHARD A. RONZIO COLLECTION

This was probably Lost Canyon, just south of Dolores, when photographed October 8, 1951.

RICHARD A. RONZIO COLLECTION

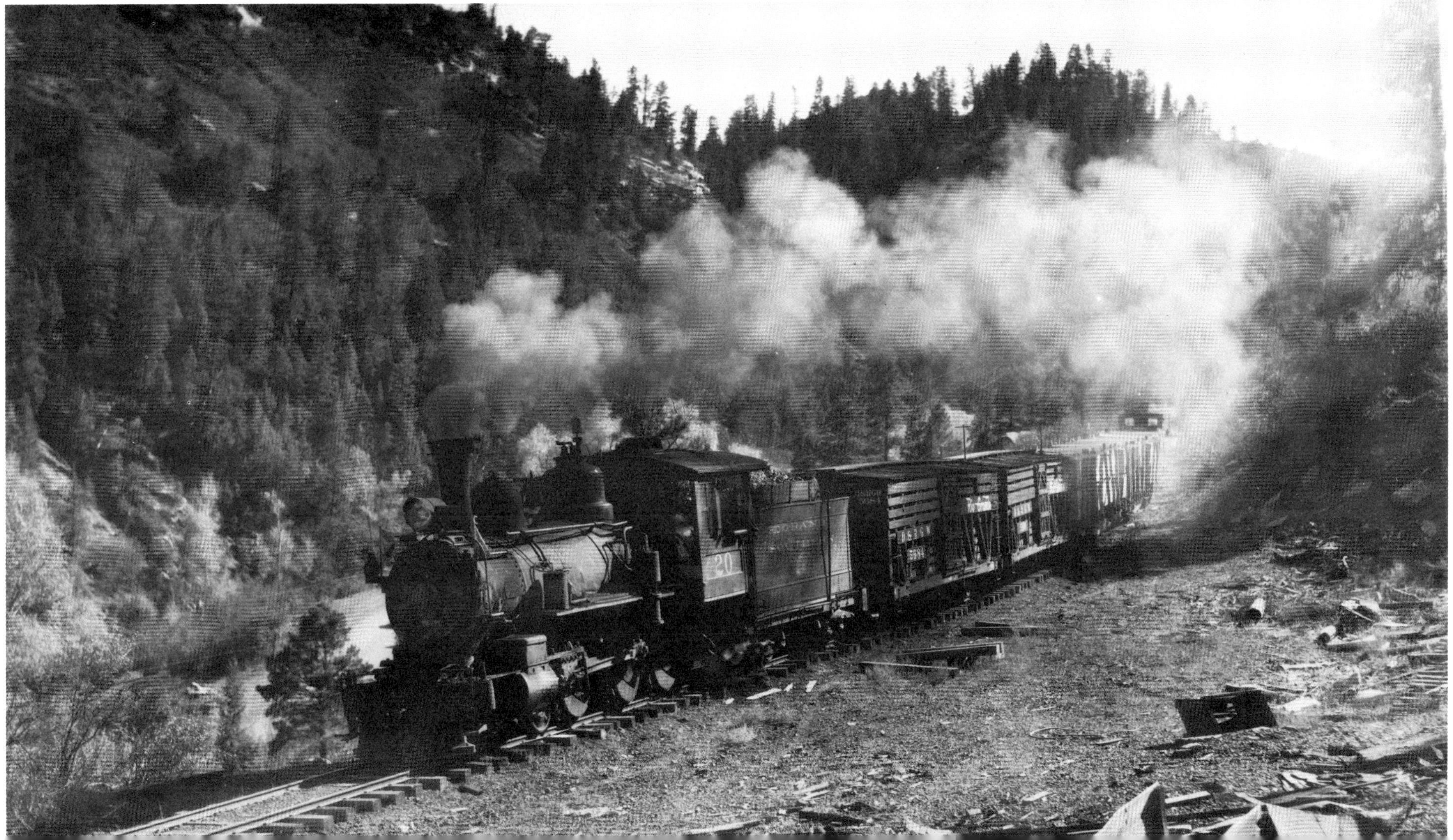

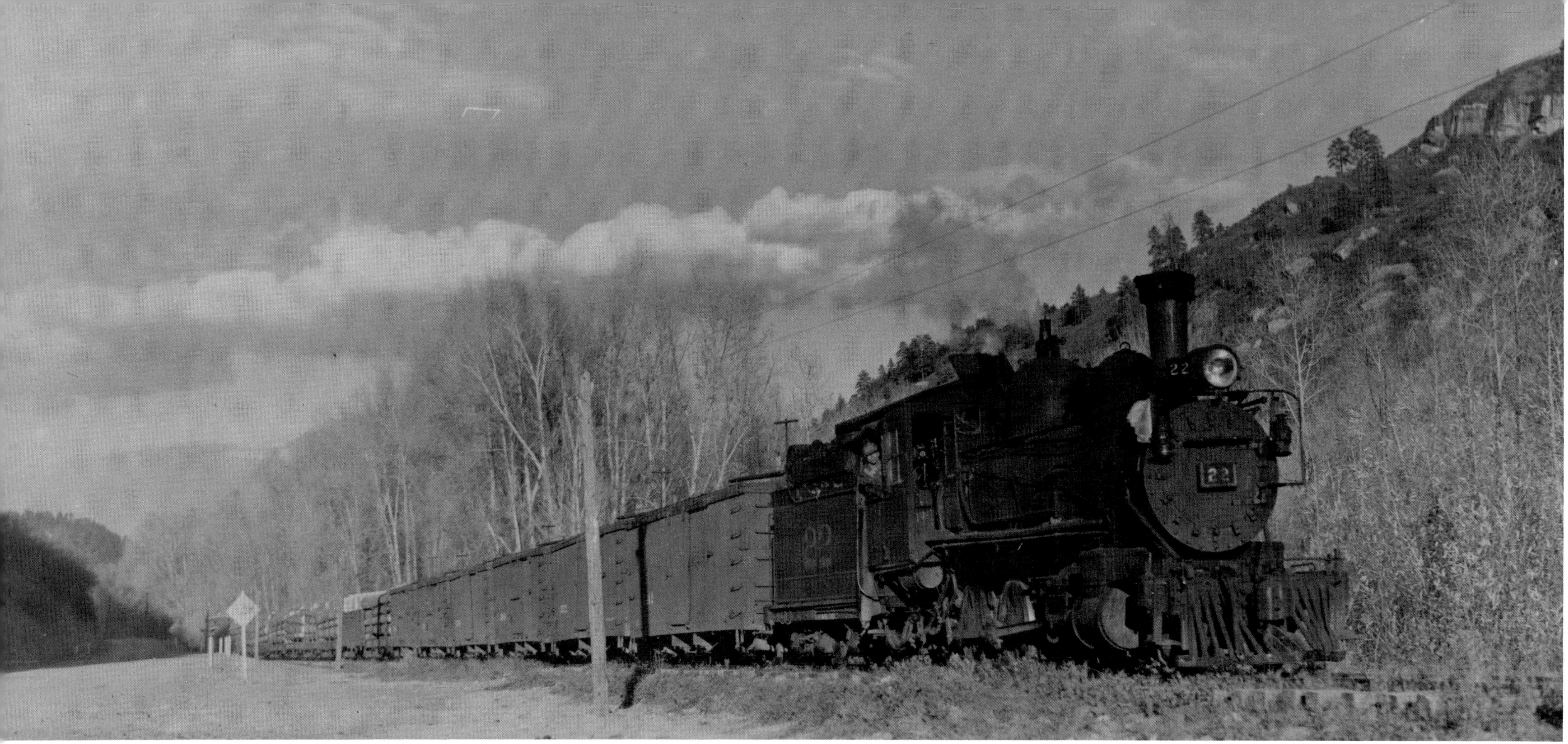

RICHARD A. RONZIO COLLECTION

RICHARD A. RONZIO COLLECTION

DOLORES

In the late fall, October 25, 1940, tenwheeler Number 22 was drifting south near Dolores, out of Rico.

The 227 appeared to need attention with a cab door propped on the gangway, while at Dolores in 1923. This locomotive had been the Chama switcher in the 1900s.

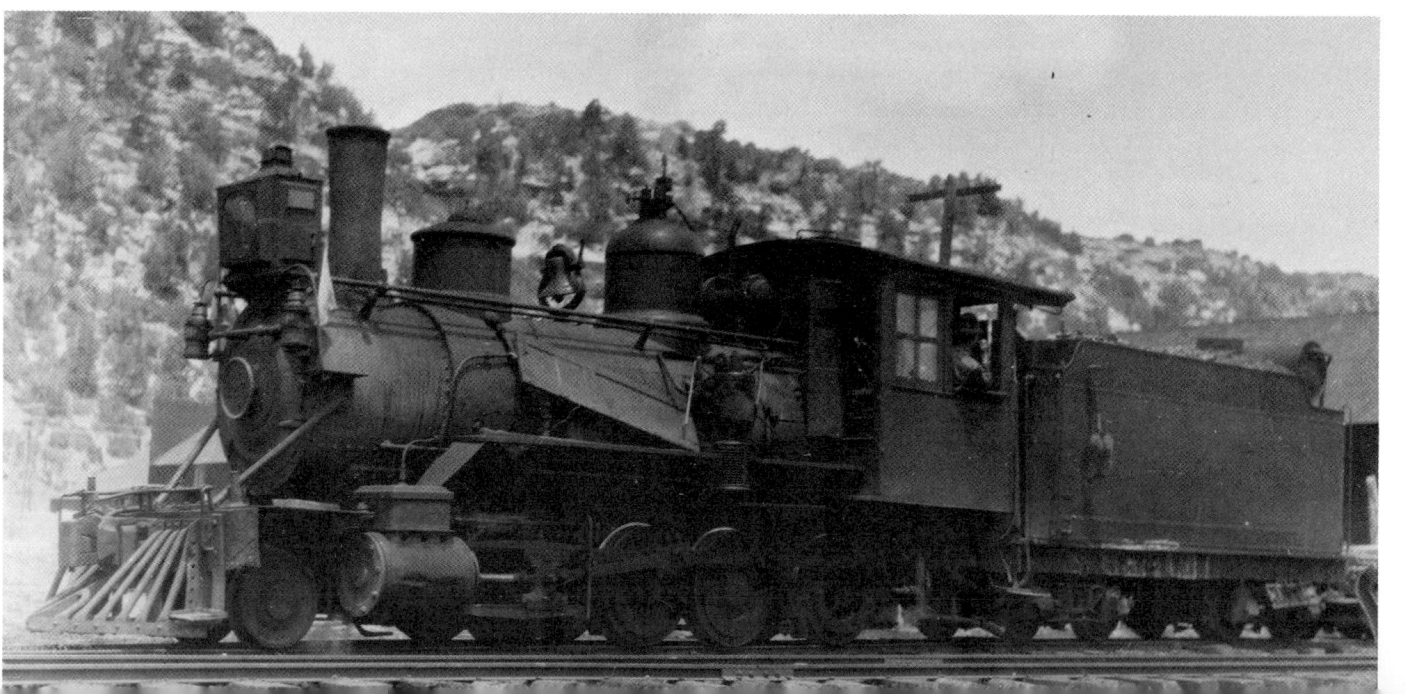

The same freight out of Rico was photographed drifting downgrade beside the Dolores river.

ELMORE FREDERICK COLLECTION

MORRIS W. ABBOTT COLLECTION - WM. R. JONES

A Civilian Conservation Corps special was running past Coke Ovens on June 30, 1940. This was the last large passenger train to run on the RGS.

The Rico sheep pens show up behind a stock train movement in this fall view of October 1, 1951. The engine is a 2-8-2, No. 461, purchased from the D&RGW in 1950.

Burns canyon, between Rico and Lizard Head Pass, was the scene of this Civilian Conservation Corps passenger special, June 30, 1940.

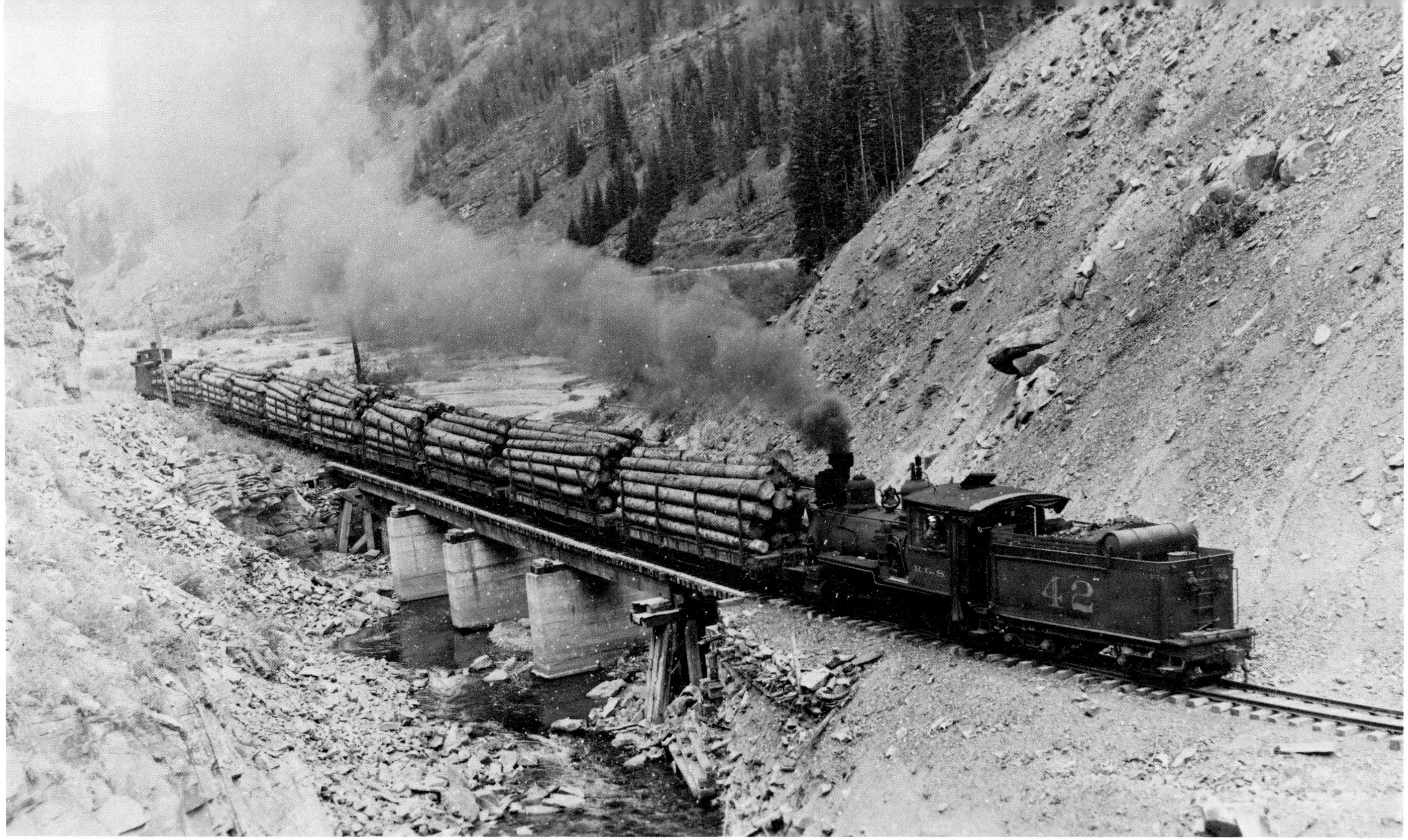

RICHARD A. RONZIO COLLECTION

ELMORE FREDERICK COLLECTION

RGS locomotive Number 42 was backing southward toward Rico with a solid load of spruce logs from Matterhorn. The scene was in Burns Canyon, September 1, 1940.

At that same viewpoint Otto Perry had stopped on October 5, 1951 to photograph engine 461 hauling a RGS freight across the Dolores River.

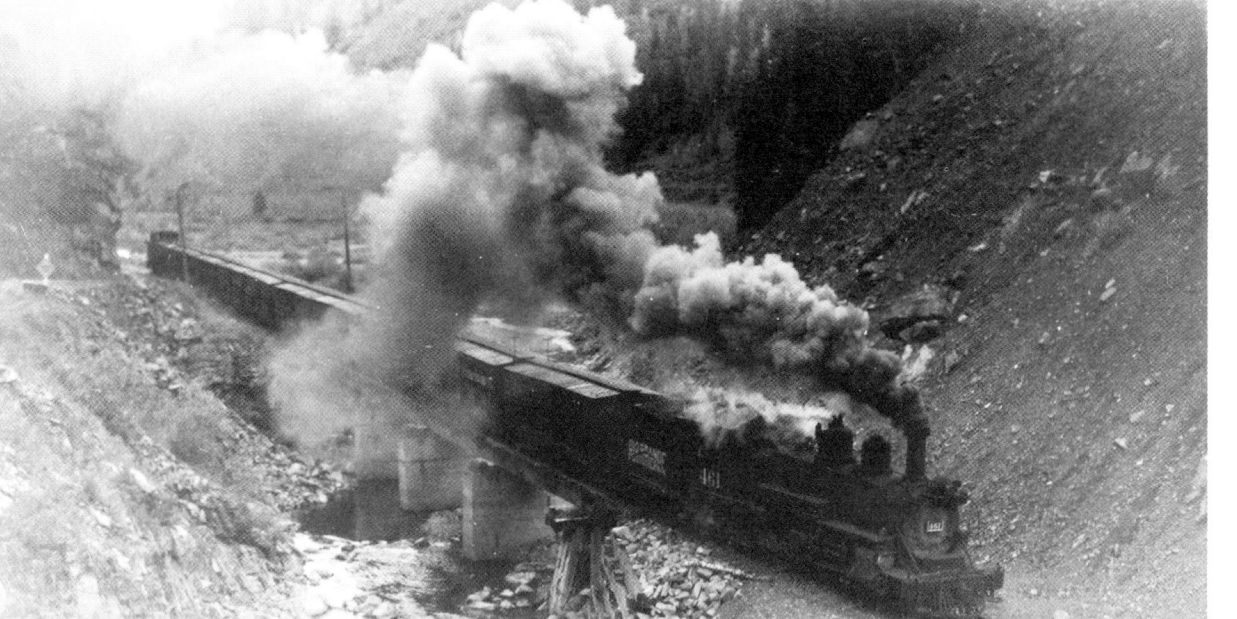

"Galloping Goose No. 4 was grinding its way up the 3% grade to Lizard Head Pass near Gallagher June 28, 1944. This is the Meadow Creek trestle.

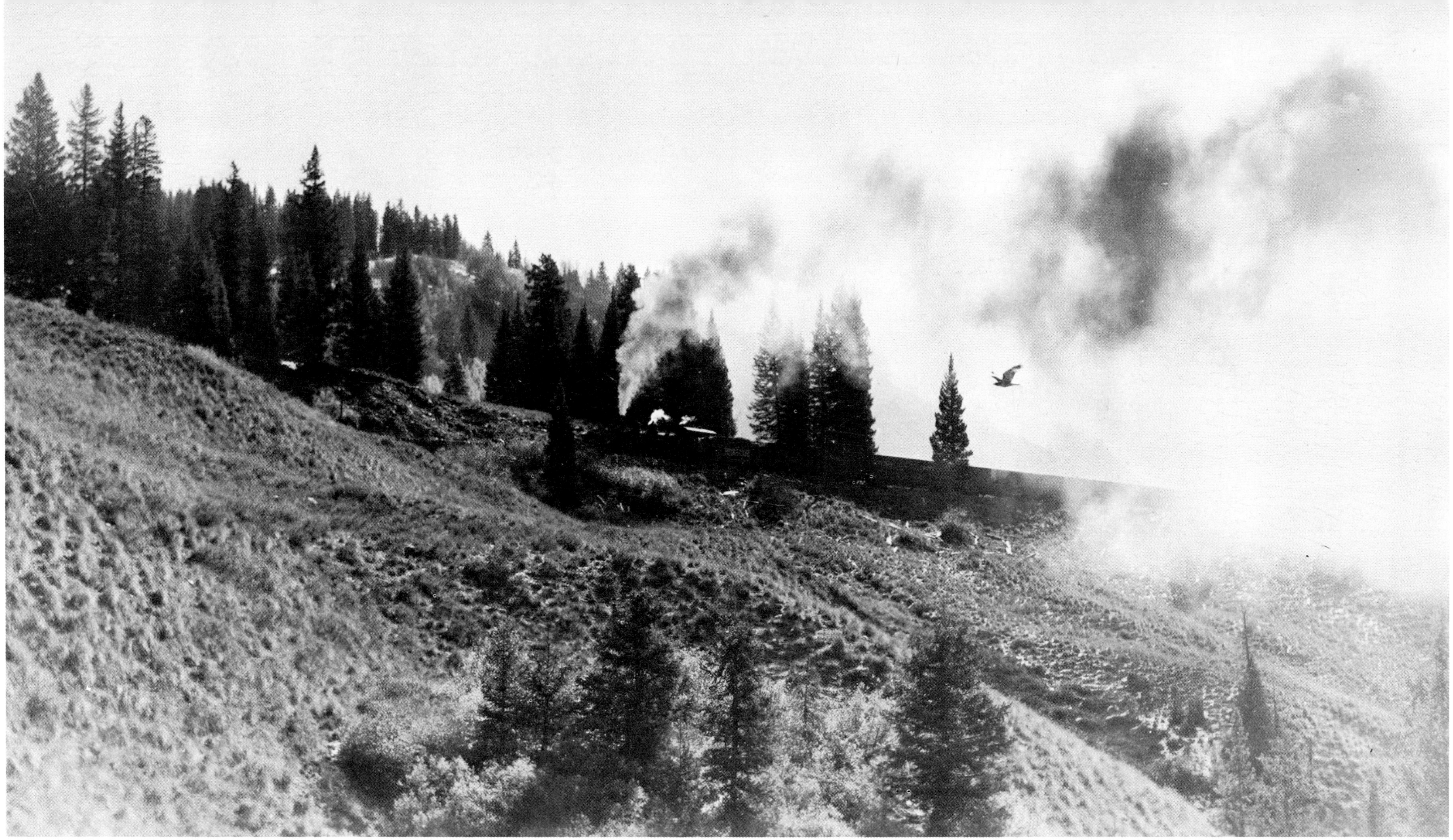

MORRIS W. ABBOTT COLLECTION - WM. R. JONES

ELMORE FREDERICK COLLECTION

LIZARD HEAD PASS

''As the Eagle flies, Gallagher, up Lizard Head Pass, Colorado'' wrote Otto on the back of his postcard October 6, 1951. Note the eagle in flight above the stock train pulled by 2-8-2 No. 461.

This fall stock extra had just cleared the snowsheds on top of Lizard Head Pass, 10,250' above sea-level. This same train appears on page 56.

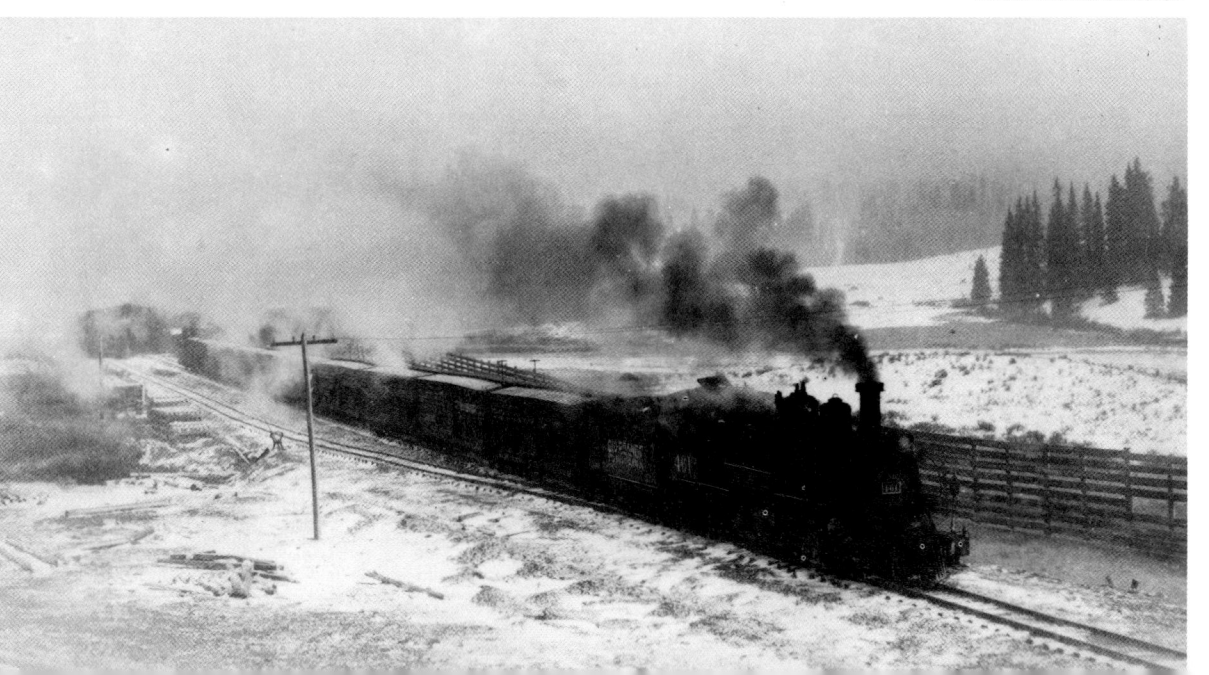

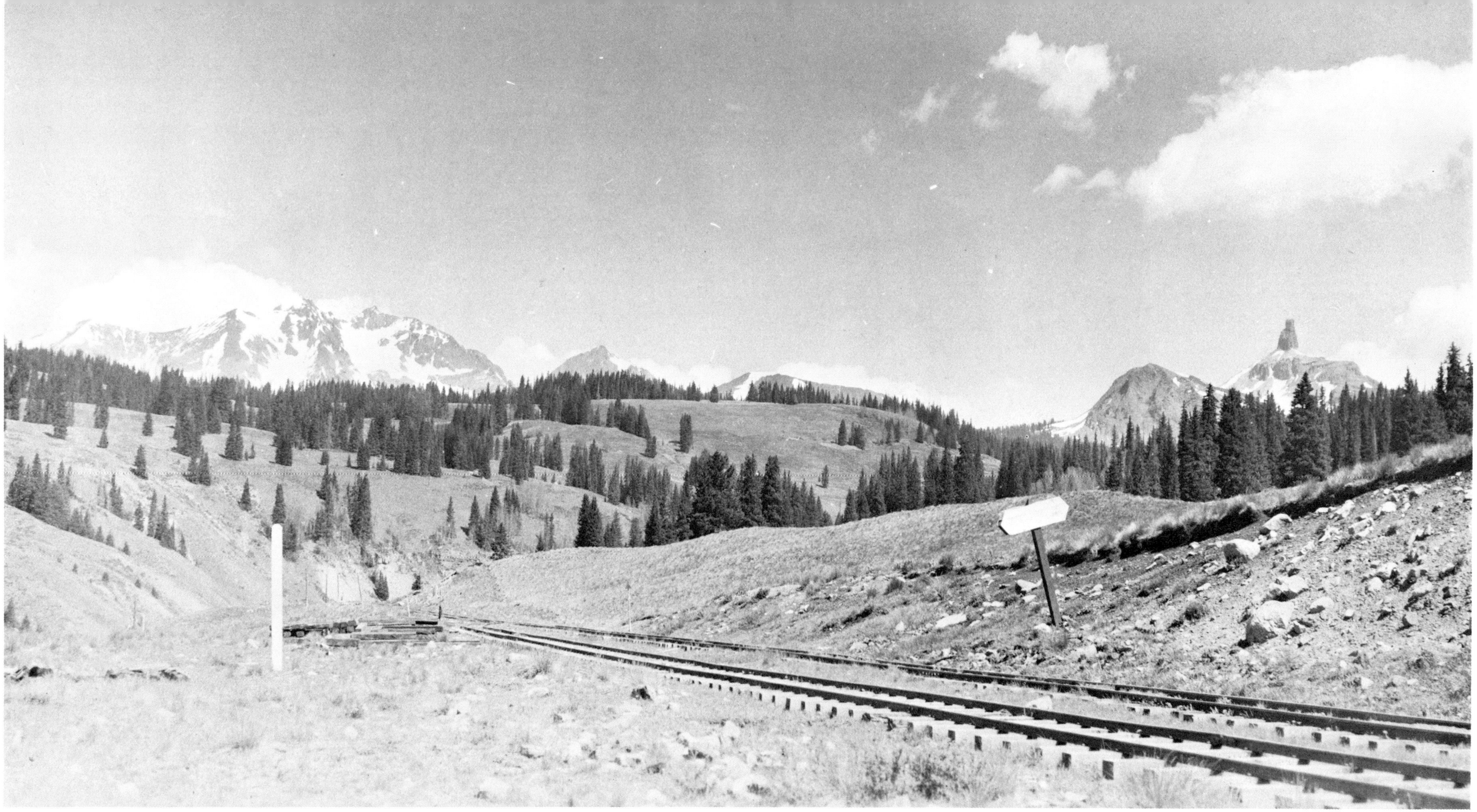

RICHARD A. RONZIO COLLECTION

RICHARD A. RONZIO COLLECTION

In this view, looking toward the distinctive rock formation named Lizard Head, seen to the right, the faded sign once read "Gallagher."

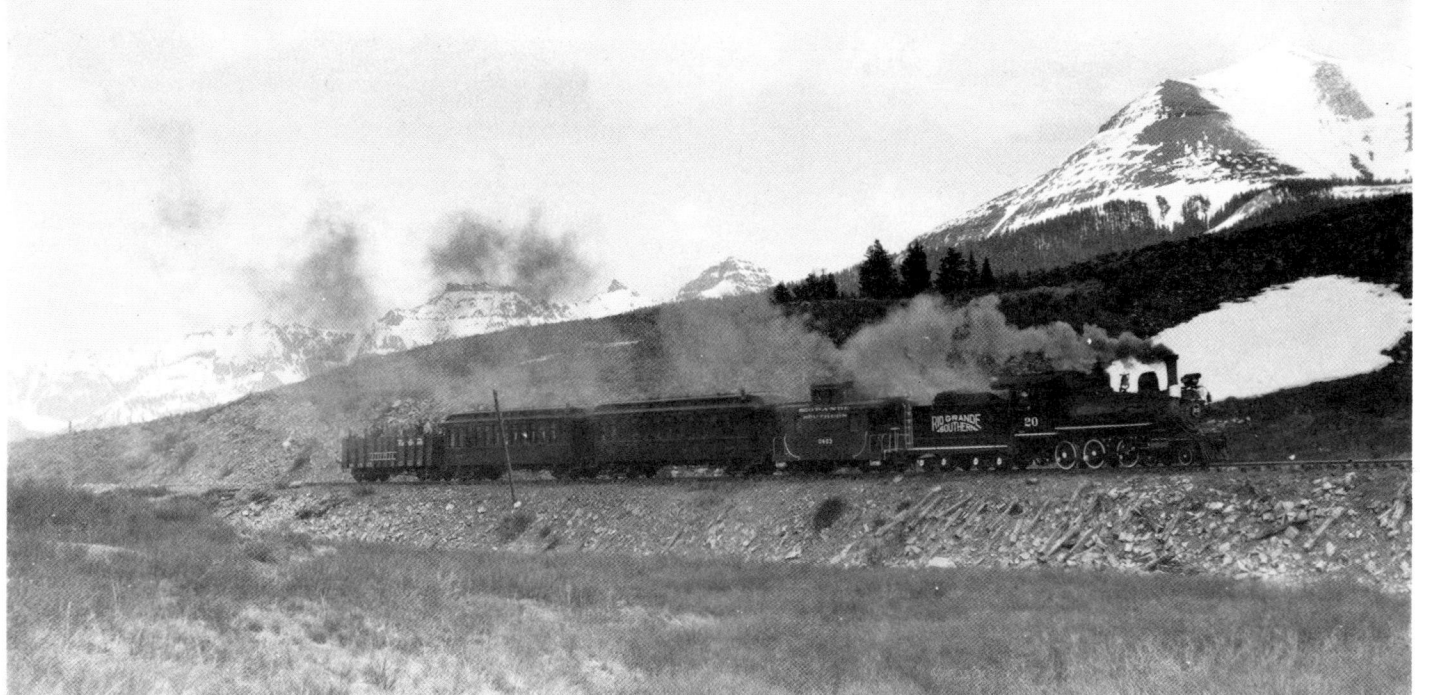

On a blustery May 30, 1947 members of the Rocky Mountain Railroad Club stopped just below the summit of Lizard Head Pass. The two coaches still feature the conductor's windows that identified them for Chili Line service.

Rio Grande Southern Locomotive Number 40 was in the vicinity of Trout Lake pulling Conoco oil tankers that soon would be obsolete.

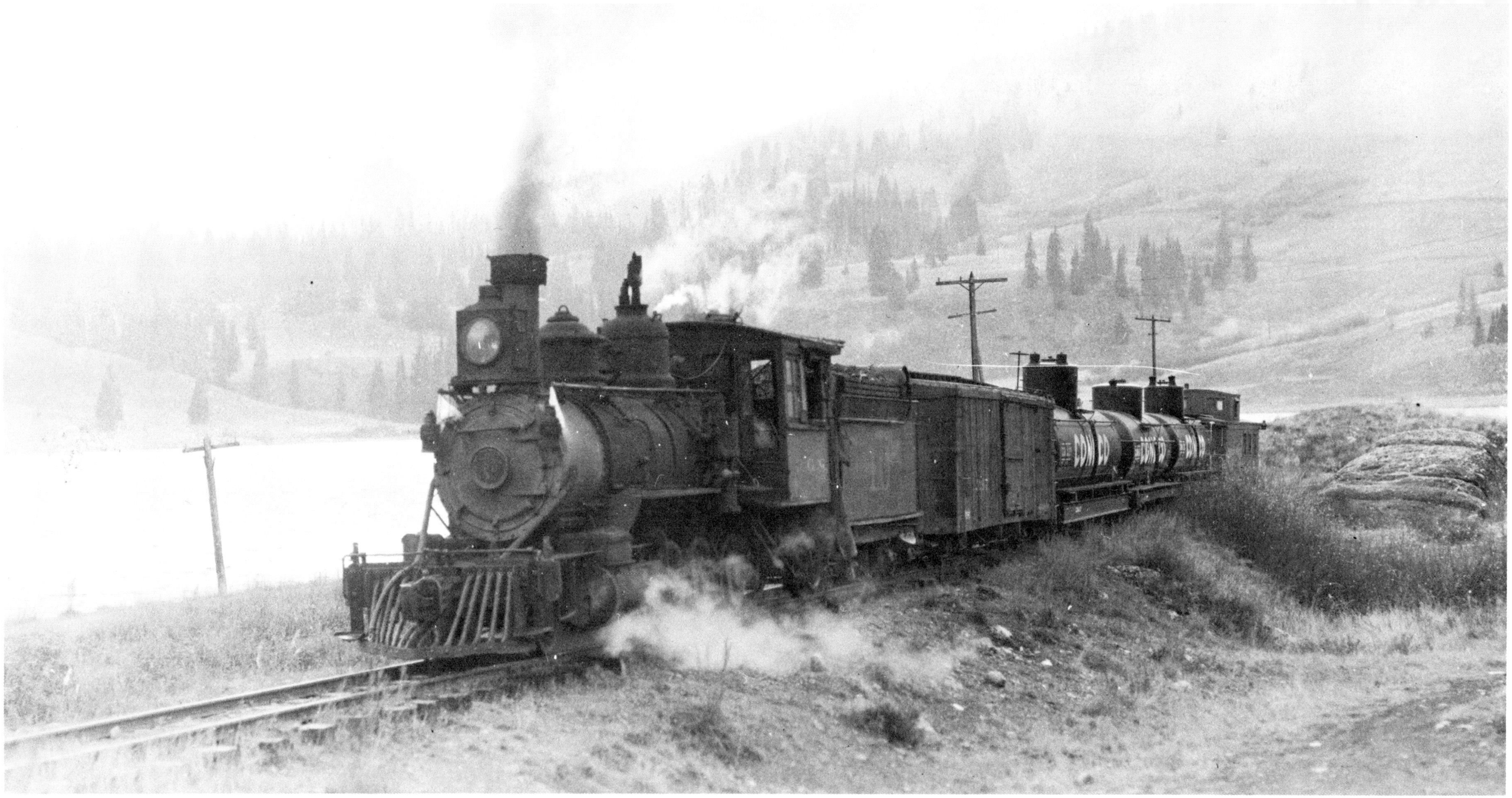

MORRIS W. ABBOTT COLLECTION - WM. R. JONES

RICHARD A. RONZIO COLLECTION

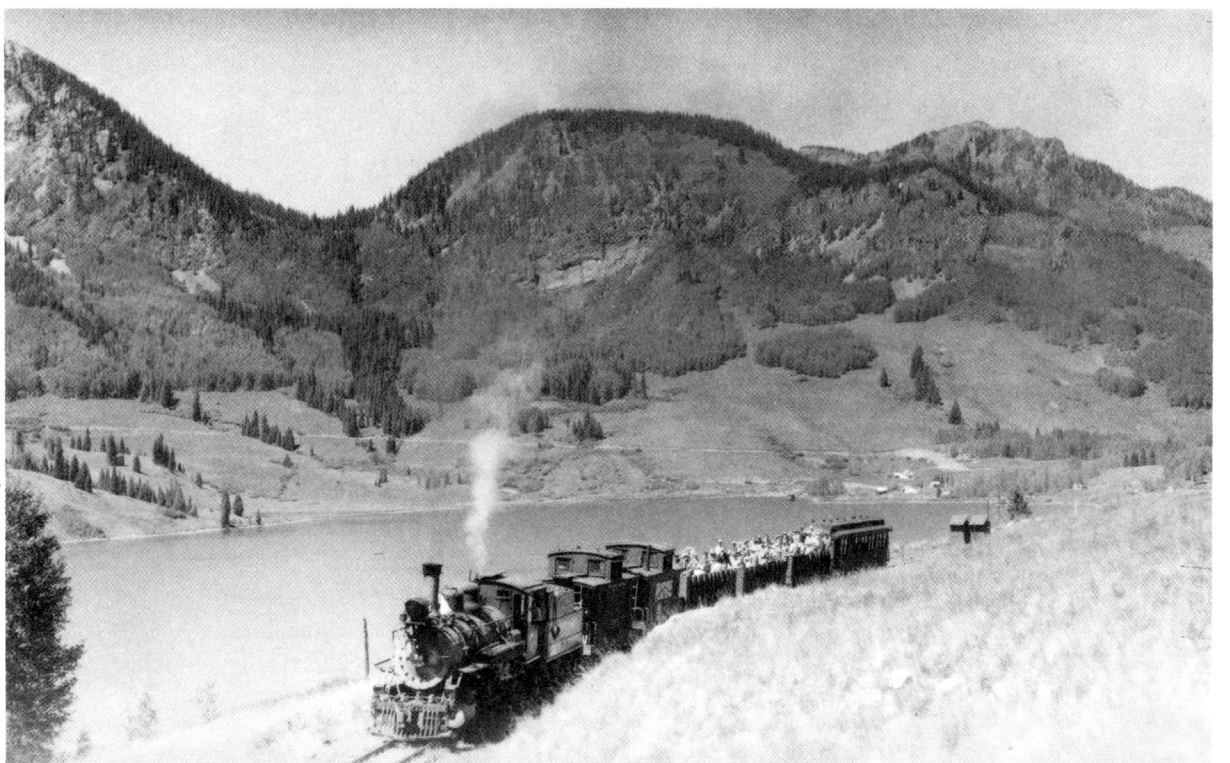

TROUT LAKE

A short, but heavy, freight was found rounding Trout Lake October 26, 1940. Low clouds with occasional snowflakes were making photography difficult for Otto on this occasion.

Another Rocky Mountain Railroad Club excursion found RGS locomotive Number 74 pulling the unusual consist on September 2, 1951. The small settlement of Trout Lake may be seen to the right. This was the final passenger run on the railroad.

A railroad legend was fading along with the autumn colors as the 461 eased a stock train down the spectacular trestles of Ophir, October 6, 1951. The same train appeared previously in Burns Canyon.

At Windy Point below Ophir the same stock train movement drifts downgrade toward Vance Junction.

RICHARD A. RONZIO COLLECTION

ELMORE FREDERICK COLLECTION

A southbound train had stopped at Sawpit, October 5, 1951 to switch out cars. The engine was No. 461.

Fall Creek made up the panorama behind this same stock train movement.

PLACERVILLE

The Rocky Mountain Railroad Club excursion of May 30, 1947 had stopped at Placerville. Engine 20, a former Florence & Cripple Creek 4-6-0, had been specially decorated for the occasion.

Otto Perry captured much of the excitment of mountain railroading when these two ancient locomotives struggled up Dallas Divide out of Placerville, beside Leopard Creek. The train was a special Civilian Conservation Corps movement on June 30, 1940.

RICHARD A. RONZIO COLLECTION

RICHARD A. RONZIO COLLECTION

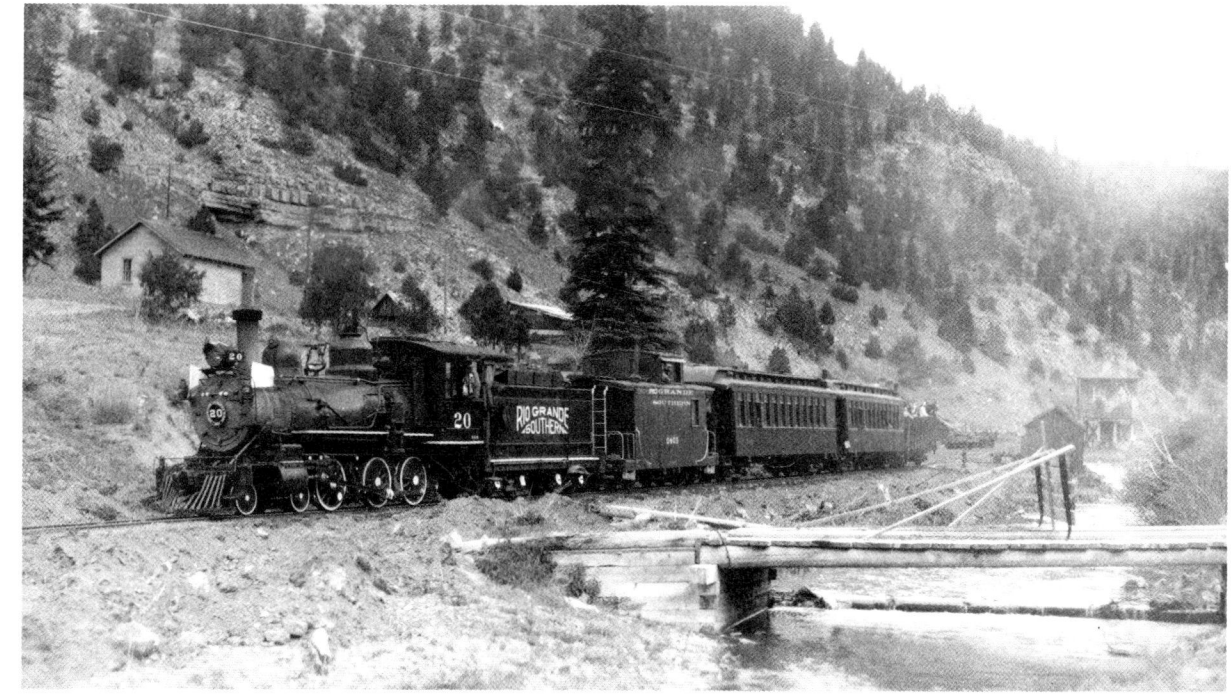

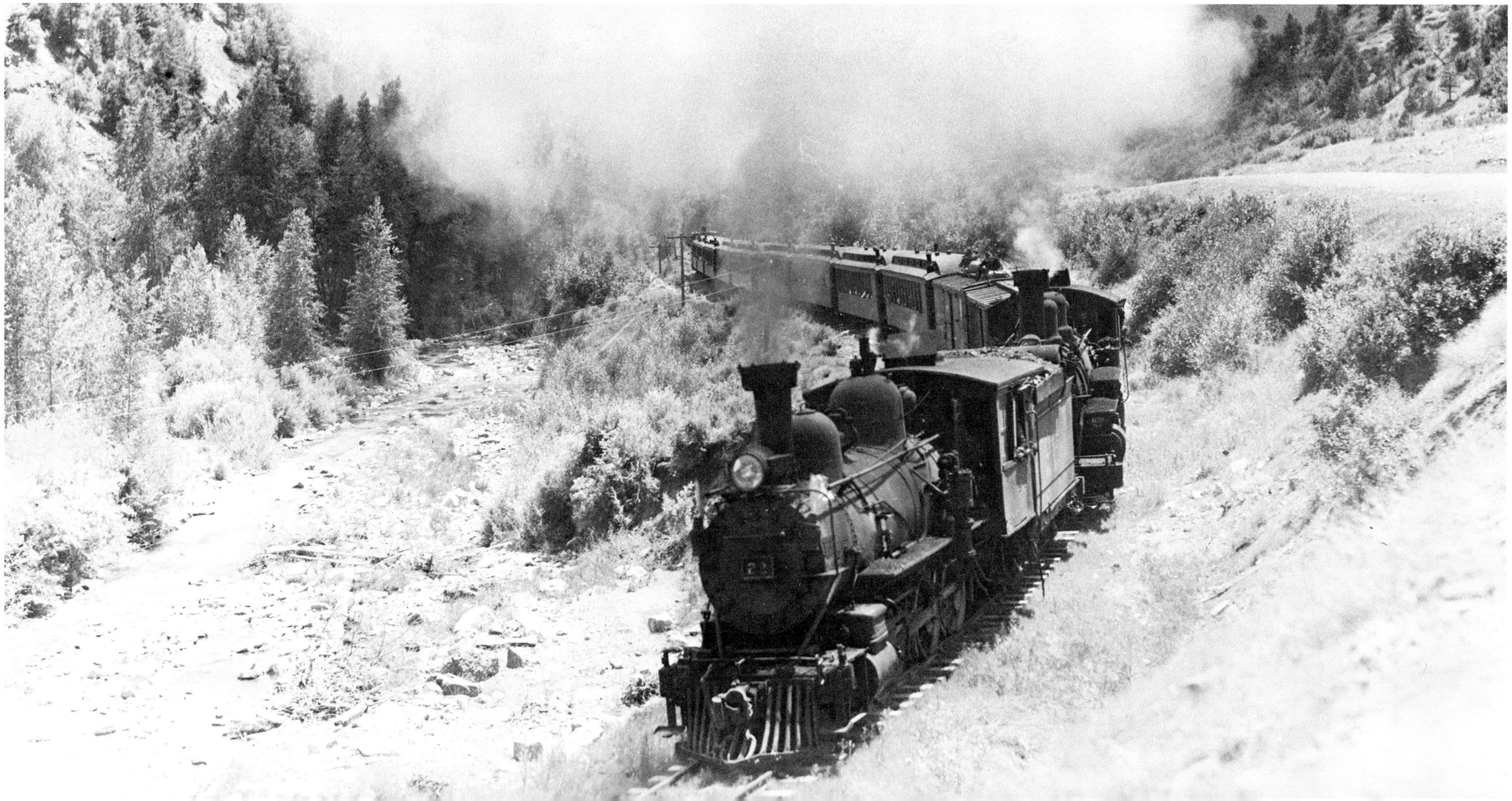

The 42 was assisting D&RGW 455 over Dallas Divide with a long string of stock cars during the fall of 1940.

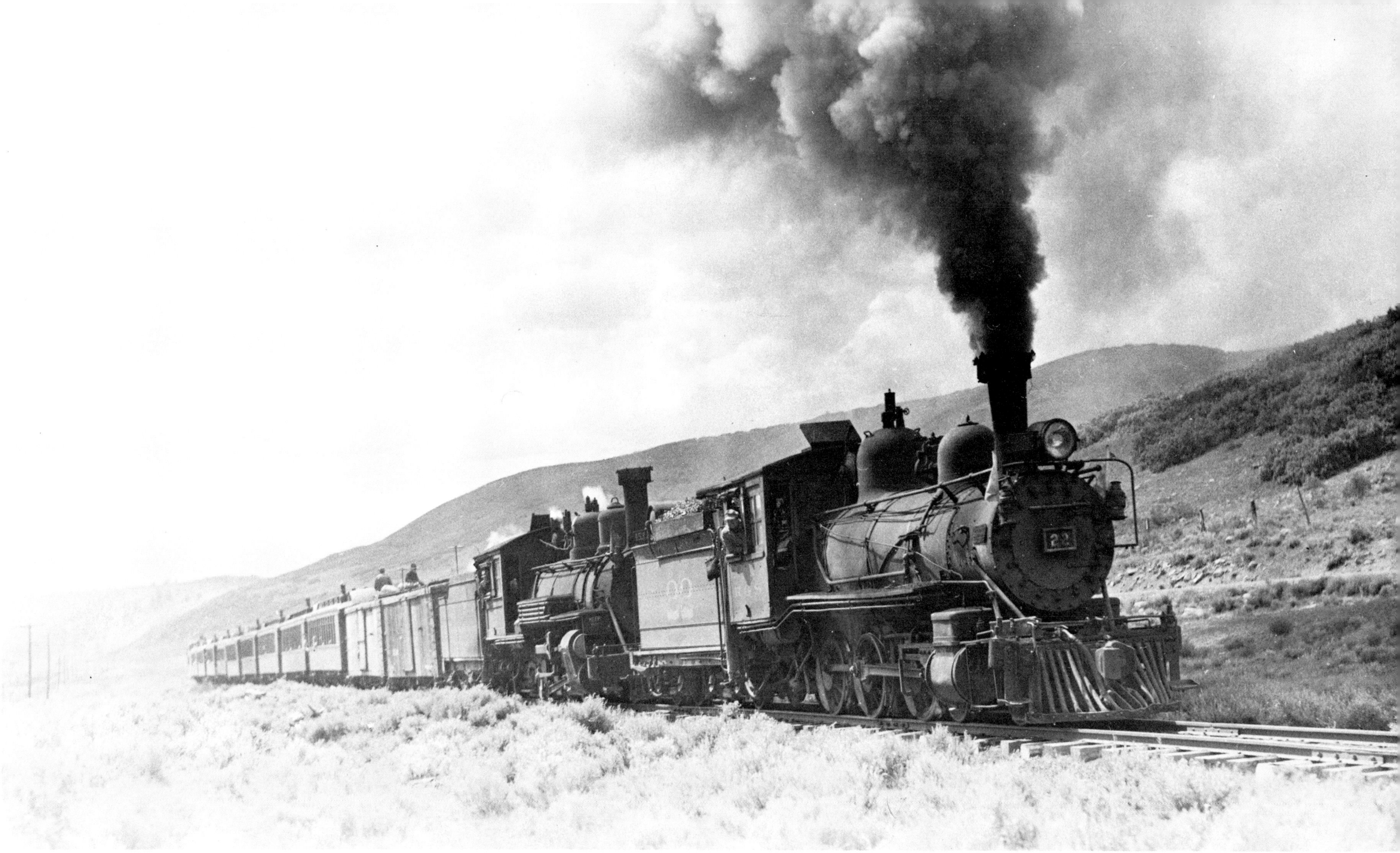

RICHARD A. RONZIO COLLECTION

DALLAS DIVIDE

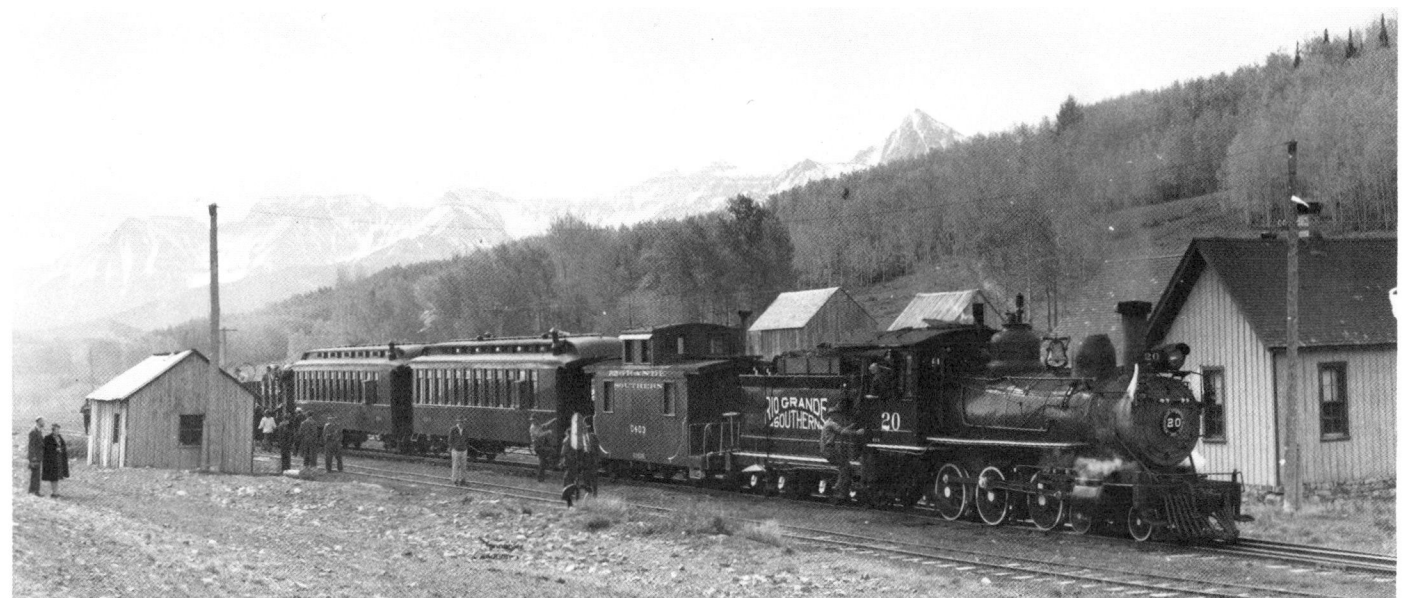

The Civilian Conservation Corps special was nearing the summit of Dallas Divide in this view taken June 30, 1940. The tools for the workmen were carried in the two boxcars.

RICHARD A. RONZIO COLLECTION

Gleaming paint and varnish were unusual on the RGS, but not when the Rocky Mountain Railroad Club chartered their excursions. The spring of May 30, 1947 found a group of famous old friends together on Dallas Divide. The San Miguel Range is seen in the distance.

The snows of late spring had left Mears Peak by October 2, 1951, when this stock train departed the Dallas Divide yard limit.

Leased D&RGW locomotive Number 464 handled boxcars of lead, zinc and vanadium over Dallas Divide on June 27, 1945.

The fall stock rush of October 24, 1940 found Otto Perry at one of his favorite locations along the 3% grade of Dallas Divide. The fireman waved, while beyond a brakeman rode the tops to turn up retainers once the top was reached.

Here the mixed CCC train of June 29, 1940, was steaming up the 4% grade toward Dallas Divide, near the summit.

Cresting the top of Dallas Divide, the mixed CCC consist of June 29, 1940 will drop down Leopard Creek to Placerville, thence over Lizard Head Pass to Dolores.

The 453 was thrashing upgrade from Ridgway with three coaches on the CCC mixed train June 29, 1940.

Originally a D&RG locomotive, engine No. 41 was simmering at Ridgway in the early 1940s. These light 2-8-0s and the heavier 2-8-2 K-27 class locomotives were the mainstay of RGS motive power.

At Ridgway on the morning of June 29, 1940, "Mudhen" 453—leased from the D&RGW awaited the conductor's highball to pull out for Dallas Divide with the CCC mixed train.

RIDGWAY

Colorado & Southern locomotive Number 70 was being readied for a morning trip up Clear Creek, out of Golden, for the mountain communities of Black Hawk and Idaho Springs. North Table Mountain forms the background on April 16, 1941 near the present Coors beer brewery.

Three Foot Narrow-Gauge Lines of Colorado

CHAPTER III

tto Perry made a great many trips to photograph the tiny Colorado & Southern, 3 foot narrow-gauge line, running up Clear Creek from Golden to Black Hawk, Central City and Georgetown. The area covered represented the first gold rush real-estate in Colorado, which in turn brought about the need for reliable transportation. The Colorado Central began laying their track toward Central City in 1872, with the tide of people from back East being overjoyed by finally having comfortable transportation into the mountains. Otto was on location with his cameras in the final days of train operations over the line to give us a glimpse of those "good old days" when life was simpler and moved a bit slower.

Based in Denver, the Colorado & Southern Railway's other 3 foot narrow-gauge line, known as "The old South Park Line," was right in Otto Perry's back yard. He lived close enough to the line to hear the diminutive locomotives whistle for grade crossings while pulling out of Denver for Leadville. This line was formally named The Denver South Park & Pacific; it reached such far away points as Leadville, Como, Breckenridge, Buena Vista and Gunnison. Otto journeyed often, along the dirt highways in search of new scenes by the South Platte River and across windy South Park, up until the last rails were pulled prior to World War II.

The Denver Boulder & Western 3 foot gauge line, running west from Boulder and the Uintah stretching north from Mack, were also the subjects of Otto's cameras. It is remarkable that Otto would make many of those trips by himself, when gasoline stations were hard to locate and an automobile breakdown could mean perhaps a week's delay in those remote areas.

GOLDEN, WESTBOUND

C&S 70 was pulling a long freight out of the Golden yard limits in this view taken May 4, 1941, as spring was arriving in the Colorado foothills. Fuel was a major source of revenue for the C&S at this time, as indicated by gondolas loaded with coal.

RICHARD A. RONZIO COLLECTION

The morning hours of May 4, 1941 were overcast, allowing Otto Perry a good photo of the 70 in shadow. The train of flat cars was headed up Clear Creek, with Golden obscured by haze beyond the caboose.

The 70 was drifting downgrade along Clear Creek in this photograph taken May 4, 1941. Having picked up loads from Black Hawk and Idaho Springs the heavy train carried ore concentrate in the boxcars and ore bearing rock inside the gondolas.

A short distance below Idaho Springs, near Floyd Hill, Otto photographed the 70 pulling a short train up grade, while backing with two boxcars and caboose.

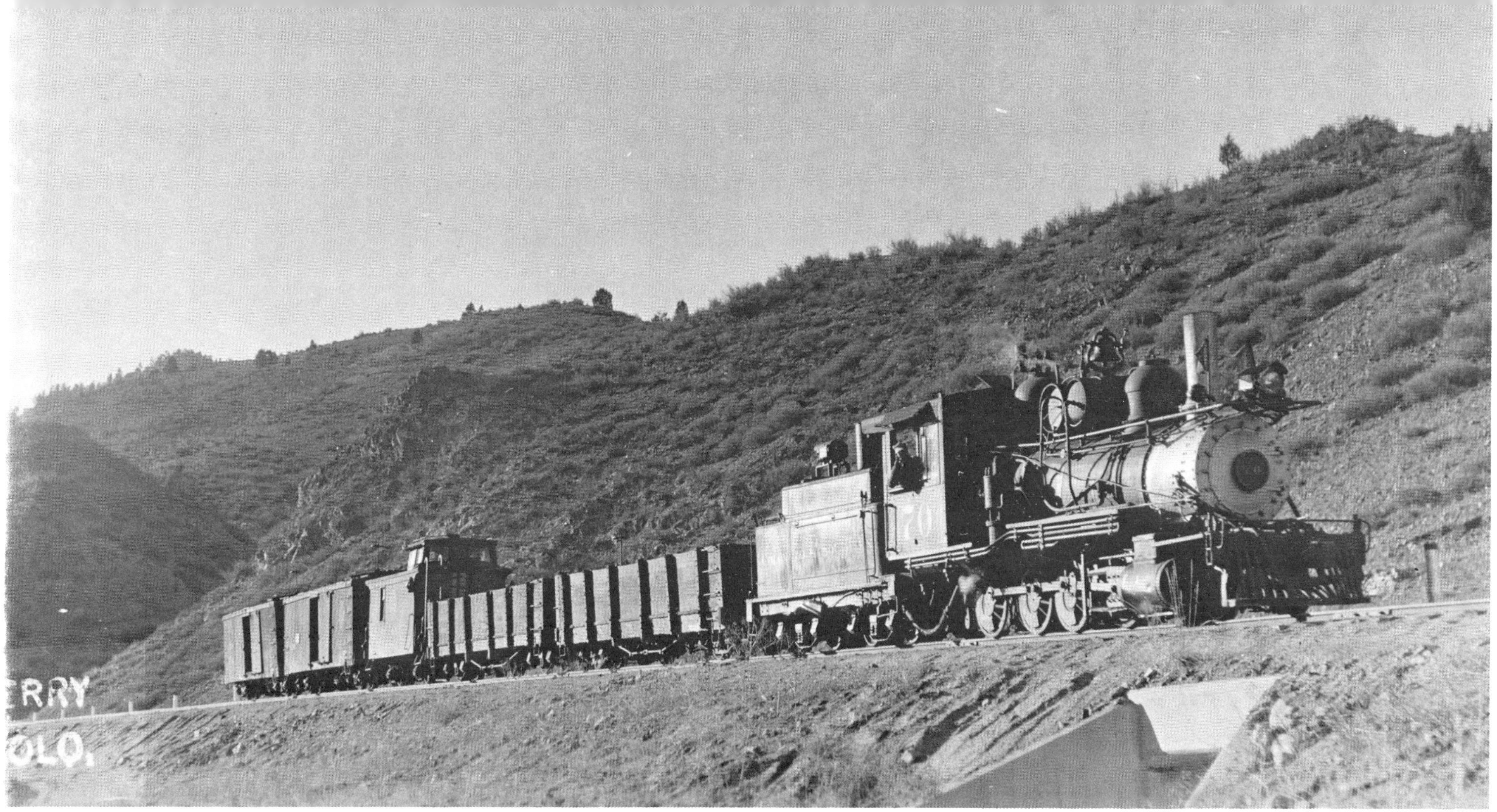

RICHARD A. RONZIO COLLECTION

The barren hills north of Beaver Brook form the scene behind the 70 as she brings a string of rolling stock down from Black Hawk April 16, 1941.

The train previously shown at Golden had reached a point just below Idaho Springs, while backing uphill, May 4, 1941.

Colorado & Southern locomotive Number 69 had the unpleasant task of hauling rail removed from the Georgetown Loop to Golden. The train was photographed leaving Idaho springs on March 21, 1939.

RICHARD A. RONZIO COLLECTION

RICHARD A. RONZIO COLLECTION

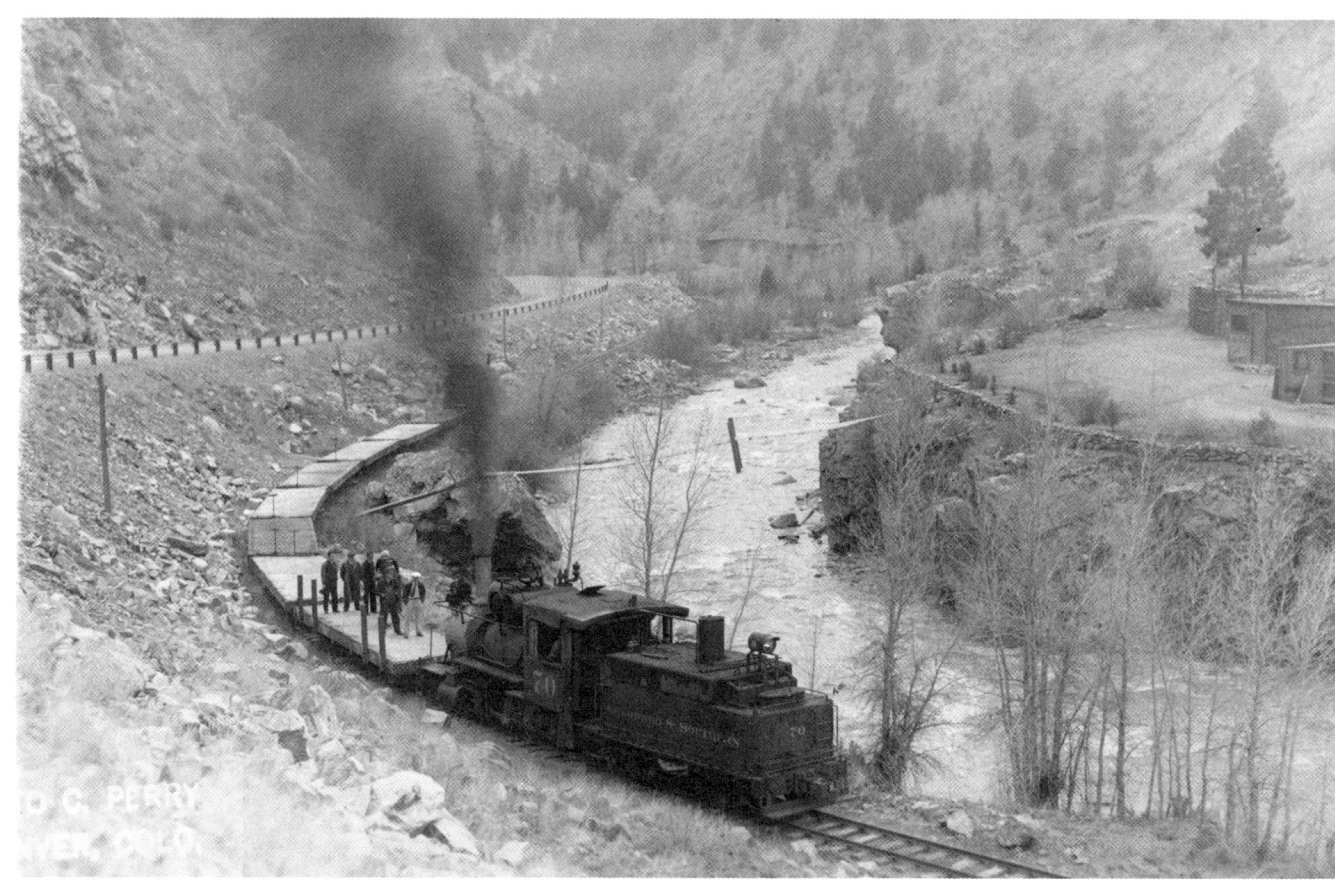

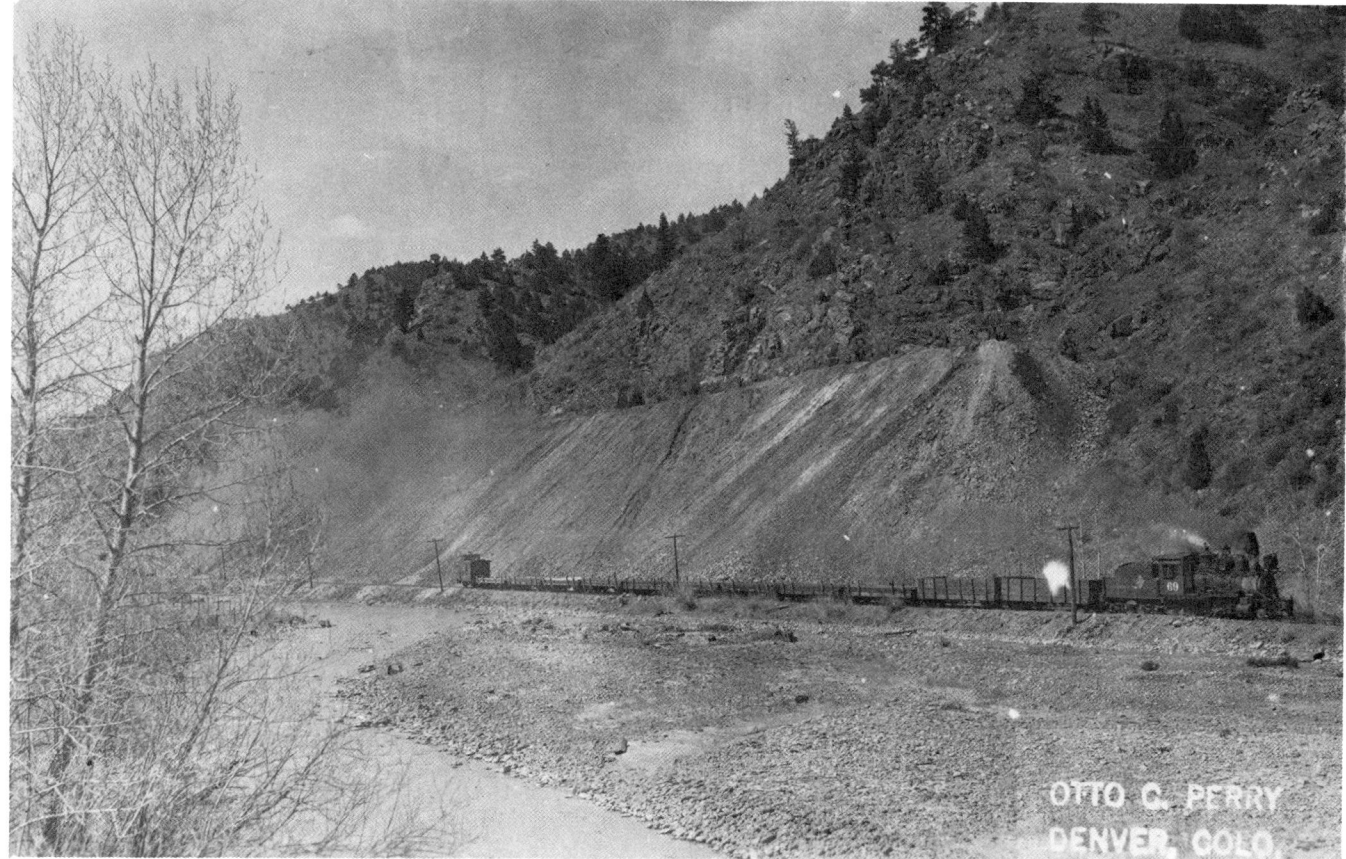

With abandonment of the C&S, mining at Idaho Springs and Black Hawk closed down. This was nearly the last train in Idaho Springs, April 16, 1941, beside the old Argo Tunnel.

Otto Perry moved in close for this shot of C&S 68 switching cars at Lawson in Clear Creek Canyon on March 13, 1939.

RICHARD A. RONZIO COLLECTION

RICHARD A. RONZIO COLLECTION

The 70 was gathering rolling stock for the last roundup west of Idaho Springs in this view taken April 16, 1941.

The Colorado & Southern Railroad set up a display of their narrow-gauge equipment at Central City. This photo shows that equipment spotted at Black Hawk in 1941.

OLD SOUTH PARK LINE

This 1918 photograph, taken in the Colorado & Southern's terminal area, showed tiny locomotive Number 21, a 2-6-0 built in 1882 for the DSP&P.

Denver Union Depot provided the setting for this rare photo Otto Perry had taken in 1916. The depot trackage still included 3-foot narrow-gauge track to accommodate passenger service to Leadville.

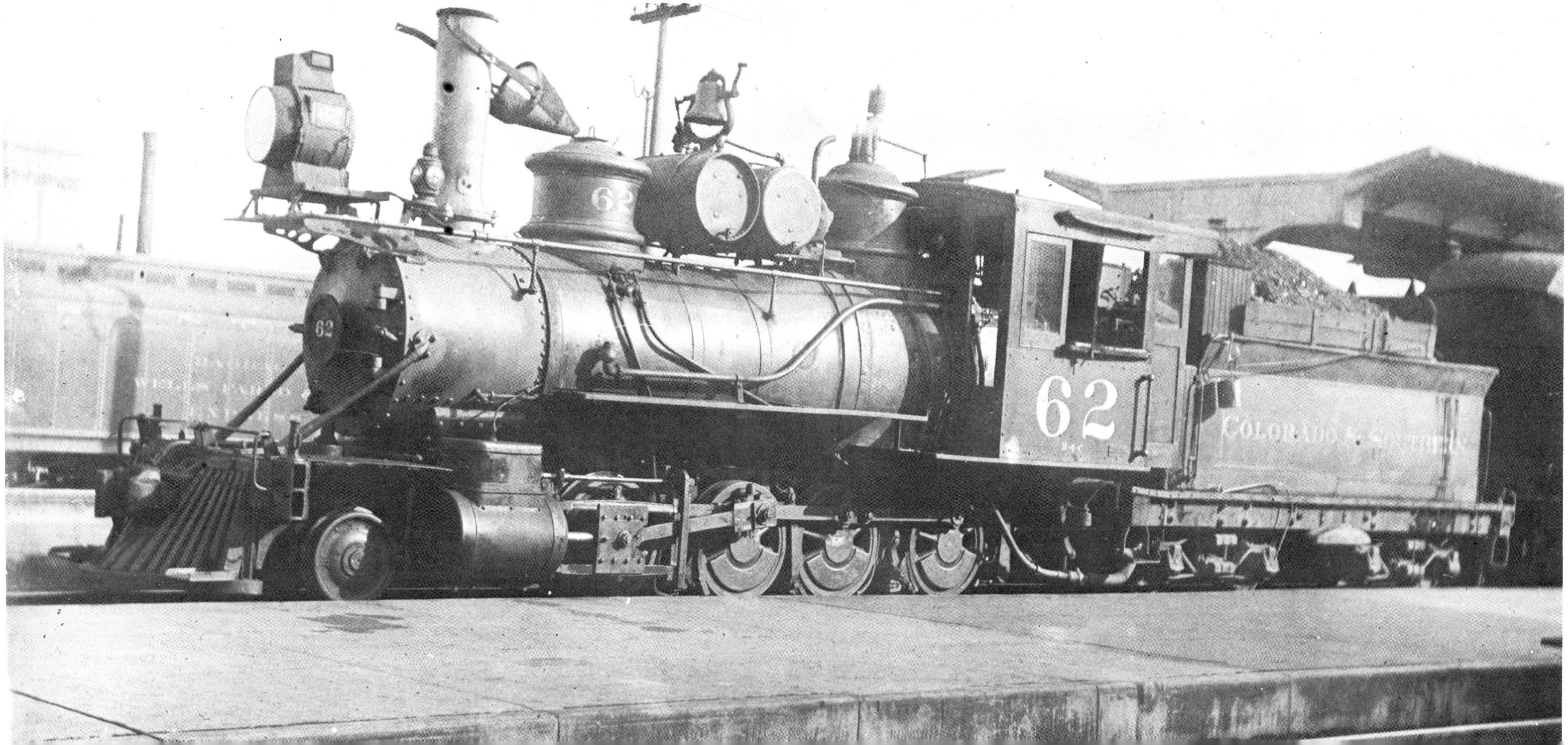

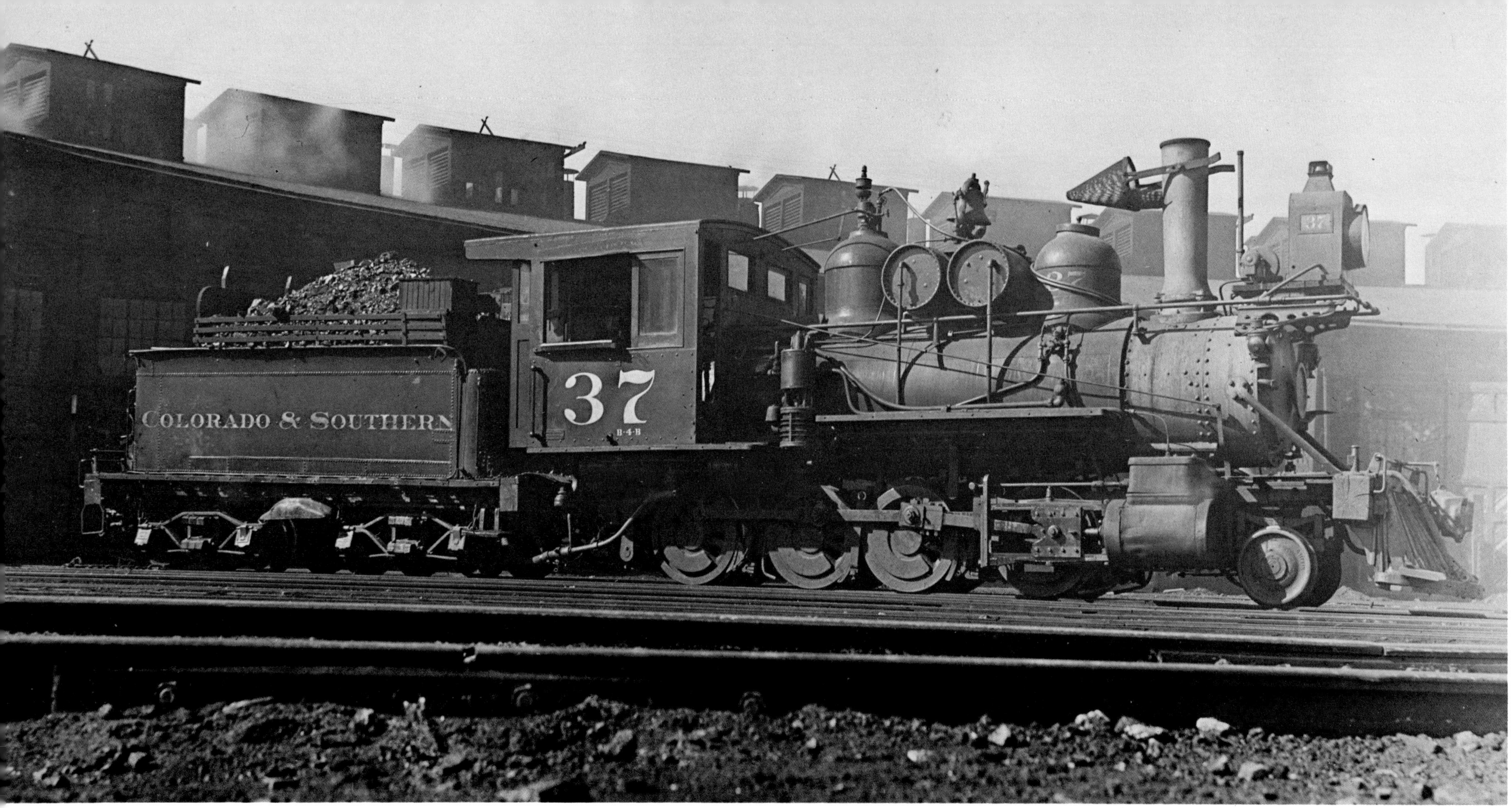

Locomotive Number 37 had her cinder screen cone tilted back, outside the Denver roundhouse in this photograph taken in 1917.

Stock cars in the background were used to transport coal in the off-season for stock movements. The 22 had stopped in sunlight that showed off running gear detail in Denver during July 1918.

The familiar "bear trap" spark arrestor of C&S narrow-gauge steam locomotives was in place on the 64 in 1921, shown here at Denver.

The 59 was steamed up ready for a freight one day back in January 1923. The dirt and grime covering this road engine proves she may need to be shopped soon.

Denver was the setting for this photograph of 1923, showing 2-6-0 No. 12 in her modernized version, which includes steel plate on the cab, air reservoir over the boiler, and "bear trap" spark arrestor, along with electric headlight.

RICHARD A. RONZIO COLLECTION

RICHARD A. RONZIO COLLECTION

RICHARD A. RONZIO COLLECTION

The 67, shown here at Denver in May 1925, was ready for a run. The fireman may have taken time to wash off the cab, since the number shows up cleaner than the remainder of the locomotive and tender.

Sunlight bathed the 61 in the Denver terminal, October 1926.

Photographed in 1931, C&S locomotive Number 10 was equipped with wedge plow for snowbucking. She was probably used in passenger service.

RICHARD A. RONZIO COLLECTION

RICHARD A. RONZIO COLLECTION

RICHARD A. RONZIO COLLECTION

Locomotive Number 5 rested her tender on the C&S turntable as the engine hostler showed her to a visitor, in July, 1918.

This southbound consist was known as the "fish train," stepping along past Overland Park, in the city of Denver, during 1918.

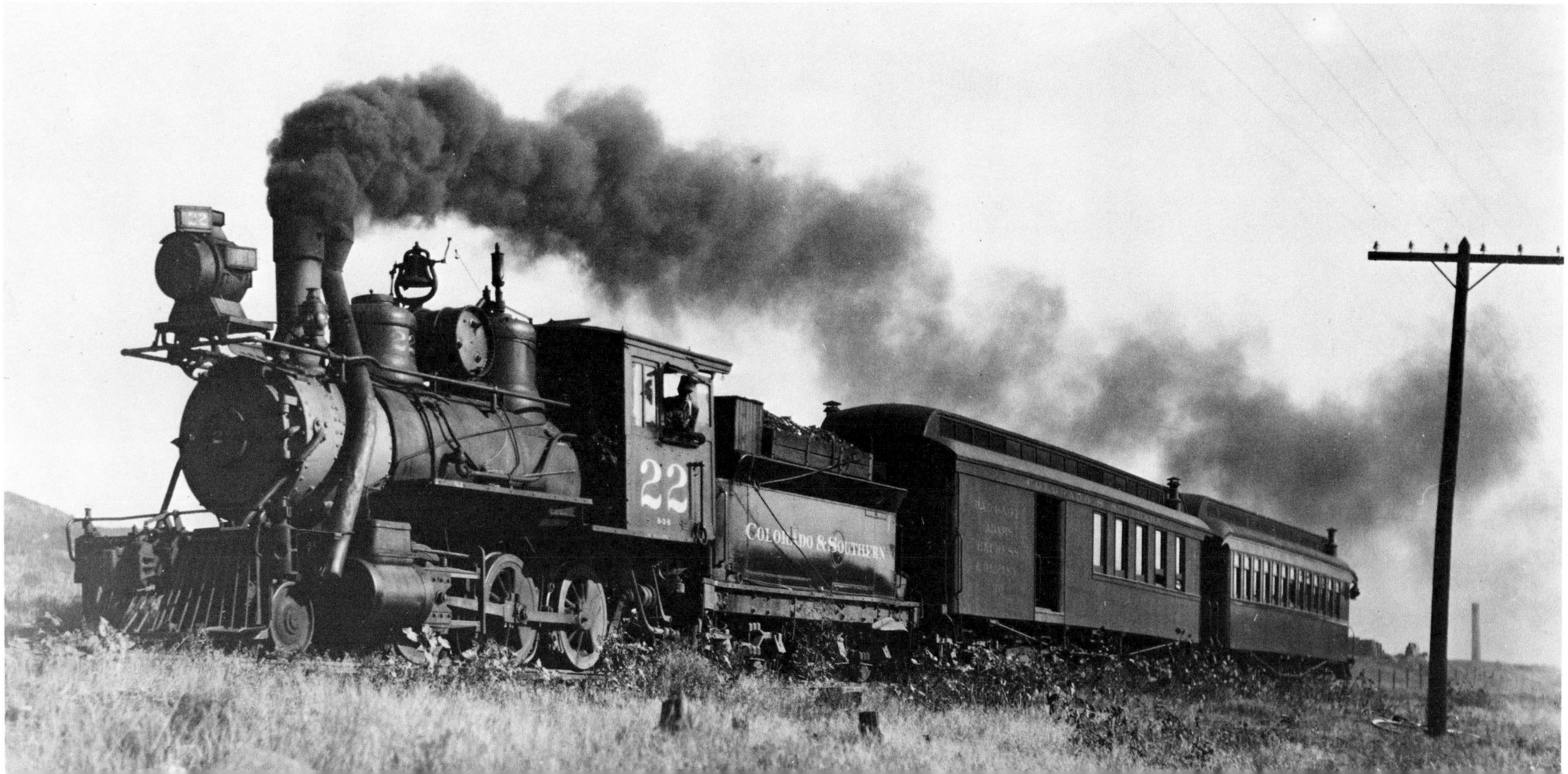

The end of the Silica branch provided the setting for this photo in 1941. Even though the branch was technically abandoned, mining activity provided carloads of mineral, making it profitable to run trains, until dismantling in 1942.

Impressive, to say the least, this photo of a freight train pulled by 4 locomotives, Numbered 68, 69, 8, and 58, was most unusual. The scene was east of Waterton, taken April 1, 1937. The South Park's last train was April 9, 1937. Thirteen revenue cars were in the first half of the train and 4 followed. Increased business at the Climax molybdenum mine accounted for these heavy trains so near the end of operations.

ELMORE FREDERICK COLLECTION

Locomotive Number 70 was pulling an unusually long train into Denver, during August of 1938. She was just north of Waterton.

Another view north of Waterton found the Leadville to Denver passenger on April 8, 1933.

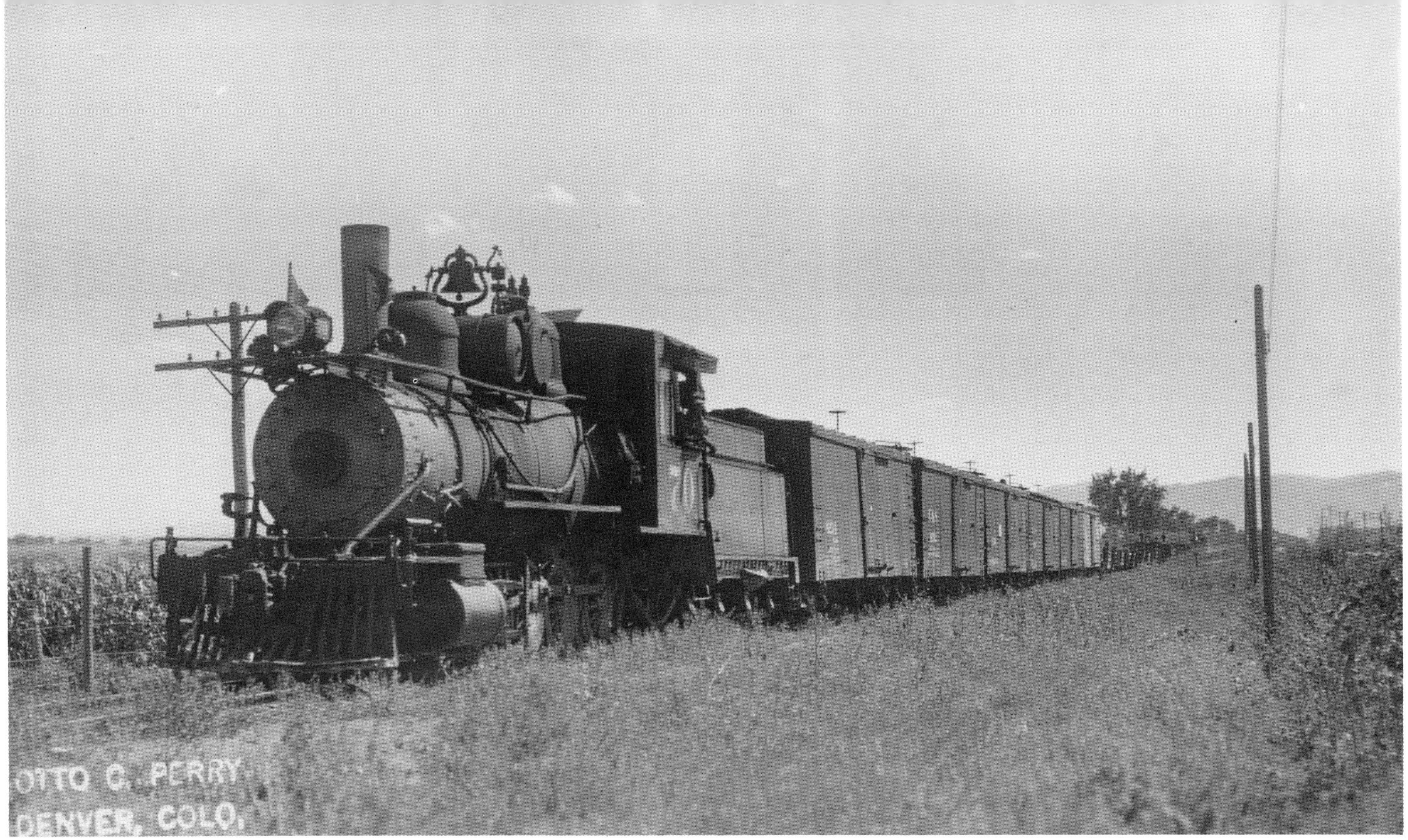

RICHARD A. RONZIO COLLECTION

RICHARD A. RONZIO COLLECTION

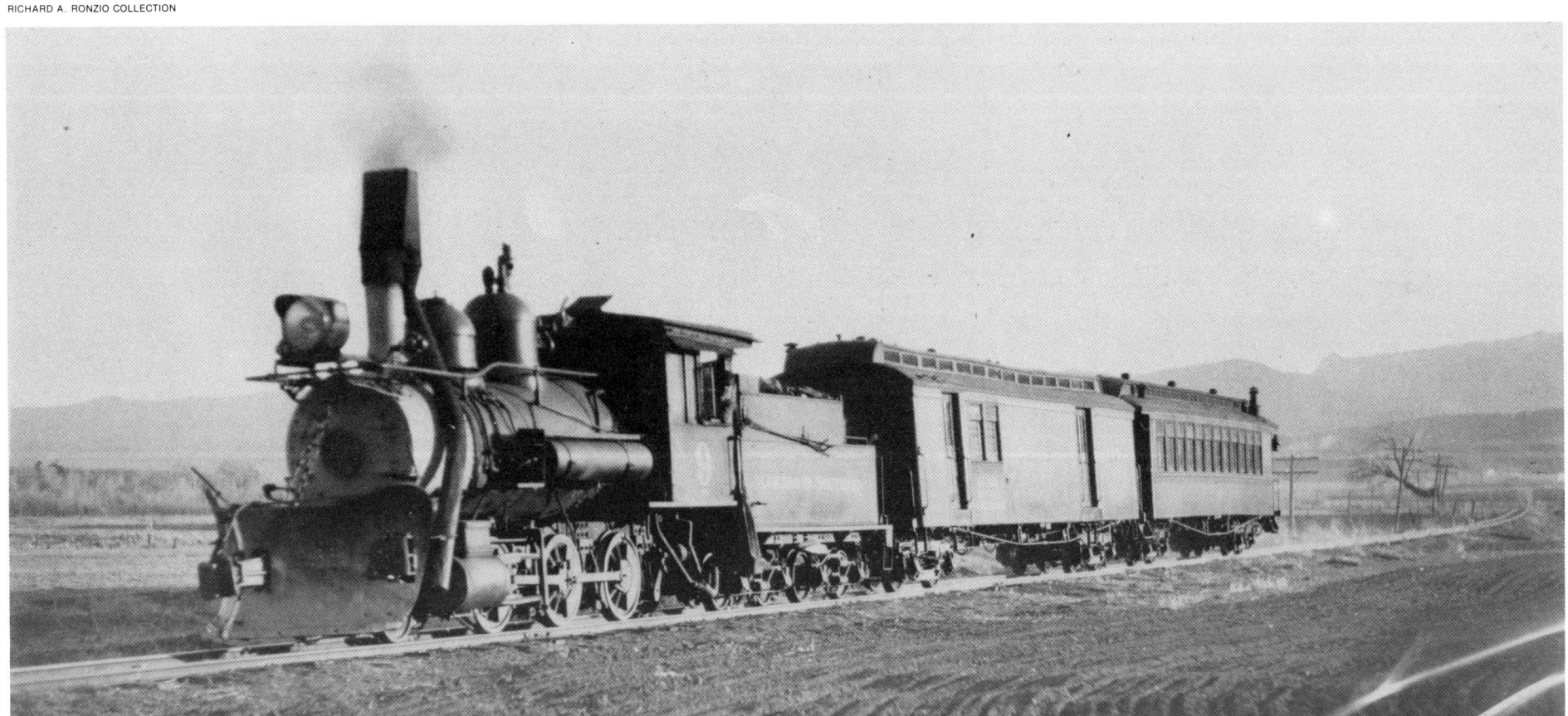

March 31, 1941 was the date of this train movement that came down from South Platte. Engines 69 and 70 had 25 cars in tow.

The 70 was pulling a scrap train near South Platte station in this view taken on October 23, 1938.

The 537, leased from the CB&Q from their Deadwood Central line, helped locomotive Number 72 with the last roundup of rolling stock on the Old South Park line. They had stopped at Webster April 11, 1937, having come off Kenosha Pass.

The locomotives uncoupled from their train in order to move more easily beneath the water spout at Webster, while one of the brakemen checked out the brake rigging beneath a boxcar.

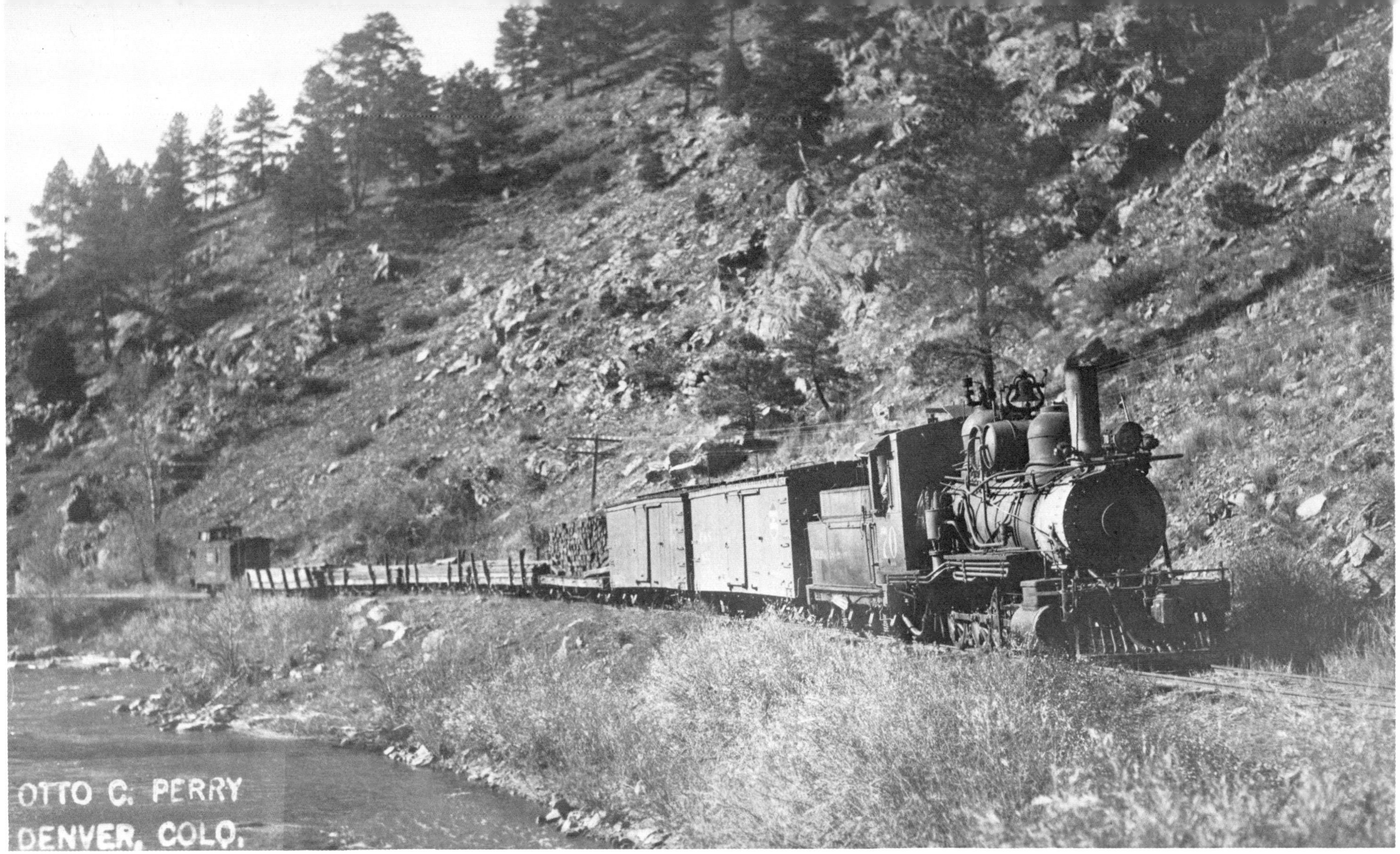

RICHARD A. RONZIO COLLECTION

RICHARD A. RONZIO COLLECTION

RICHARD A. RONZIO COLLECTION

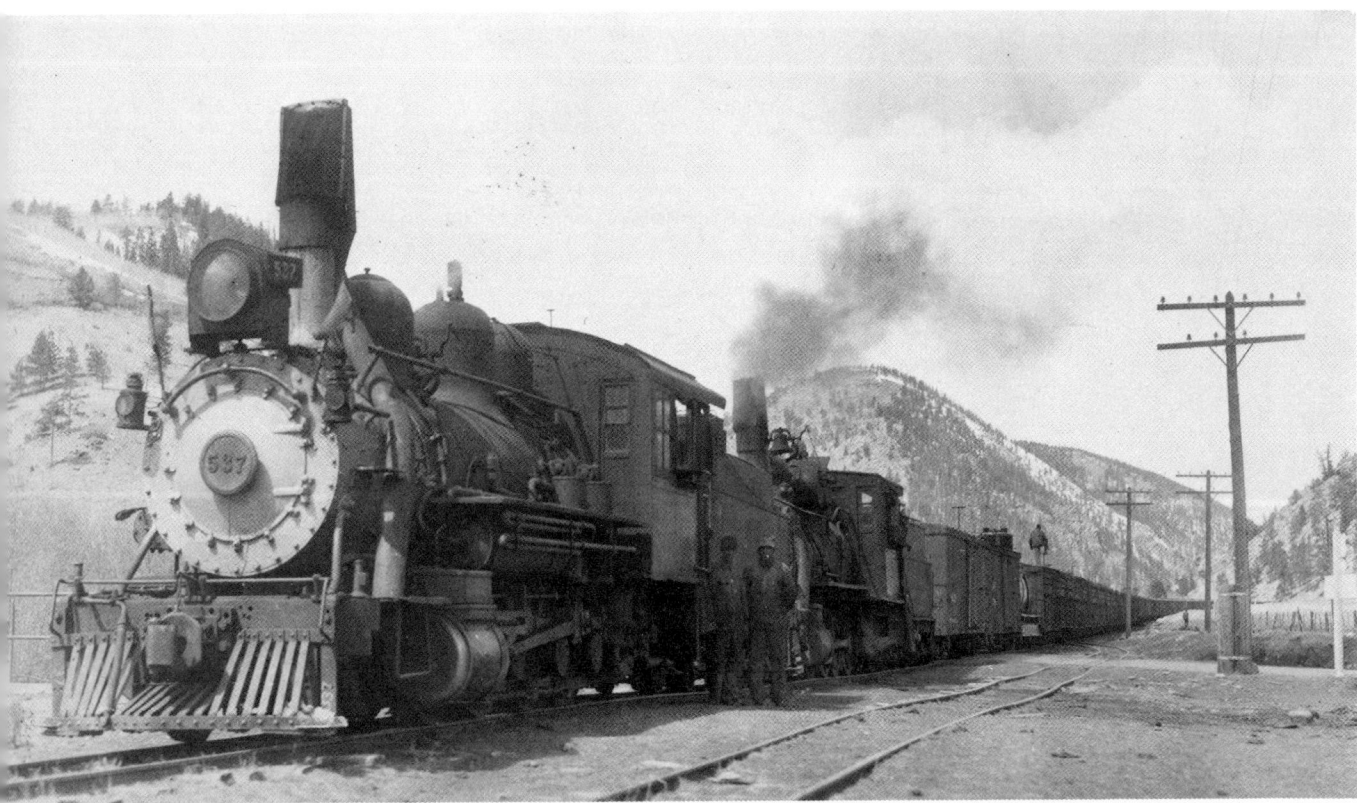

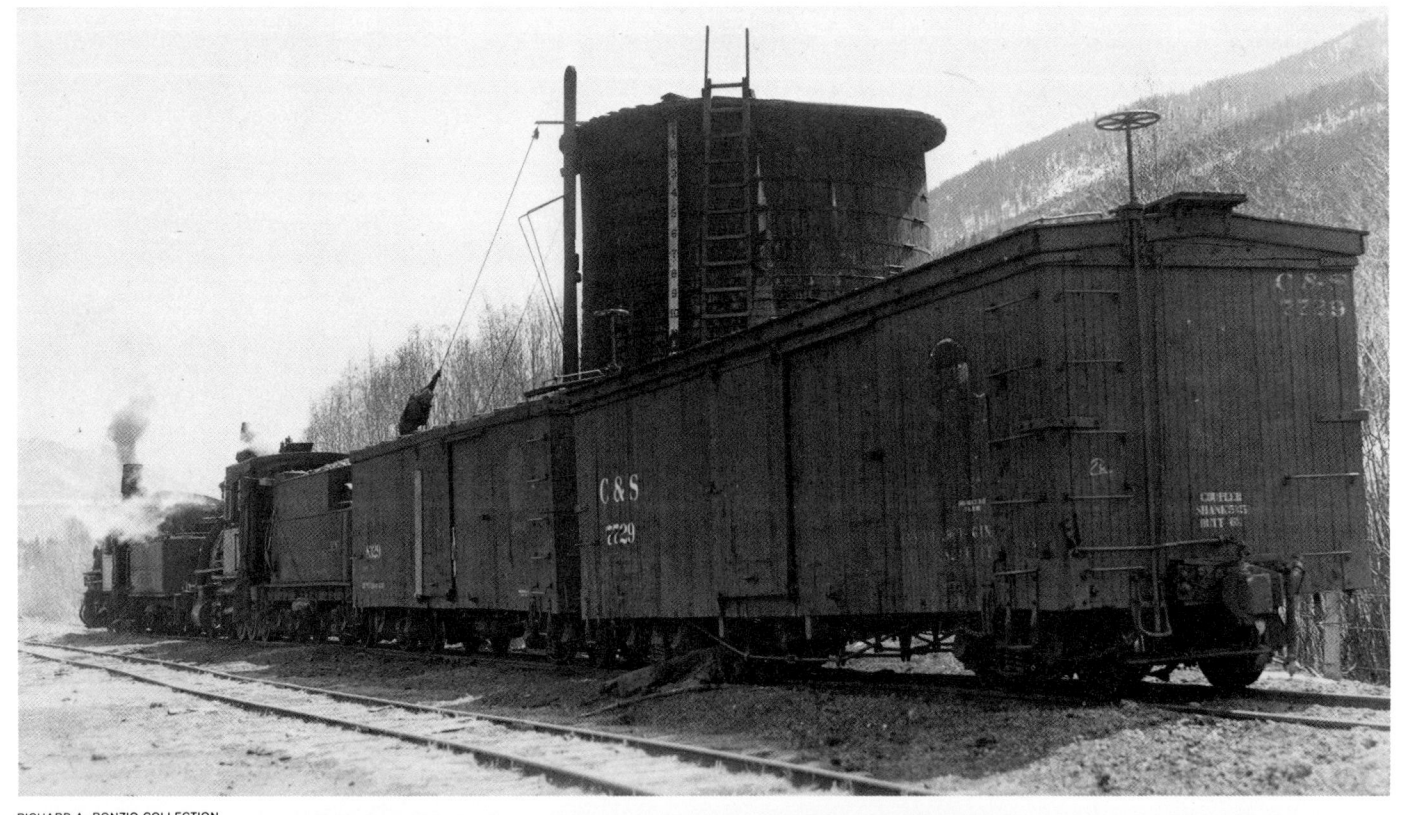

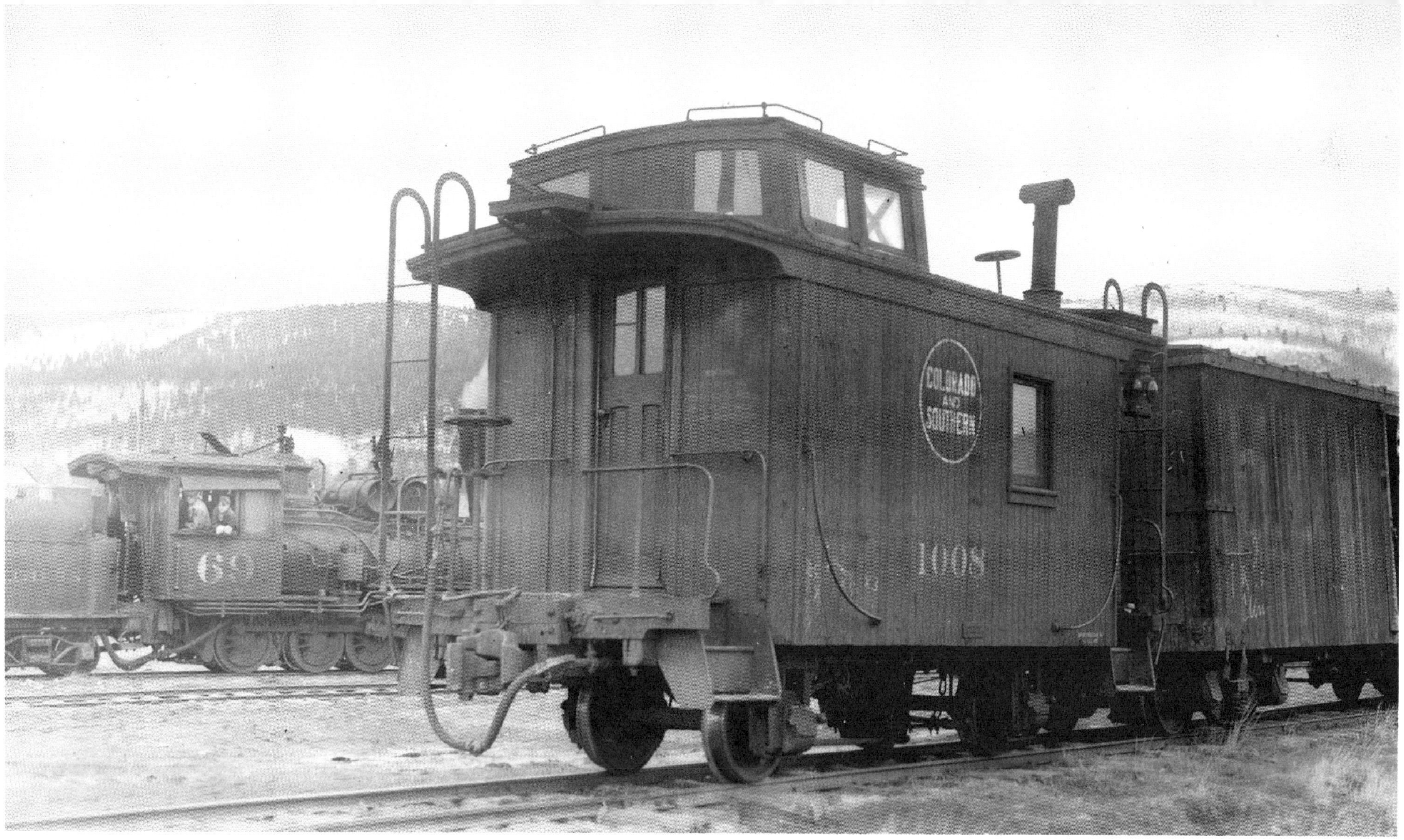

RICHARD A. RONZIO COLLECTION

Colorado & Southern bobber Number 1008 made an excellent photo on an overcast day at Como, a division point for the system.

Snow was one of the old South Park's worst enemies, especially in South Park. These two views, taken at Como in 1937, show part of the problem with snow packing into every crevice of the running gear. Otto had probably taken a train ride to Leadville and back.

RICHARD A. RONZIO COLLECTION

RICHARD A. RONZIO COLLECTION

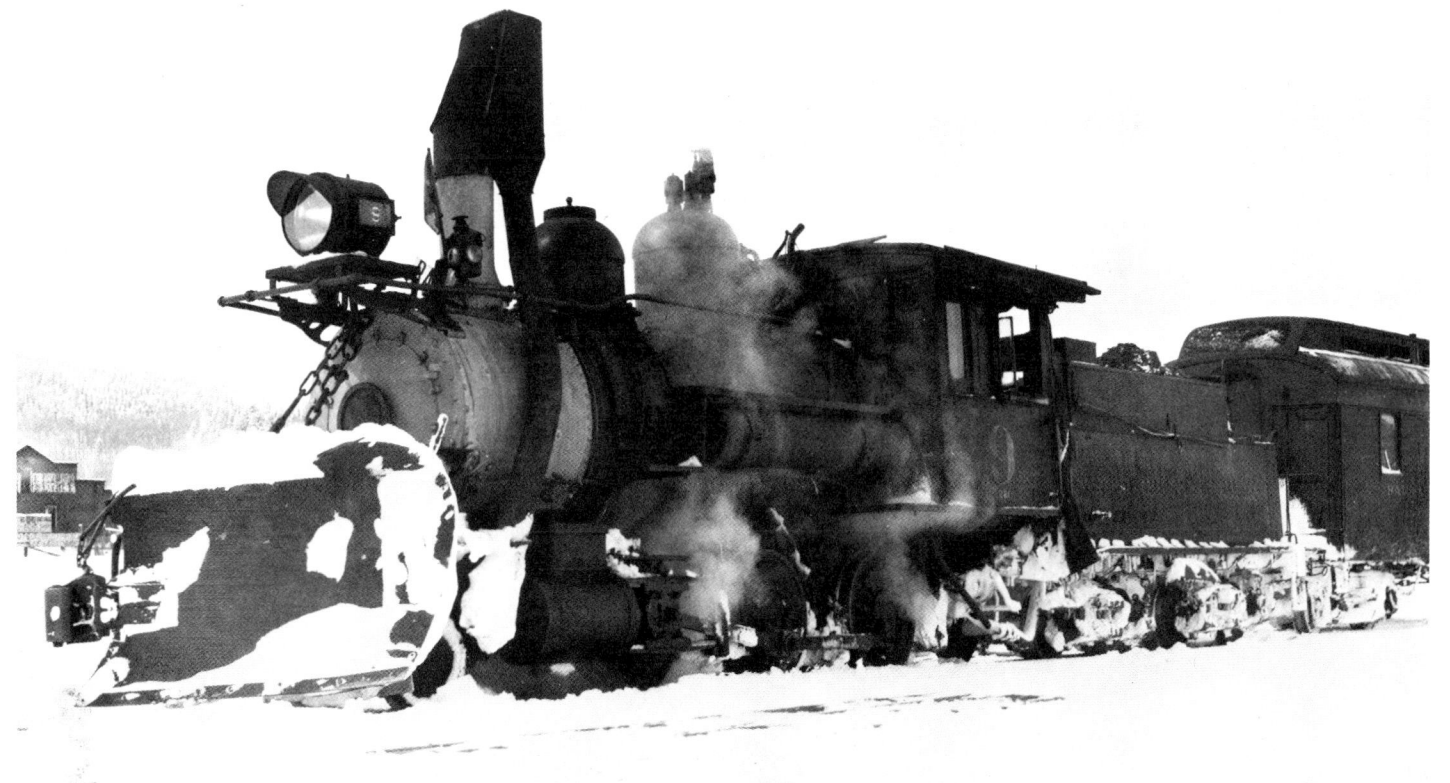

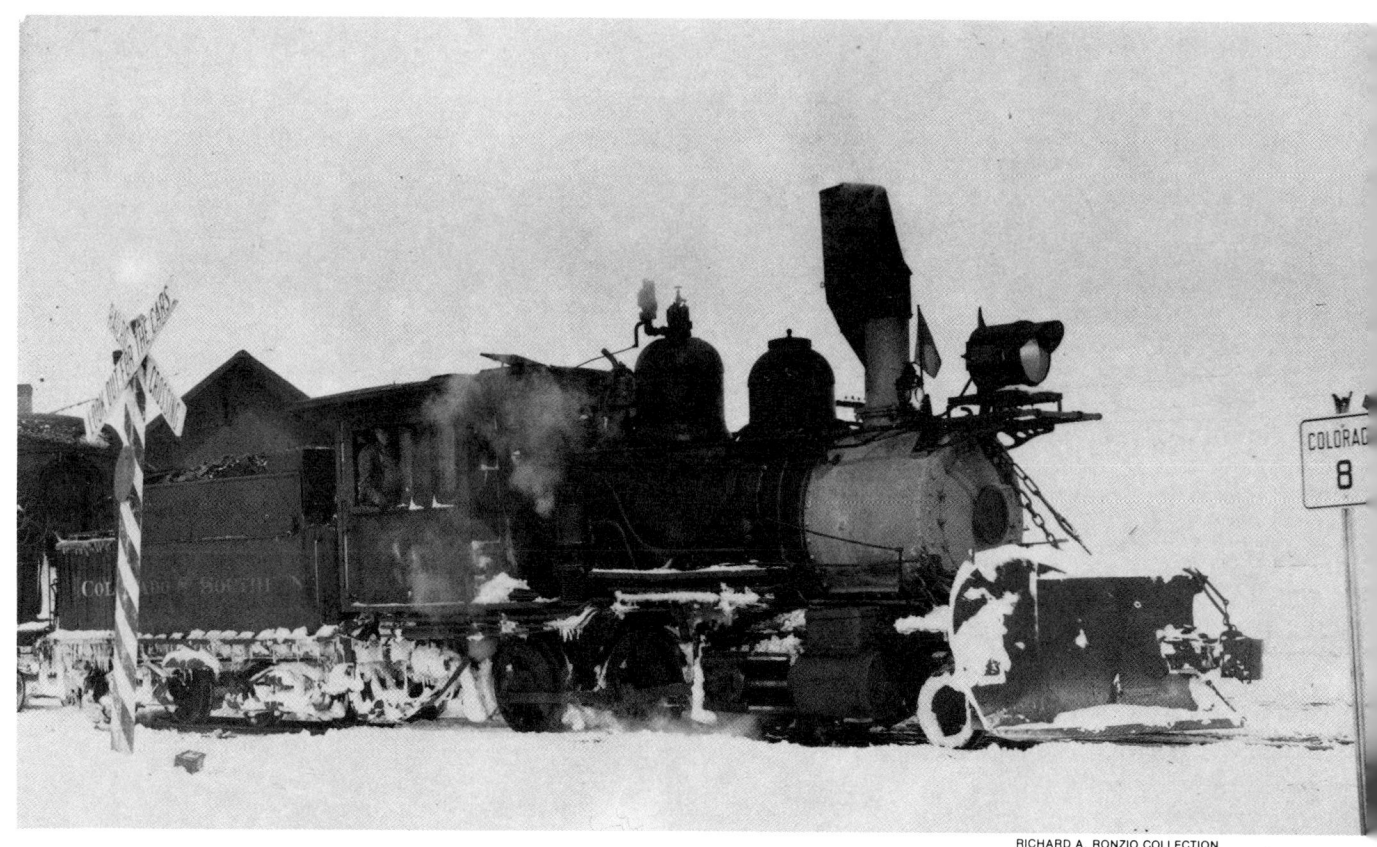

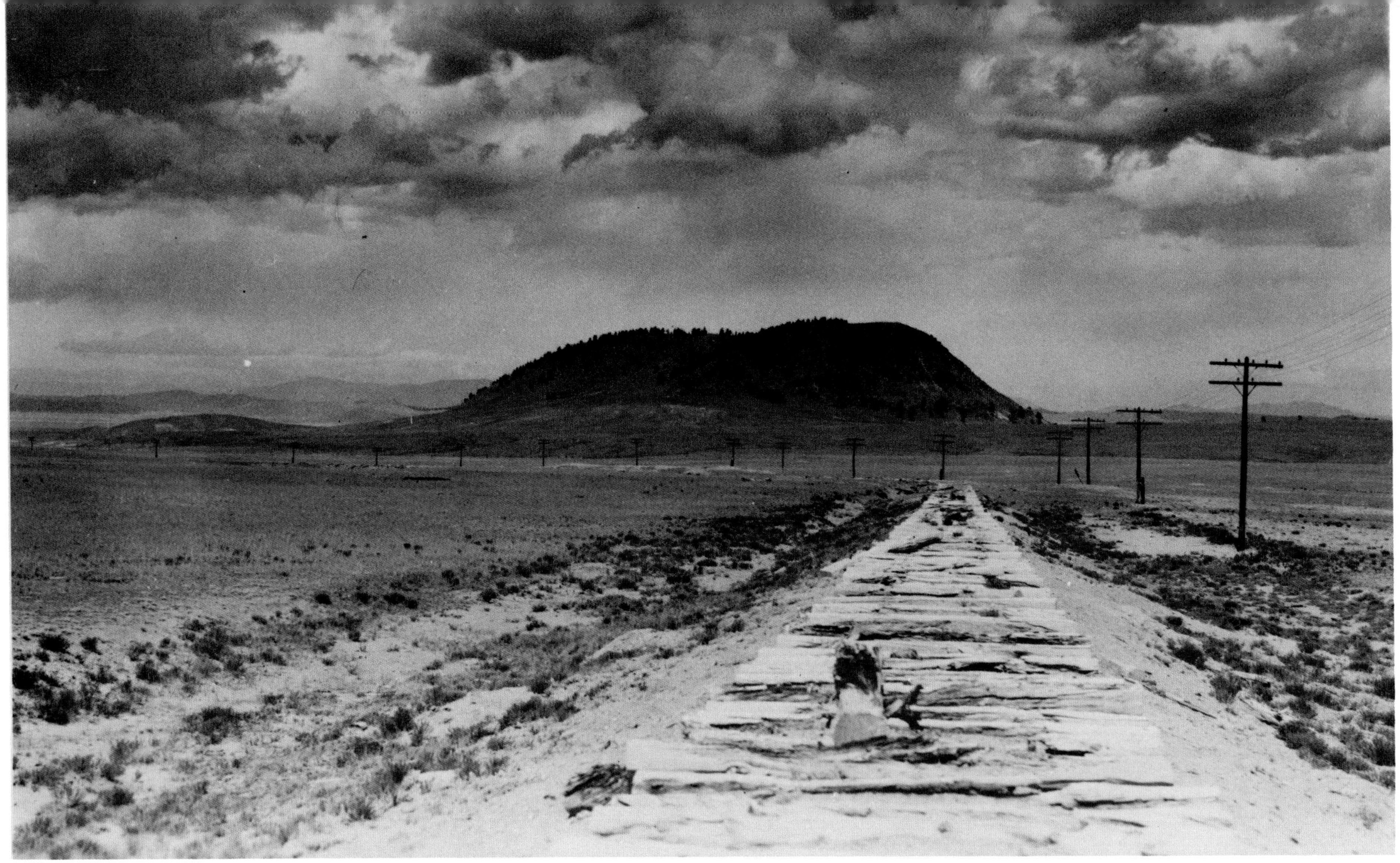

ELMORE FREDERICK COLLECTION

The sun bleached ties of the South Park line stretched for miles in this view looking toward Garos.

Train Number 90 was near Garos, in South Park during 1926. The junction at this point served the towns of Fairplay and Alma to the north.

RICHARD A. RONZIO COLLECTION

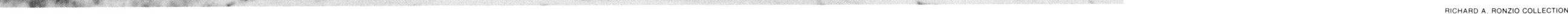

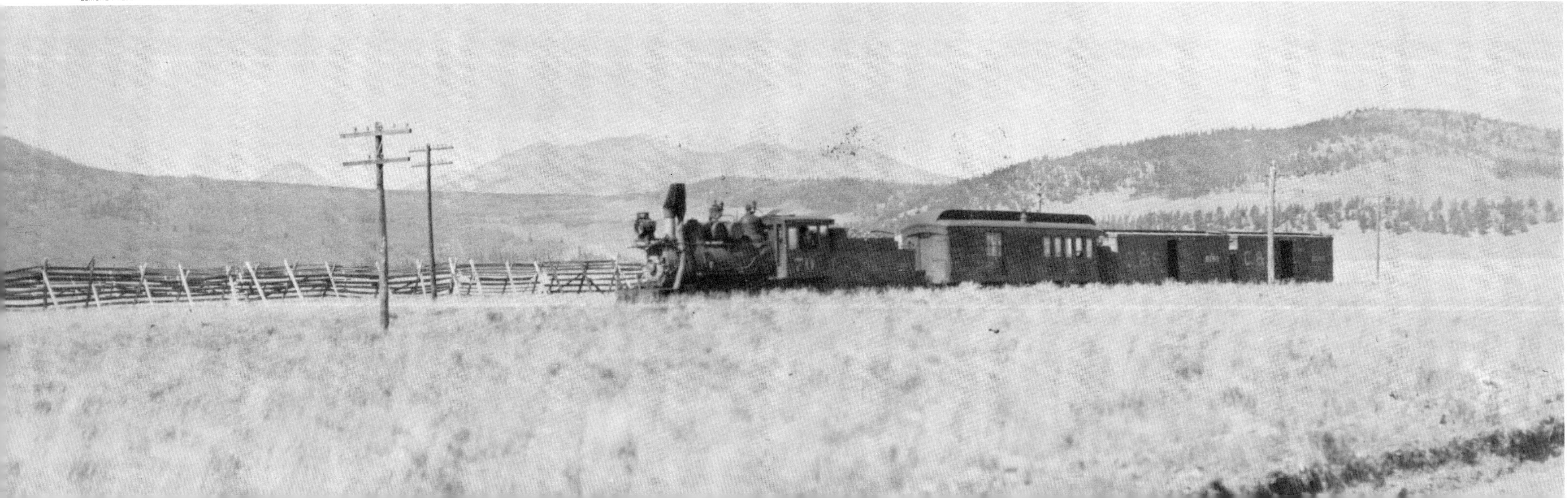

Summer of June 15, 1943 found a narrow-gauge freight on Fremont Pass, below Climax. Locomotive Number 74 originally ran on the Denver, Boulder & Western.

Locomotive Number 74 was pulling a string of boxcars and gondolas loaded with lumber out of Leadville, for Climax in the early 1940s.

RICHARD A. RONZIO COLLECTION

ELMORE FREDERICK COLLECTION

Approaching Climax, the 74 bladed away windblown snow at the high altitude of 11,320 feet above sea level.

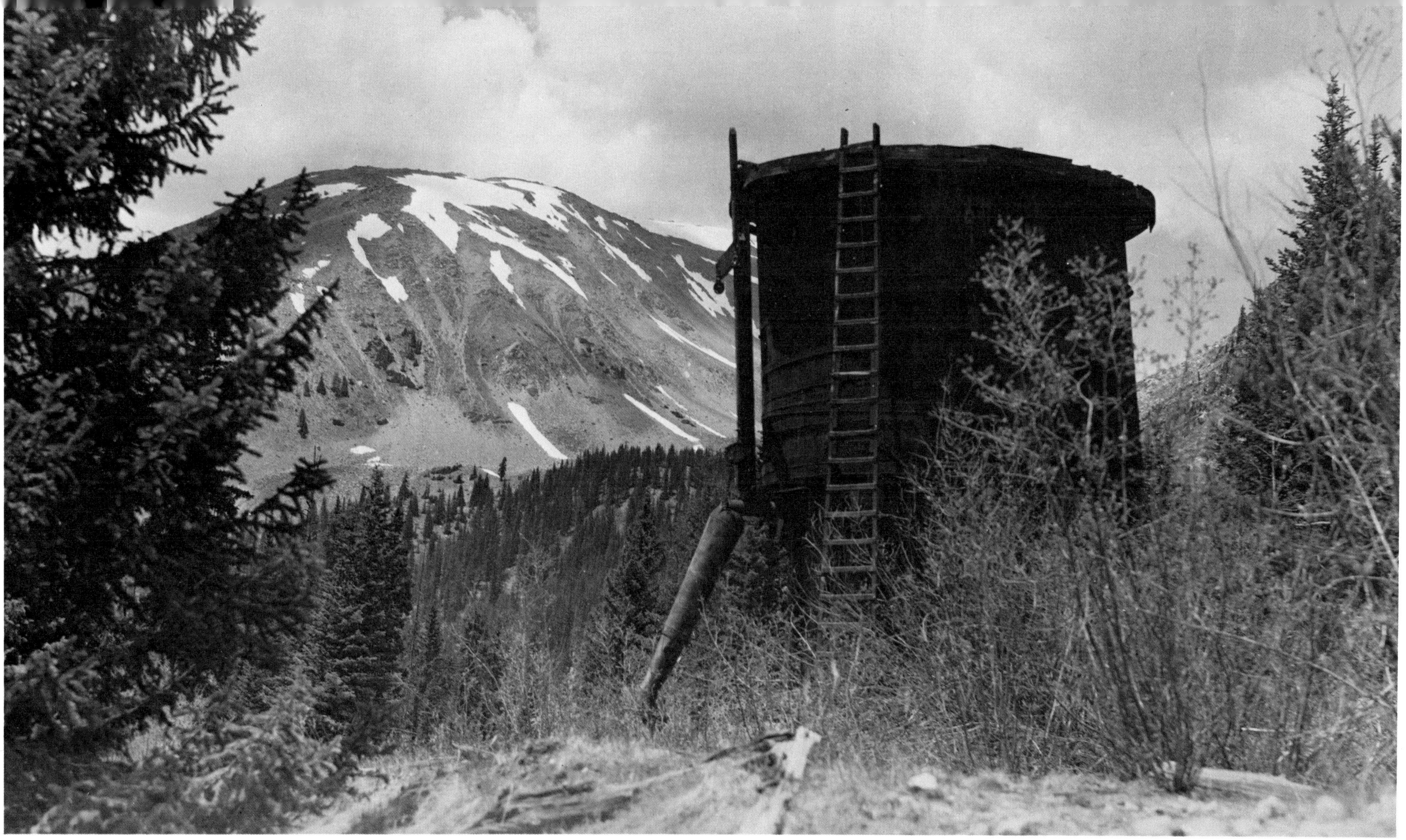

ELMORE FREDERICK COLLECTION

ELMORE FREDERICK COLLECTION

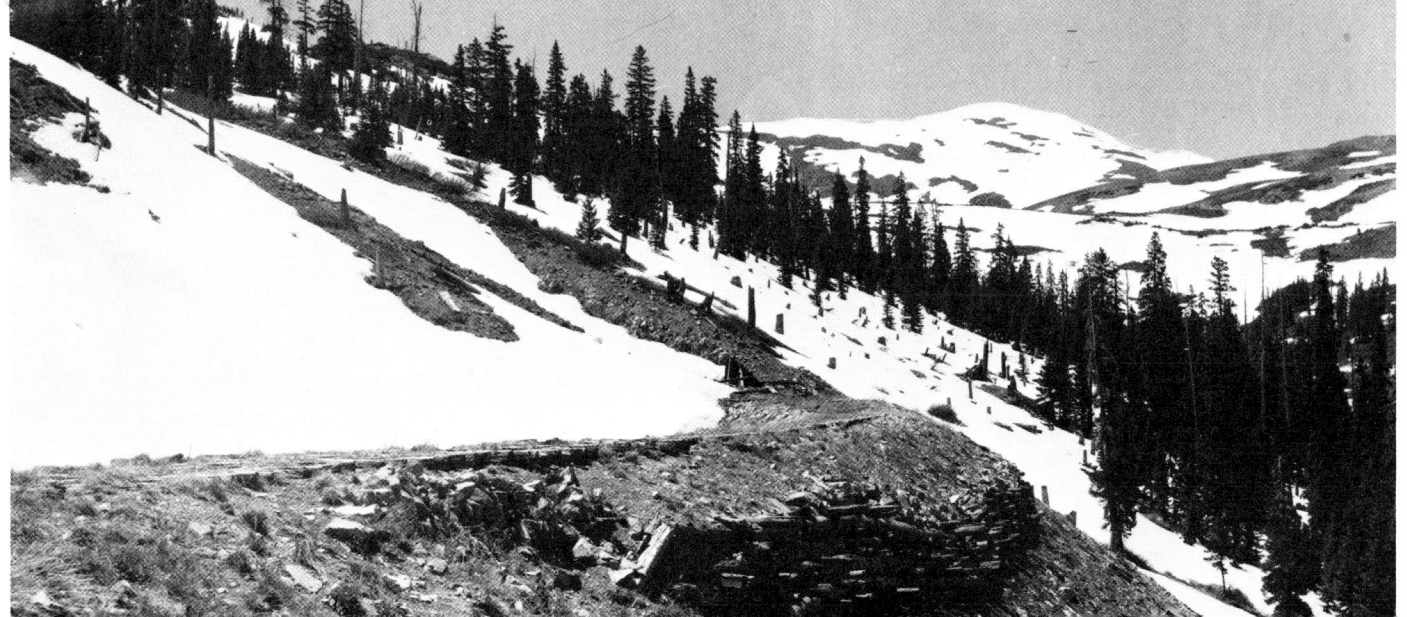

Otto Perry occasionally took scenic photographs as shown on this page. Subject of the top photo was the Woodstock Tank, below Alpine Tunnel on the west side of the Continental Divide. The lower photo was taken of the east portal of Alpine Tunnel, on the old South Park line, as it looked in 1943.

This page contains 3 views of Denver Boulder & Western locomotives that Otto Perry had photographed on one of his trips to Boulder. Locomotive Number 30 had unusually high running boards and was equipped with slide valves. Locomotive Number 1 was said to be too small and a poor steamer for the steep grades, and it lay idle for long periods. Locomotive Number 31 still had the old style steam chests with extended piston rods. A spark arrestor capped her stack when ever it made a run up Boulder Canyon.

The DB&W terminal and shops are illustrated in this photo showing the 32 being overhauled outdoors. The one stall carpenter's shop was to the right. These scenes were taken a few blocks west of the corners of Broadway and Canyon in today's downtown Boulder.

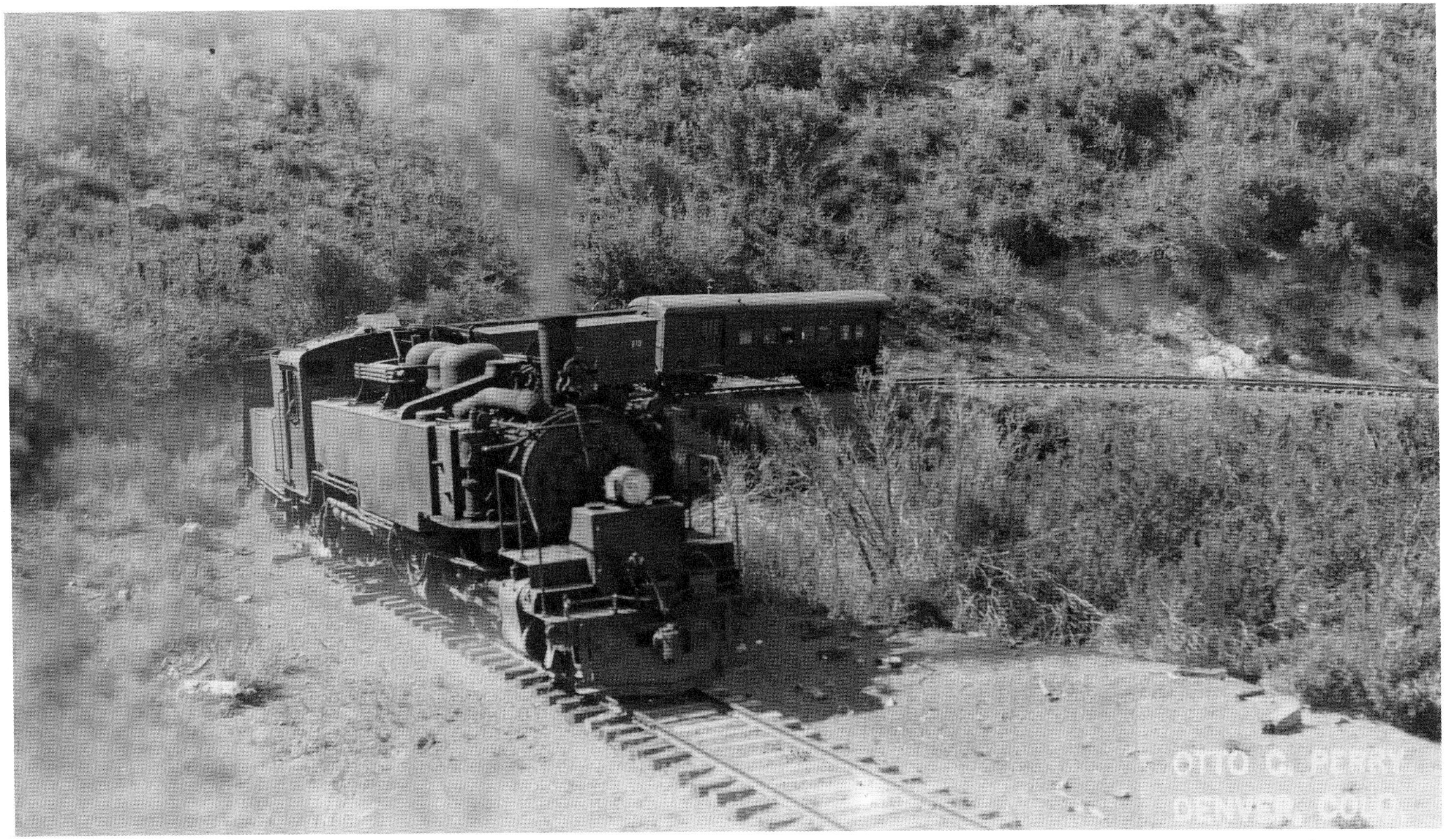

RICHARD A. RONZIO COLLECTION

RICHARD A. RONZIO COLLECTION

The Uintah Railway, running north from Mack, Colorado, was visited by Otto Perry before the line closed down in 1939. Locomotive Number 50 was rounding the 65° curves on Baxter Pass in the top photo. Below, the same train was photographed north of Carbonera. Engines 50 and 51 were the only narrow-gauge mallets used in the U.S.A.

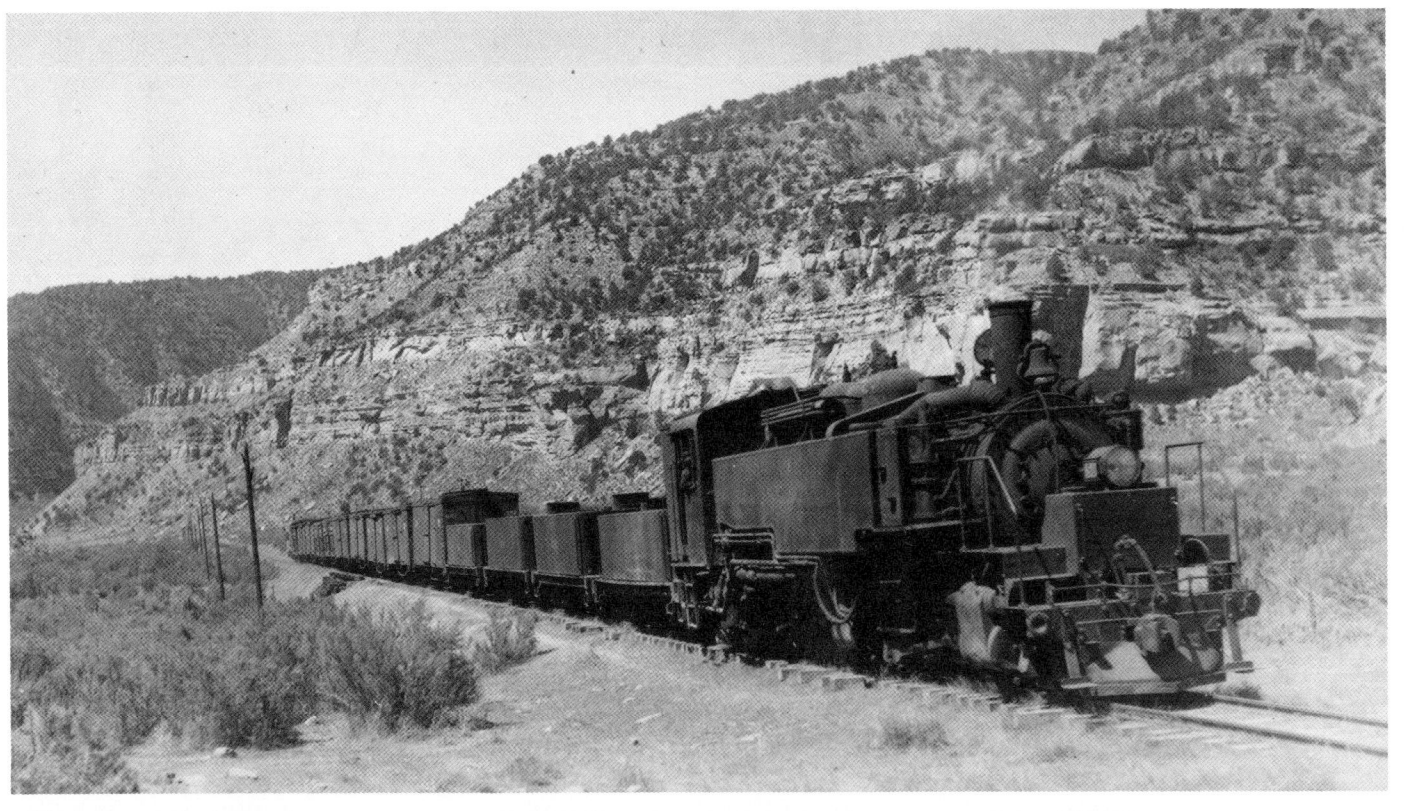

The rugged canyon north of Cooley echoed with the passing of locomotive Number 50 as she pulled the next-to-the-last scheduled weekly train out of Mack.

Train Number 1, the "Scenic Limited" Denver to Salt Lake City and Ogden, Utah, was photographed August 24, 1930. The train was leaving Hanging Bridge, deep within the Royal Gorge of the Akansas. The bridge was suspended 1,053 feet above the river.

Standard-Gauge Railroads of the Rocky Mountain Region

CHAPTER IV

This chapter attempts to cover a small portion of the photographs Otto Perry took of heavy mainline and standard gauge branchline railroads in the Rocky Mountain region. This includes the D&RGW, the Moffat Road, the Cripple Creek area, [Midland Terminal, Colorado Springs and Cripple Creek District], Colorado & Southern, Chicago Burlington & Quincy, and the Union Pacific. The Santa Fe system will follow in the next chapter.

A majority of these railroads had their terminals in Denver which was most convenient for Otto Perry to be on the scene of action. His favorite haunts were in fact the terminals of these monstrous pieces of locomotive machinery. And around the terminals there was no perfume that could compare with that aroma of hot grease, coal smoke, creosote and steam. Otto Perry's house was within walking distance of Burnham Shops where the D&RGW repaired locomotives and cars, and rebuilt locomotives from standard gauge to narrow gauge. It was here the Silverton passenger train equipment was rebuilt with steel and aluminum.

At the time of World War II the wartime ban on railroad photography kept Otto away from the terminal areas. Otto managed to continue his photography out along the mainlines and of course he was most cautious, making sure no one noticed his actions. Even after the war it was often difficult for him to walk through a terminal area without having the railroad police question his actions.

DAVID S. DIGERNESS COLLECTION

DENVER & RIO GRANDE WESTERN

Waiting for the green eye, the engineer was looking up the right-of-way, back when the 1700's were the biggest passenger power on the D&RGW. Many Rio Grande engineers did not wear the usual blue-stripped caps, which were an almost universal mark of their profession.

Fourteen handsome 4-8-4's were built by Baldwin for the D&RGW in 1929 to replace two and three-cylinder 4-8-2's in passenger service. The 1700's operated without change between Denver and Salt Lake City. Here, at Burnham engine terminal, the valve motion and machinery were being washed.

DAVID S. DIGERNESS COLLECTION

RICHARD A. RONZIO COLLECTION

DAVID S. DIGERNESS COLLECTION

The 1706 was photographed at Denver, during 1934. She was one of the first group of 4-8-4's purchased by the D&RGW for passenger service on it's main lines. Note the Elesco feedwater heater located beneath the smoke box.

Otto photographed the "Scenic Limited" found near Struby, moving along at 55 MPH, September 18, 1932. This passenger train carried through cars between Chicago-St. Louis and San Francisco.

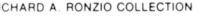

The southbound mail-passenger train named "The Westerner" provided Otto Perry with this vista, near Castle Rock on March 13, 1932. The train was traveling on Santa Fe rails at a speed of 40 MPH, climbing a 1.4% grade.

The D&RGW's last two 4-6-2's, Numbers 801 and 804, were assigned to the daily local trains, running between Denver and Craig. They offered RPO, express, baggage and buffet facilities. This scene was at Tunnel Number 1, 24 miles from Denver.

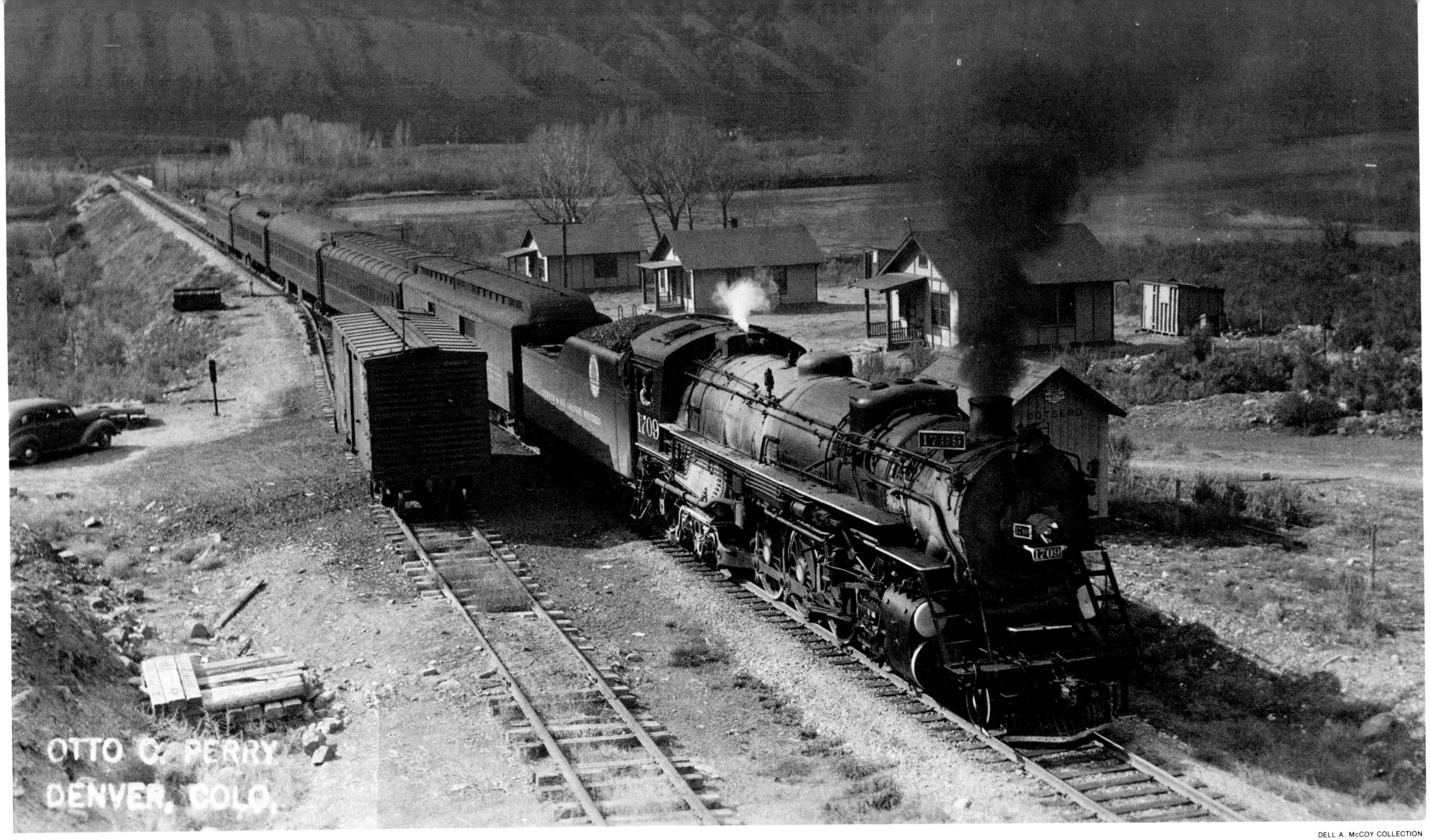

DELL A. McCOY COLLECTION

DELL A. McCOY COLLECTION

"The Panoramic" was headed toward Denver April 30, 1939. This passenger train ran between Denver and Salt Lake City, via the Moffat Tunnel and Dotsero cutoff. The section houses at Dotsero are located just north of the wye joining the cutoff with the original main line.

The setting for this dramatic photograph was taken near Pinecliffe, February 9, 1936. The freight was pulled by one of 16 Mallet articulated 2-8+8-2's built for the D&RG in 1913 by American Locomotive Company. At this time the Rio Grande had running rights over the D&SL to reach the Dotsero Cutoff.

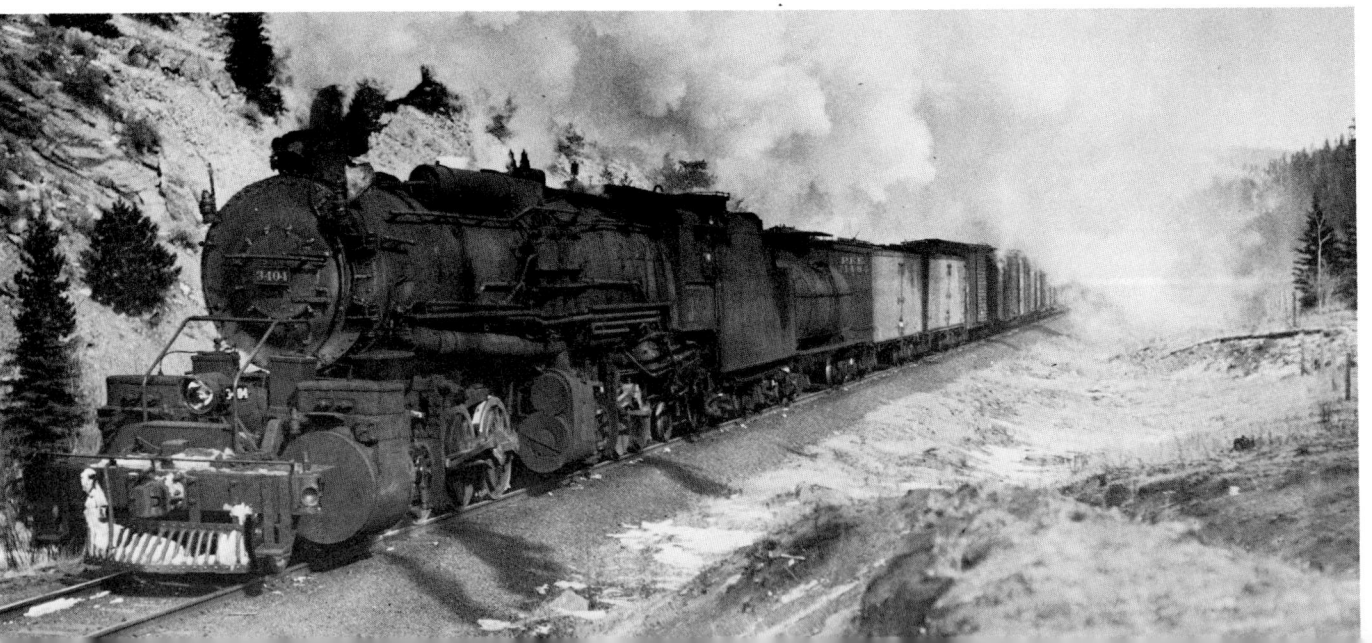

RICHARD A. RONZIO COLLECTION

RICHARD A. RONZIO COLLECTION

Near Creede, a D&RGW stock train was photographed crossing the Rio Grande river, September 15, 1956. The 1136, based in Alamosa to serve this mining branch, was one of the last few still operating prior to the end of Standard-gauge steam power in December.

A rare view of "The Mountaineer," the daily passenger mail train between Grand Junction and Montrose, photographed south of Delta. The 760 was one of two heavy 4-6-0's rebuilt with smaller drivers.

One of Otto Perry's early photographs shows Colorado Springs & Cripple Creek District locomotive Number 8 being prepared for a run to Cripple Creek. The Colorado Midland roundhouse at Colorado City was the location in 1918.

CS&CCD

A year later in 1919, Otto Perry photographed Colorado Springs & Cripple Creek District locomotive Number 1 at Colorado Springs. These locomotives hauled both freight and passenger trains on the steeply graded short line around the southern flanks of Pikes Peak.

COLORADO SPRINGS & CRIPPLE CREEK DISTRICT RAILROAD

Colorado Springs & Cripple Creek District locomotive Number 103 was idle at Colorado Springs on June 22, 1919; and all operations were suspended just a little more than a year later.

Otto Perry again visited the Colorado Springs & Cripple Creek District railroad on July 5, 1920 at Colorado Springs. He found locomotive Number 102, a switcher, under steam. This locomotive lacked its original trailing truck, which had been necessary on sharply curved trackage in the mining district.

MIDLAND TERMINAL

Dropping down the 4% grade, a Midland Terminal freight train was photographed in Ute Pass March 31, 1935. She was hauling ore concentrate to the mill at Colorado City.

RICHARD A. RONZIO COLLECTION

Called "doodlebugs" by locals, Motor 102 of the Midland Terminal was crossing the Colorado Midland steel trestle at Manitou Springs June 23, 1941. She was built by William McKay in Colorado City shops in 1937 from an old Colorado Springs streetcar body. The Motor was used for passengers, LCL freight and mail to Cripple Creek. The paint scheme was bright yellow with aluminum and black lettering. She held 8 passengers.

It was not uncommon for the Midland Terminal to operate long trains of empty ore cars powered by 5 locomotives, up Ute Pass. The 61, a 2-8-2, had been cut into the consist of 60 cars in this view taken July 9, 1939.

RICHARD A. RONZIO COLLECTION

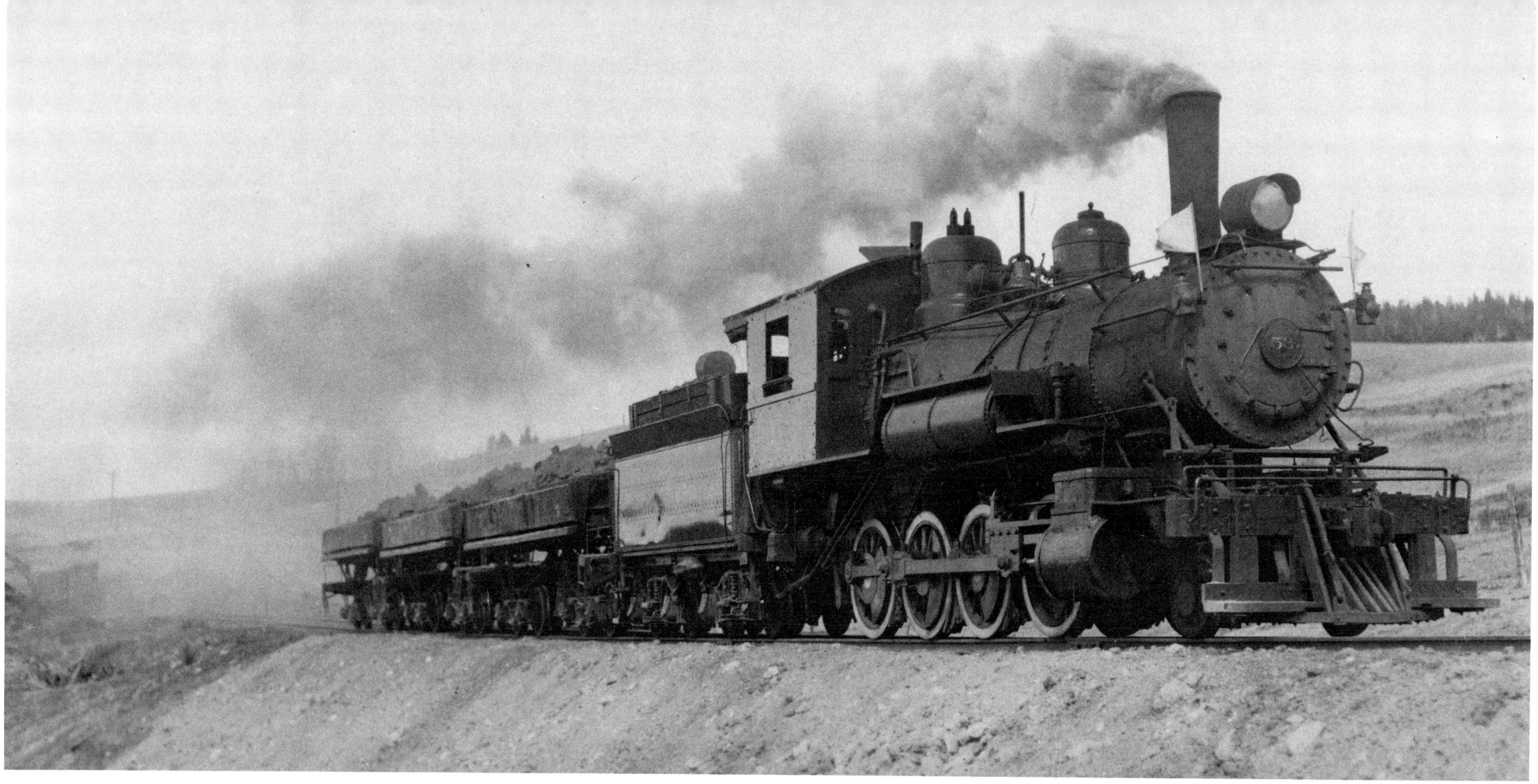

RICHARD A. RONZIO COLLECTION

RICHARD A. RONZIO COLLECTION

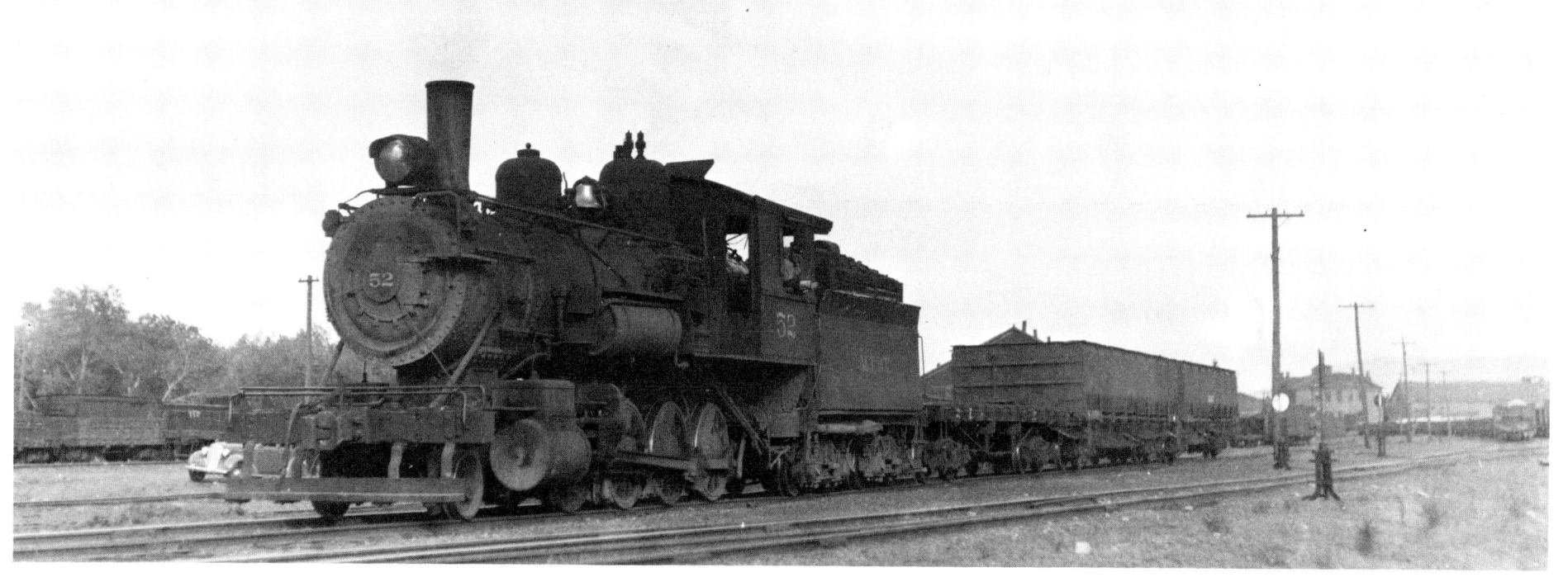

Midland Terminal work extra 53 was near Divide April 7, 1935. The locomotive Number 53 came originally from the Colorado Midland.

Locomotive Number 52 was switching the yards at Colorado City May 28, 1941. This was the Midland Terminal connection with The Rio Grande and Santa Fe railroads.

The locomotive Hostler was peering from the cab window of C&S standard-gauge locomotive Number 422 when Otto took this photograph in Denver in 1919. Despite its age, the locomotive was well maintained, having been built for the Union Pacific Denver & Gulf Ry. in 1897.

COLORADO & SOUTHERN

Colorado & Southern locomotive Number 649 was awaiting major repairs at the Denver shops in 1919.

A typical Colorado & Southern passenger train, hauled by one of five small 4-6-2's, made an excellent study of locomotive types for Otto Perry. This was taken March 19, 1932, near Westminster, Colorado.

Colorado & Southern locomotive Number 309 was photographed at the Denver Union Station, May 23, 1924. This locomotive was a relic from the U.P.D.&G. Ry., having been built in 1896.

CHICAGO BURLINGTON & QUINCY

The 522 was in dead storage when photographed in the Denver yards on May 16, 1936. She was a light 2-8-0, originally delivered in 1902 as a tandem-compound.

Although the CB&Q's 4-8-2's had been ordered for heavy passenger service, they were demoted to secondary status when 4-6-4's and 4-8-4's arrived. After having been repaired in Denver shops, the 7014 was broken-in on a local freight.

DAVID S. DIGERNESS COLLECTION

DAVID S. DIGERNESS COLLECTION

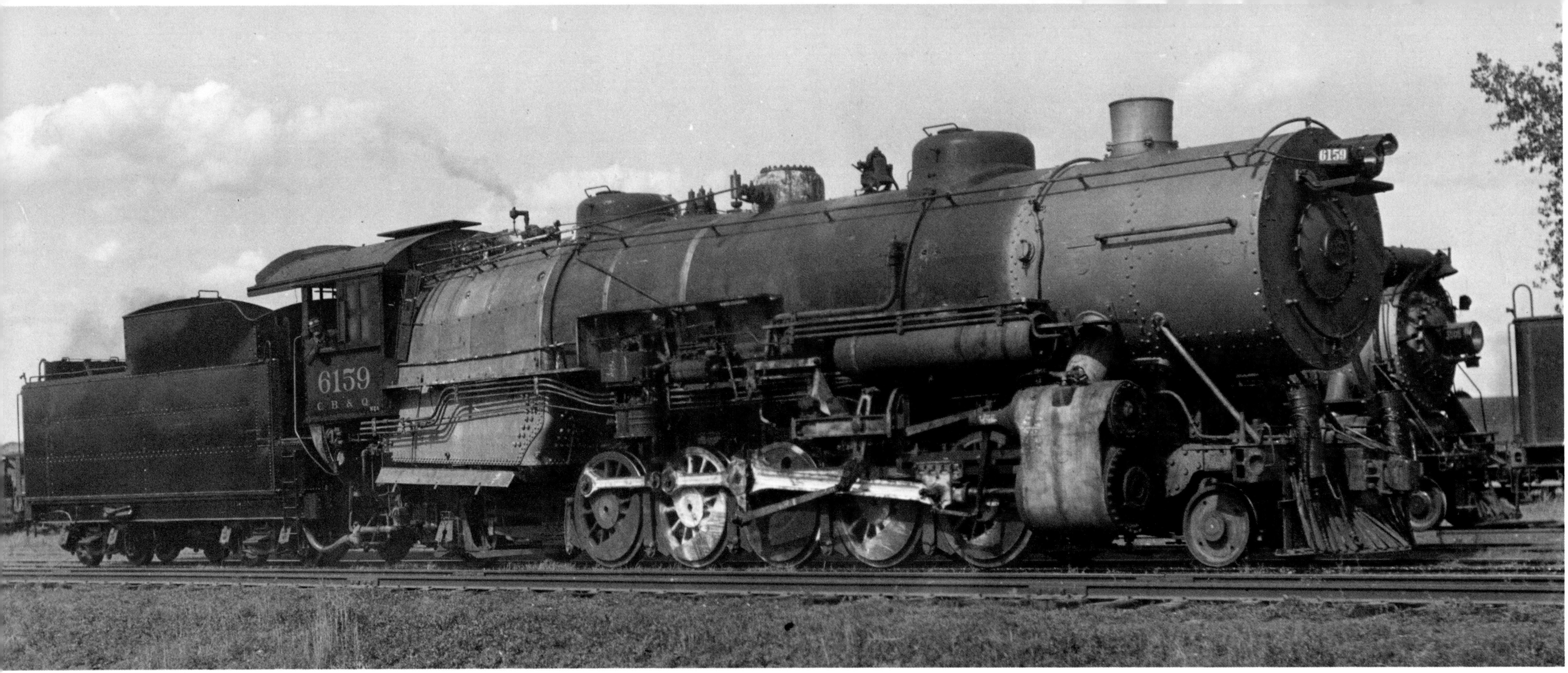

DAVID S. DIGERNESS COLLECTION

DAVID S. DIGERNESS COLLECTION

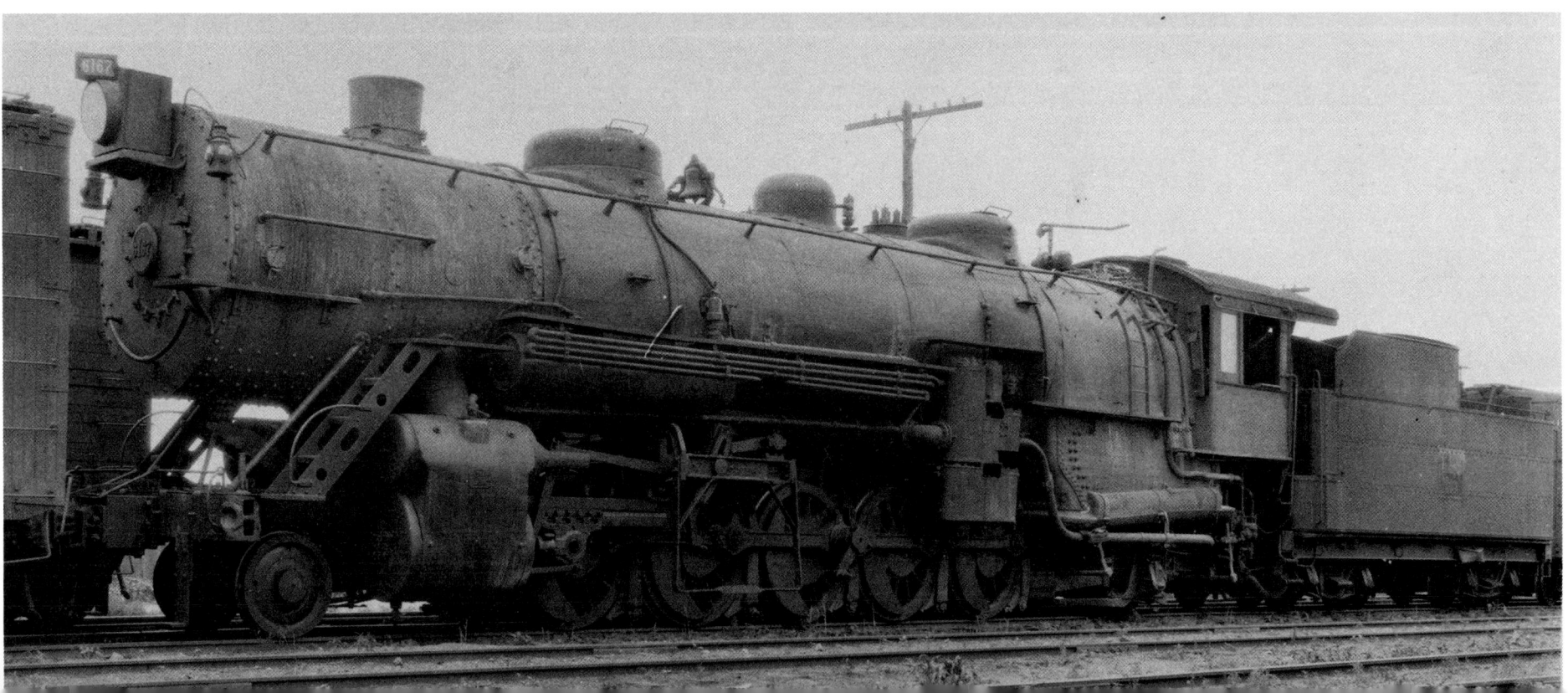

CB&Q Number 6159 was a massive piece of machinery, one of a fleet of 71 2-10-2's designed for slow, heavy freight service.

The fireman's side of locomotive Number 6167 reveals an antique carbon arc headlight mounted on a greatly extended smokebox, and a modern feedwater heater mounted just forward of the firebox.

A 2-year-old 4-8-4, designed for fast long-distance freight service, at the Denver terminal in 1932. This was CB&Q locomotive Number 5605 one of eight delivered by Baldwin in 1930.

FW&D 2-8-0 Number 251 appears to have just emerged from the paint shop, and it was equipped with a new cab. The engineer of this locomotive was taking advantage of the shade inside the cab, while he was switching cars in the yard at Wichita Falls in 1931.

This 2-8-0 freight hauler still retained its unusual arched-window cab, to which the fireman had attached an awning to shade him from the blistering heat of Texas. The Fort Worth & Denver was a CB&Q subsidiary operating entirely in Texas.

A grimy road engine, locomotive Number 404 was waiting orders at Childress, Texas in 1930. FW&D locomotives burned oil because it was so plentiful at that time.

Bridgeport, Nebraska, was a stop for Otto Perry in 1931 where he found CB&Q locomotive Number 4109. In need of repairs, this 2-6+6-2 compound was enroute to the shops at Denver.

DAVID S. DIGERNESS COLLECTION

DAVID S. DIGERNESS COLLECTION

UNION PACIFIC

A most unusual locomotive for the Union Pacific, Number 3310 was a "high stepper." The wheel arrangement of 4-4-2 indicated light, high-speed passenger service, and the engine had been given 81-inch drivers.

Morning haze covered Denver August 29, 1926 as Union Pacific locomotive Number 2855 hauled a heavy passenger train through interlocking trackage north of Denver Union Station.

DAVID S. DIGERNESS COLLECTION

DELL A. McCOY COLLECTION

A sleek Pacific type locomotive equipped with Vanderbilt tender was uncoupled from her passenger train at Denver in 1919. The Union Pacific always took great pride in maintaining passenger equipment in top condition as evidenced in this photo.

DAVID S. DIGERNESS COLLECTION

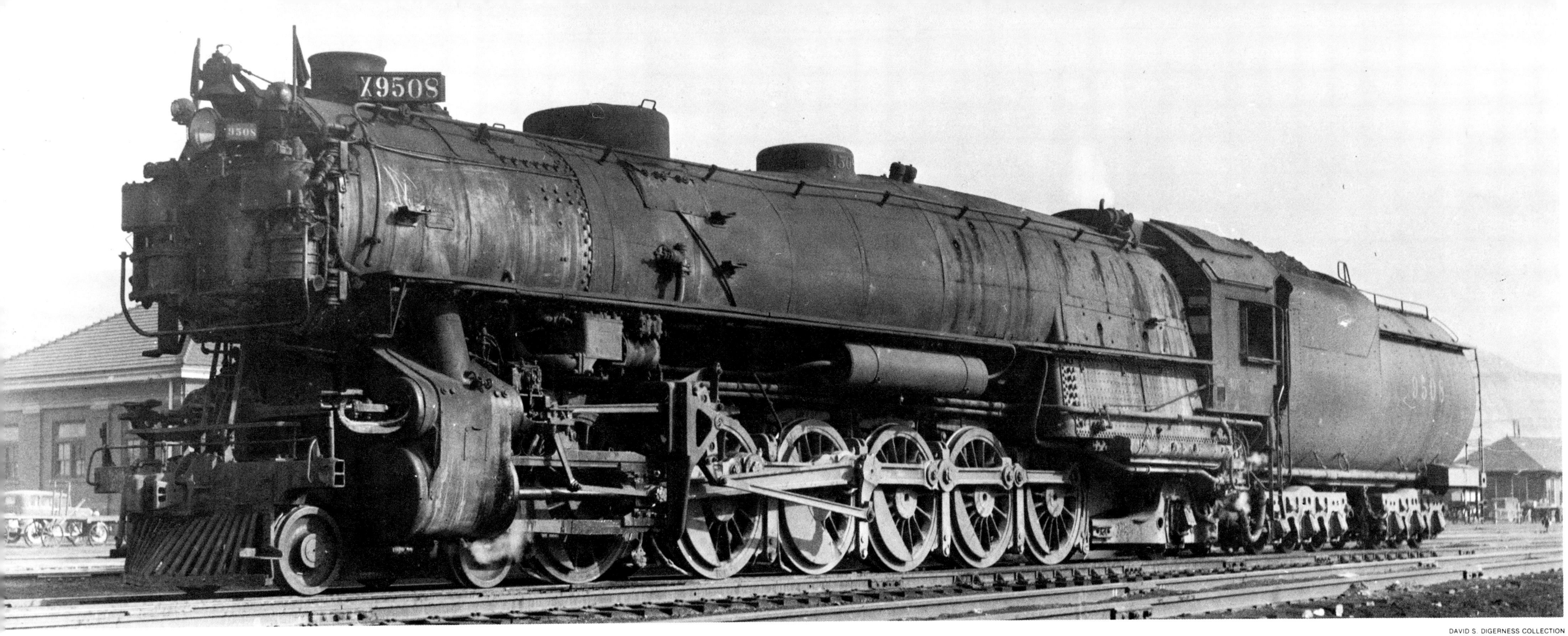

DAVID S. DIGERNESS COLLECTION

DAVID S. DIGERNESS COLLECTION

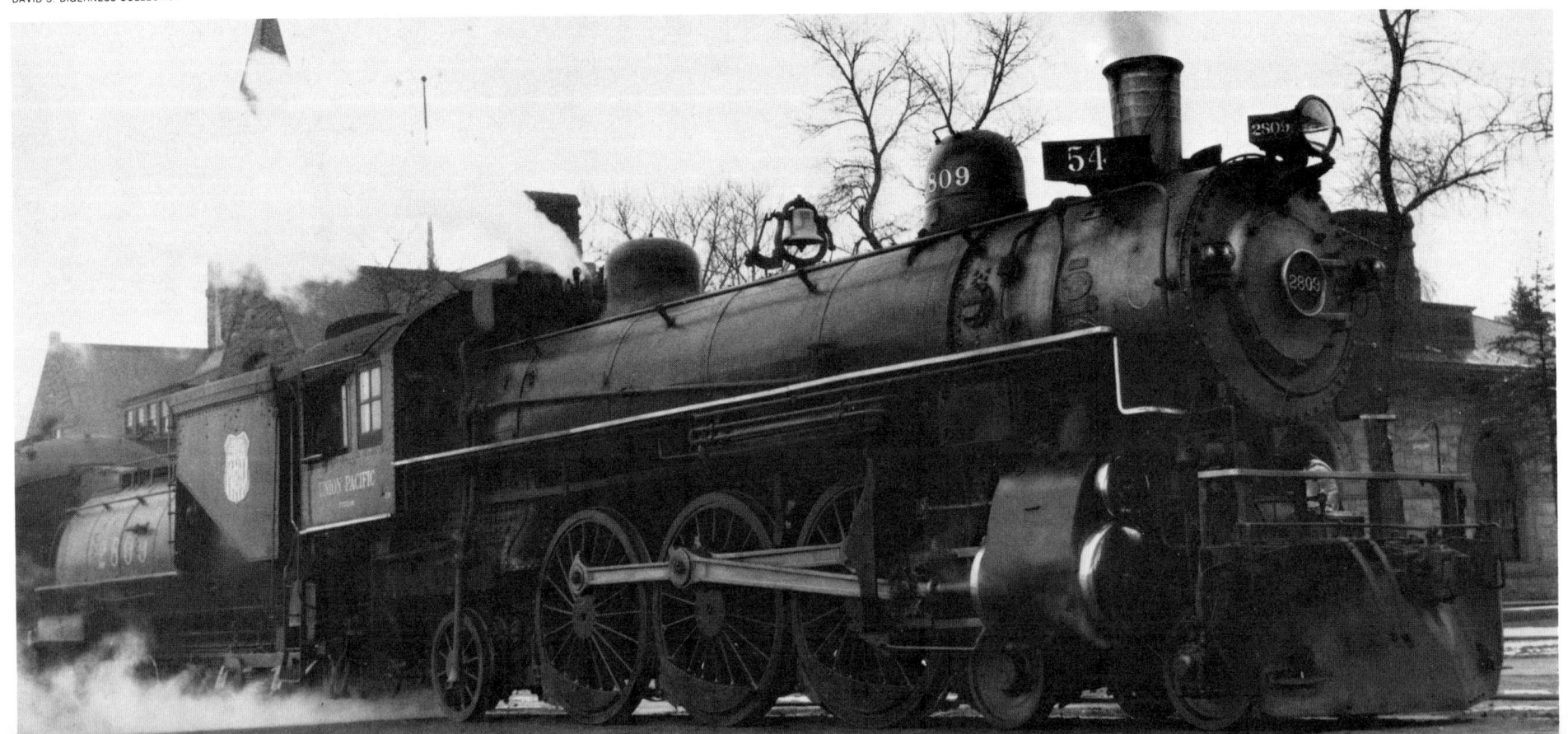

The Union Pacific was the only system to utilize six rigid driving axles in their locomotives. The 9508 was one of 15 engines assigned to the Oregon short line subsidiary. The locale is Green River, Wyoming in 1936.

Equipped with snowplow, for bucking light drifts on branch lines, locomotive Number 2809 was ready for departure at Cheyenne in 1931.

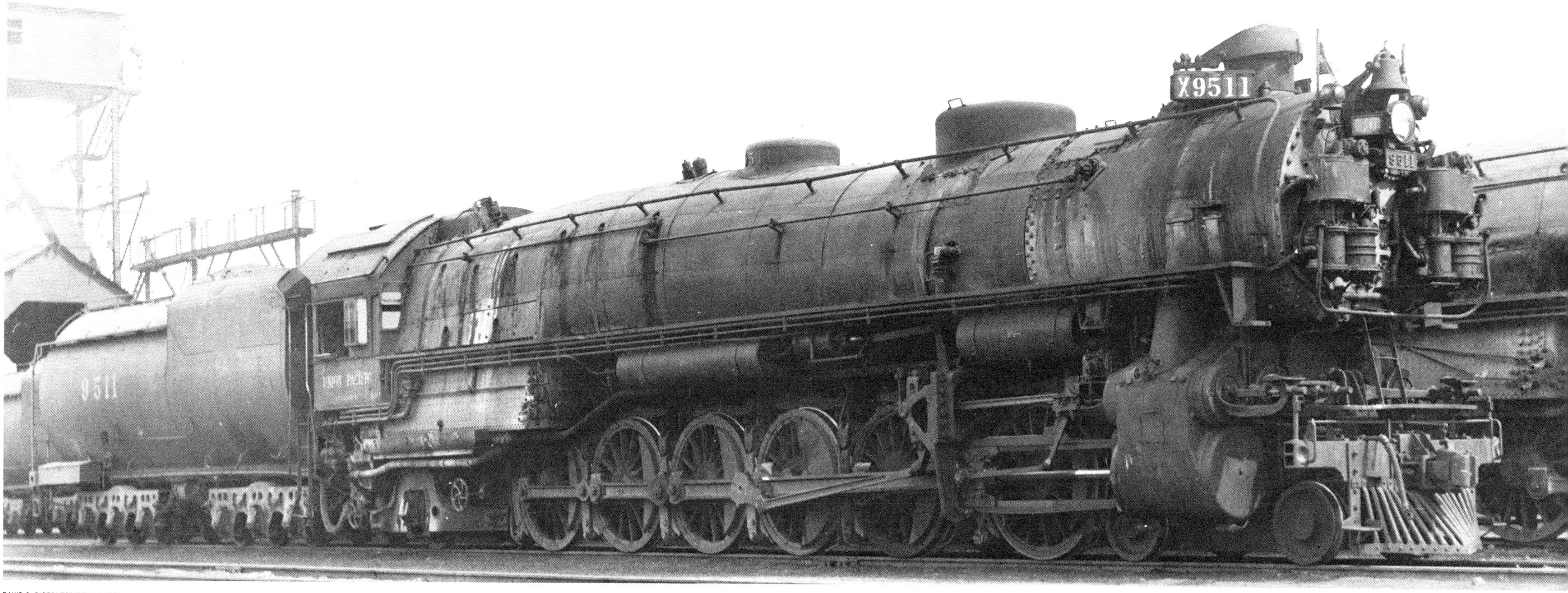

DAVID S. DIGERNESS COLLECTION

Some of the Union Pacific's 88 3-cylinder 4-12-2's worked for 30 years before they were displaced by diesel-electric units. This one's number denoted allocation to the Oregon short line.

A more-modern Pacific type locomotive was getting ready to depart Cheyenne with the first section of train No. 4, in July 1920.

DAVID S. DIGERNESS COLLECTION

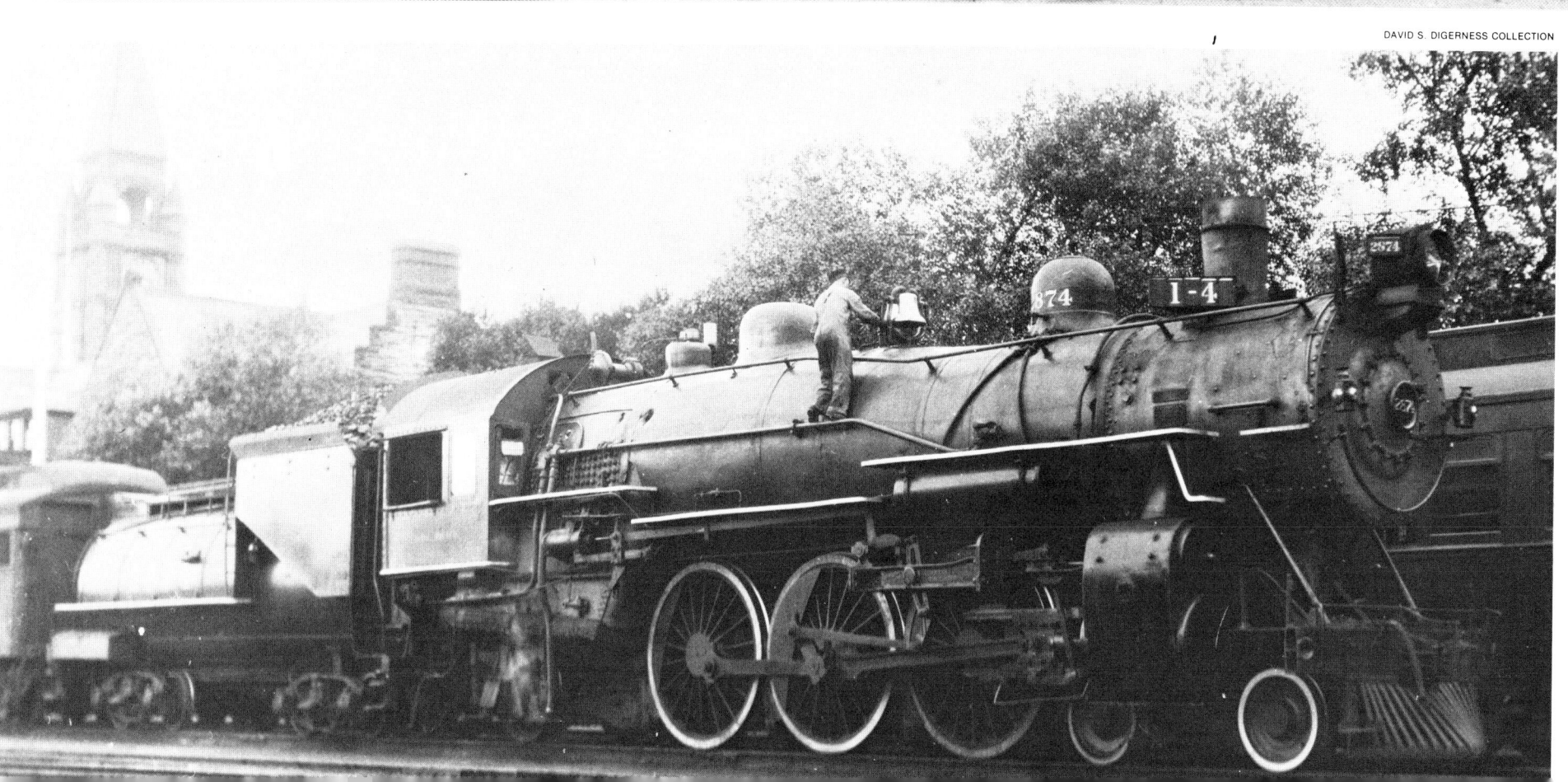

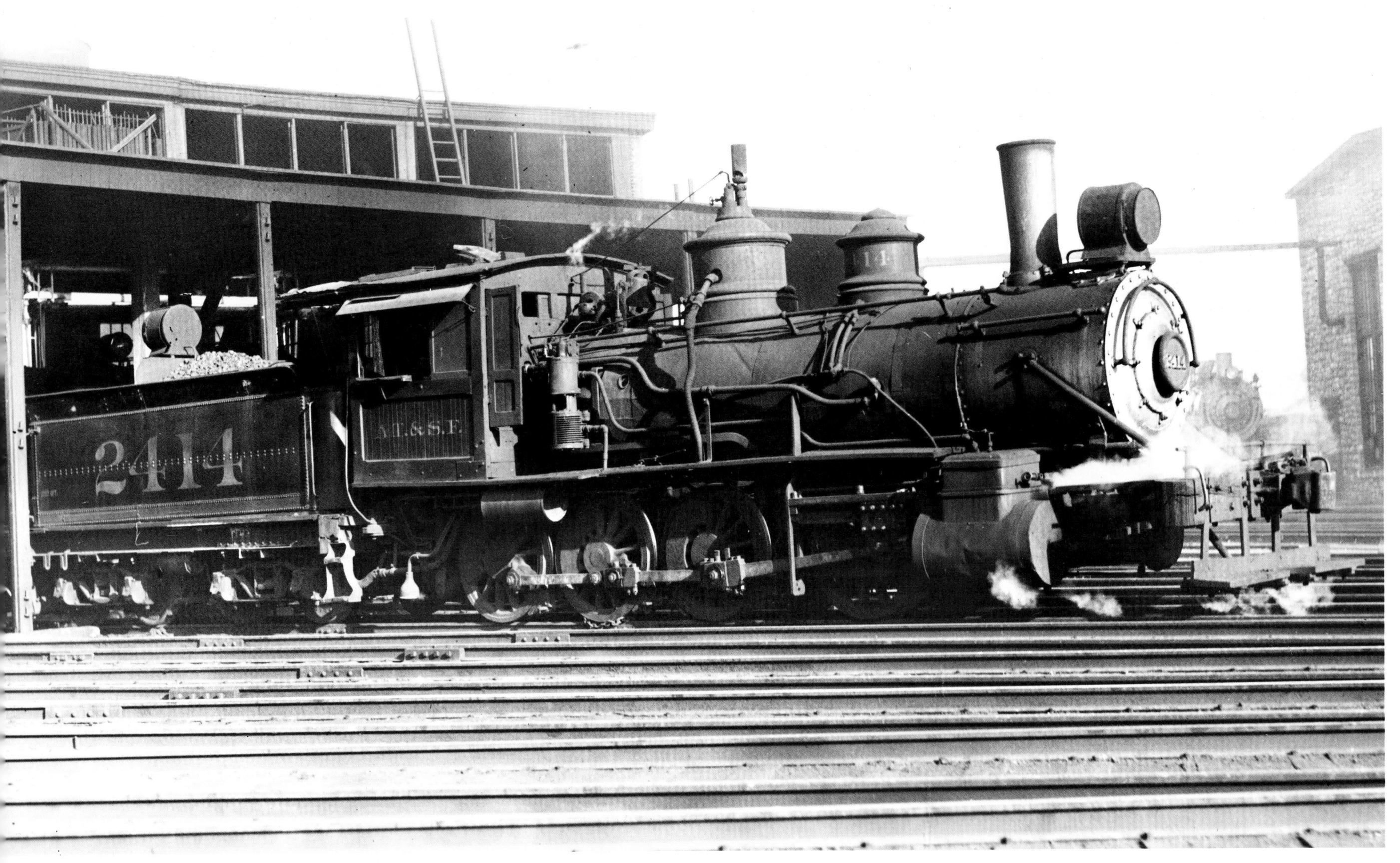

ATCHISON TOPEKA & SANTA FE

Beyond the Rocky Mountains

CHAPTER V

DAVID S. DIGERNESS COLLECTION

 lthough Otto Perry is remembered for his railroad photography in Colorado, he did not neglect other states where he found ample opportunity to record on film locomotives of both the great trunk lines and the short or obscure railroads. His travels took him to both coasts, and he was probably the only amateur photographer present at Atlantic City, N.J., in 1919, when railroads, builders and suppliers exhibited their latest achievements. Thanks to him, his photo of the Pennsylvania's sole 2-8+8-0 may be the only one existing today.

Unlike some railroad photographers, Otto photographed everything possible; he considered nothing unworthy of his efforts. Consequently, we have a remarkable photographic record of unusual locomotives, antiquated engines, diesel-electric units, motor cars, and electric locomotives. Not only did he take photographs at stations during train stops, but he found time to wander around engine terminals where there was much greater variety. He did not overlook storage tracks, where he found engines in various states of disrepair, and frequently he came upon newly repaired engines just out of the paint shop, real rarities.

Otto's residential proximity to the Rocky Mountains gave him automotive access to the spectacular scenery which formed the background of so many photos taken of trains in action. He possessed an uncanny sense of location, which took him to little-known spots for memorable scenes, and even his photos in cluttered busy yards reflect his innate artistry. Because of his meticulous recording of places and dates, another aspect of his technique was revealed. First, he would photograph an engine in a terminal, then again when it departed with a train, and finally one or two more times at interesting locations along the right of way.

The photos in this chapter depict only a minor sample of Otto's far-ranging photographic excursions along the nation's railroads.

Among the oldest locomotives on the AT&SF system were the tiny 2-8-0's built in 1880. Rare indeed, they were found only in yards where they worked as switchers. Otto snapped the 2415 at Pueblo, Colorado, shortly before it was scrapped, but the 2414 became a famous survivor. Shown here at Argentine, Kansas, in 1933, without its pilot truck, it remained in service until 1941, when it was restored to its original configuration for exhibition use as the "Cyrus K. Holliday" bearing the number 1.

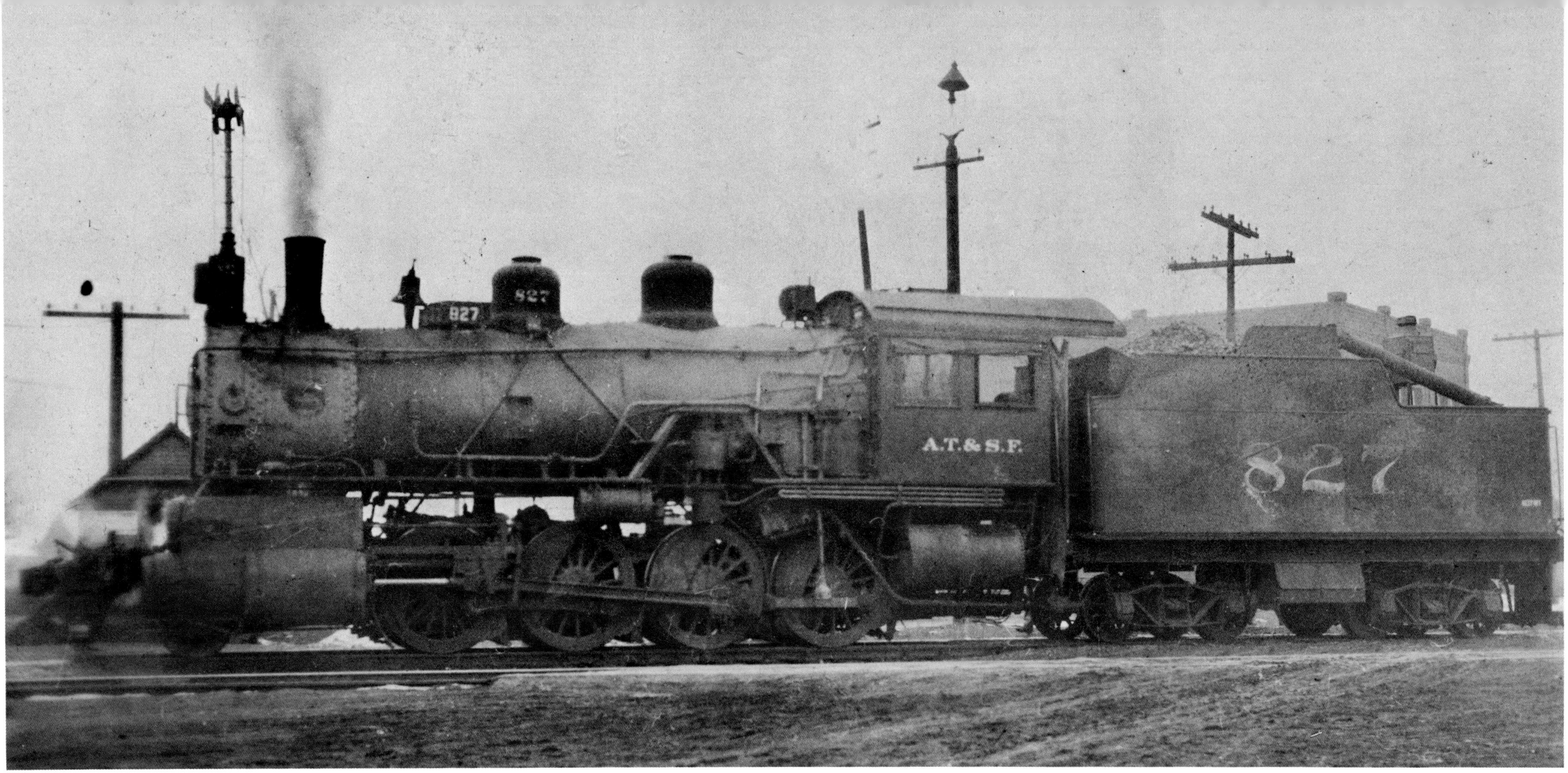

DAVID S. DIGERNESS COLLECTION

DAVID S. DIGERNESS COLLECTION

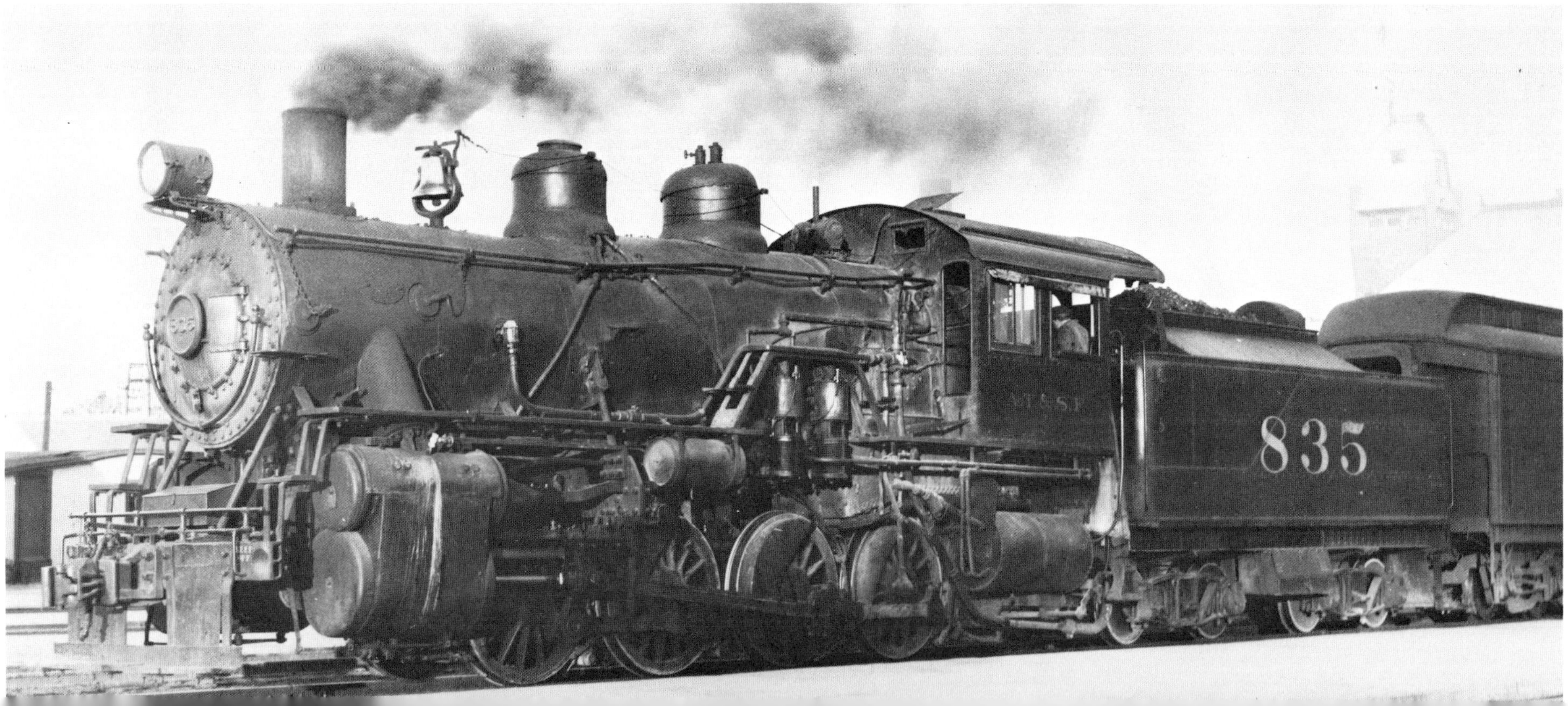

The 825-864 group of 2-8-0's had been delivered as tandem-compound engines, illustrated by the 827 at Pueblo in 1920. In the late 1920's several were modified to become 0-8-0 switchers, like the 835 at Pueblo in 1933.

Only a year before it was scrapped, the 698 posed in the small yard at Needles, California, during a break between trains. Built by Baldwin in 1899, the engine showed several changes from its previous appearance.

The 778, a 2-8-0 built in 1900, was one of 20 such engines originally built for the Santa Fe Pacific. Otto discovered it at Topeka, Kansas, in 1921, when it was working as a yard switcher.

Five Baldwin 2-8-0's came into the Santa Fe's roster from the St. Louis, Rocky Mountain & Pacific in 1915. All of them were still working in 1932 when Otto photographed the 870 [ex-StLRM&P 101] at Raton, New Mexico.

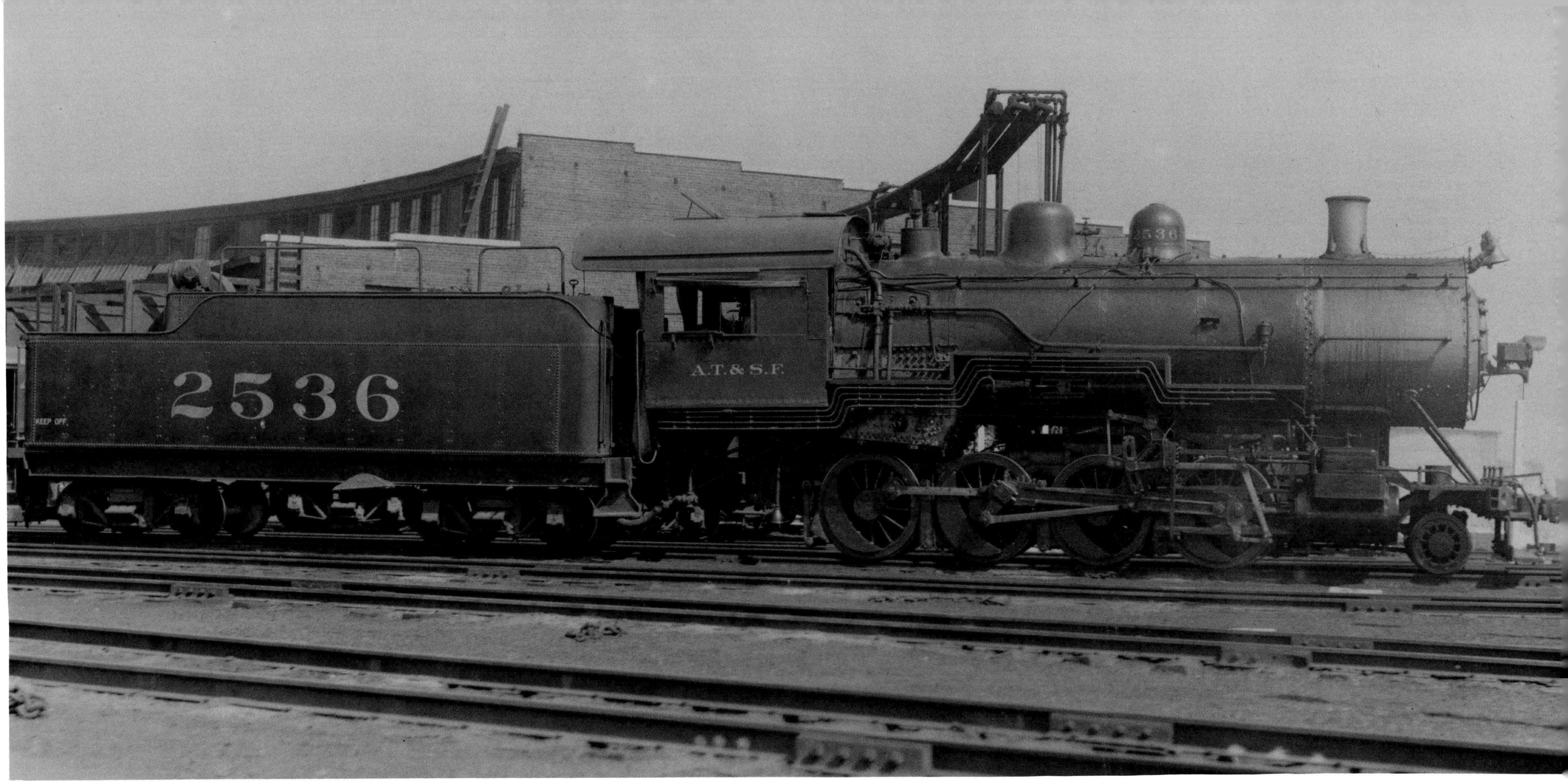

DAVID S. DIGERNESS COLLECTION

When the AT&SF absorbed the Kansas, City, Mexico & Orient in 1929 it inherited a roster of unusual locomotives, among which were 2-8-0's numbered 2504 and 2536. The former had been constructed for the New York Central railroad in 1906; the latter had been delivered to the KCM&O in 1909. The 2504 got no farther than Amarillo, Texas, where it was stored in 1930, but the 2536 [with a new boiler at Topeka, Kansas in 1931] ran until 1951.

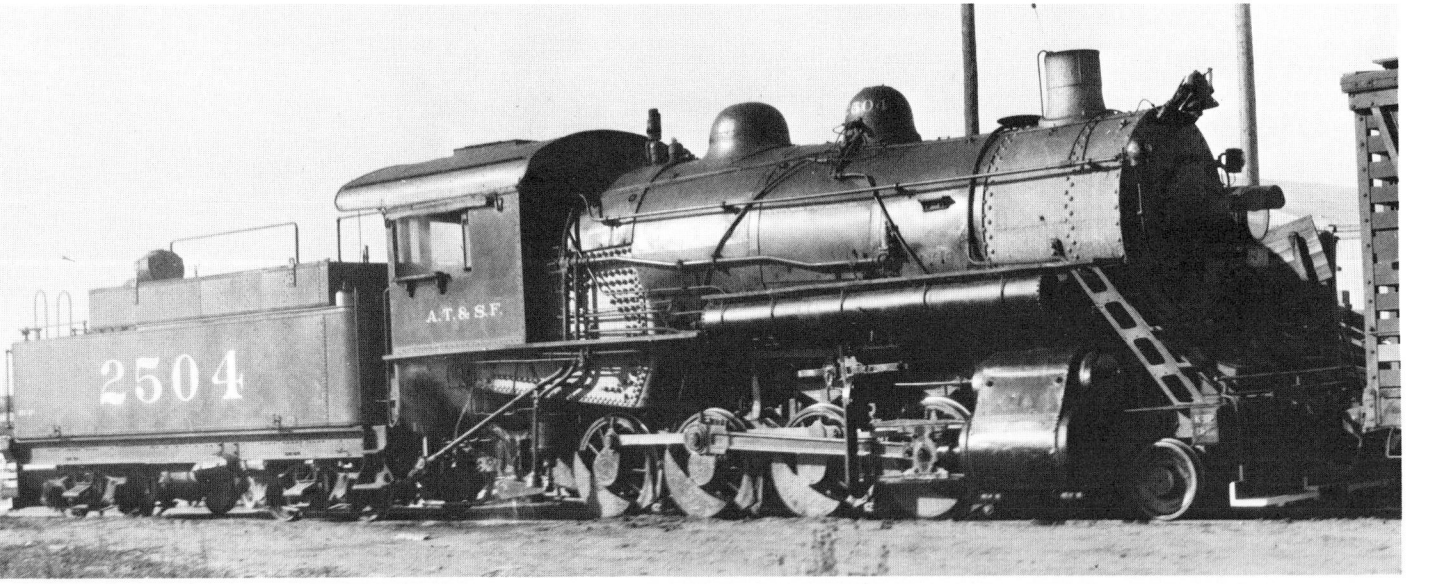

The Santa Fe was one of the earlier purchasers of the 4-6-4 type, buying 10 of them in 1927. All were rebuilt about ten years later, as illustrated by this portrait of the 3457 at La Junta, Colorado, in 1938.

Engines 885-899 had been constructed as Vauclain-compounds in 1902. Initially renumbered from 900-914 in 1903, they were rebuilt as shown during 1908-1909. Otto found the 891 at Littleton, Colorado, in 1918, the 886 at Belen, New Mexico, in 1933, and the 885 at Argentine, Kansas, in 1921. Some of them were running for more than 50 years!

AT&SF

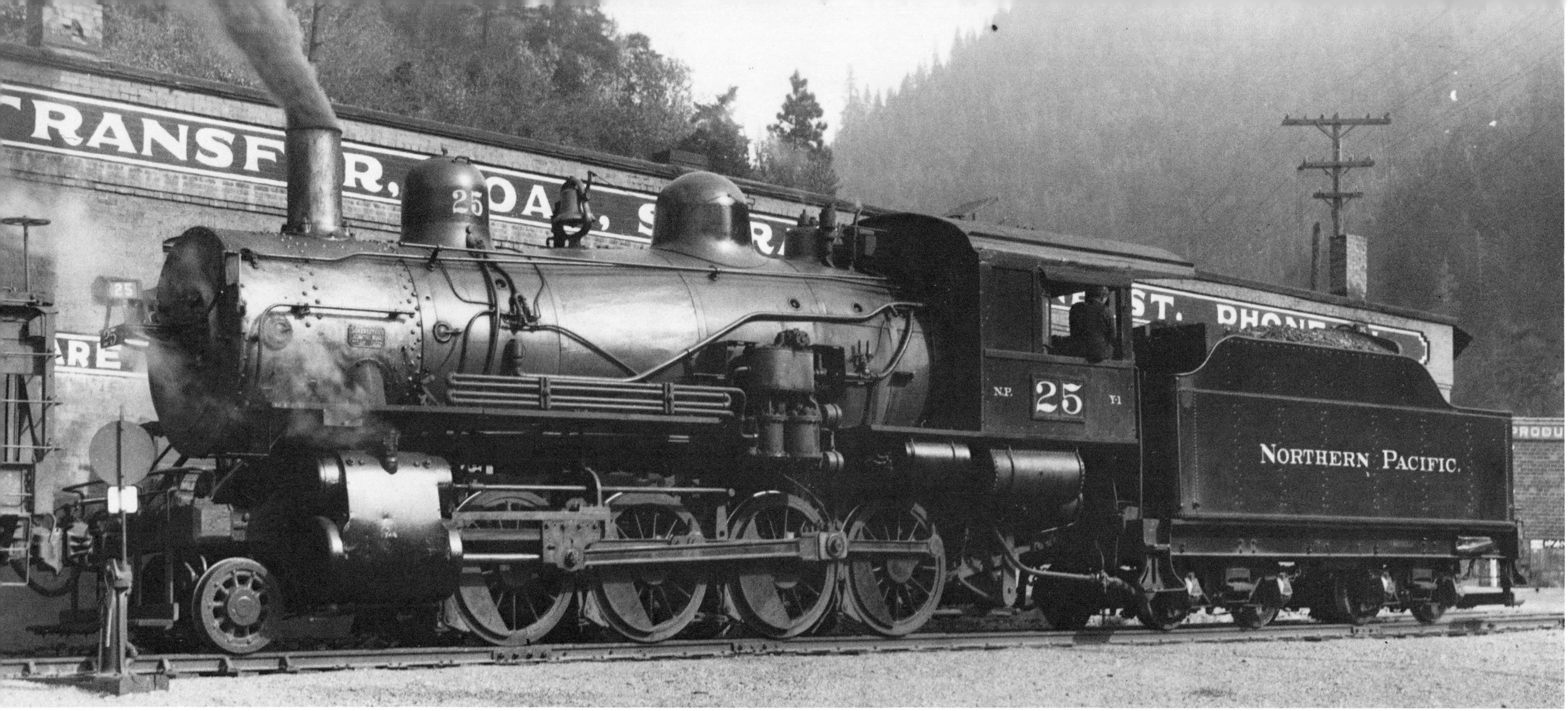

DAVID S. DIGERNESS COLLECTION

DAVID S. DIGERNESS COLLECTION

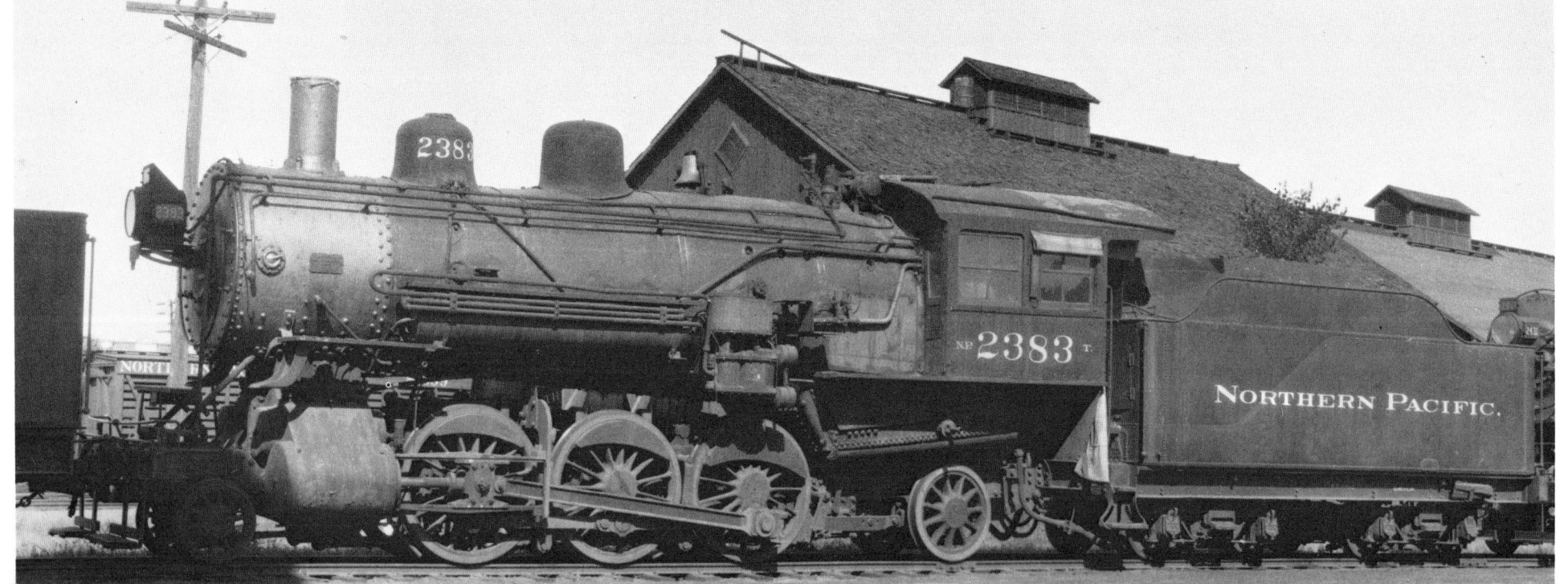

In Wallace, Idaho, the NP used ancient 2-8-0's for switching ore cars in this remote mining town at the end of a very steep branch over Mullan Pass.

Although the Northern Pacific was noted for its large sized locomotives, it retained several varieties of quite small power for use on branch lines. The 1370, working out of Tacoma, Washington, in 1931, was a 4-6-0 of 1902 vintage, while the 2383 was one of the 170-member fleet of 2-6-2s, the nation's biggest group.

NORTHERN PACIFIC

DAVID S. DIGERNESS COLLECTION

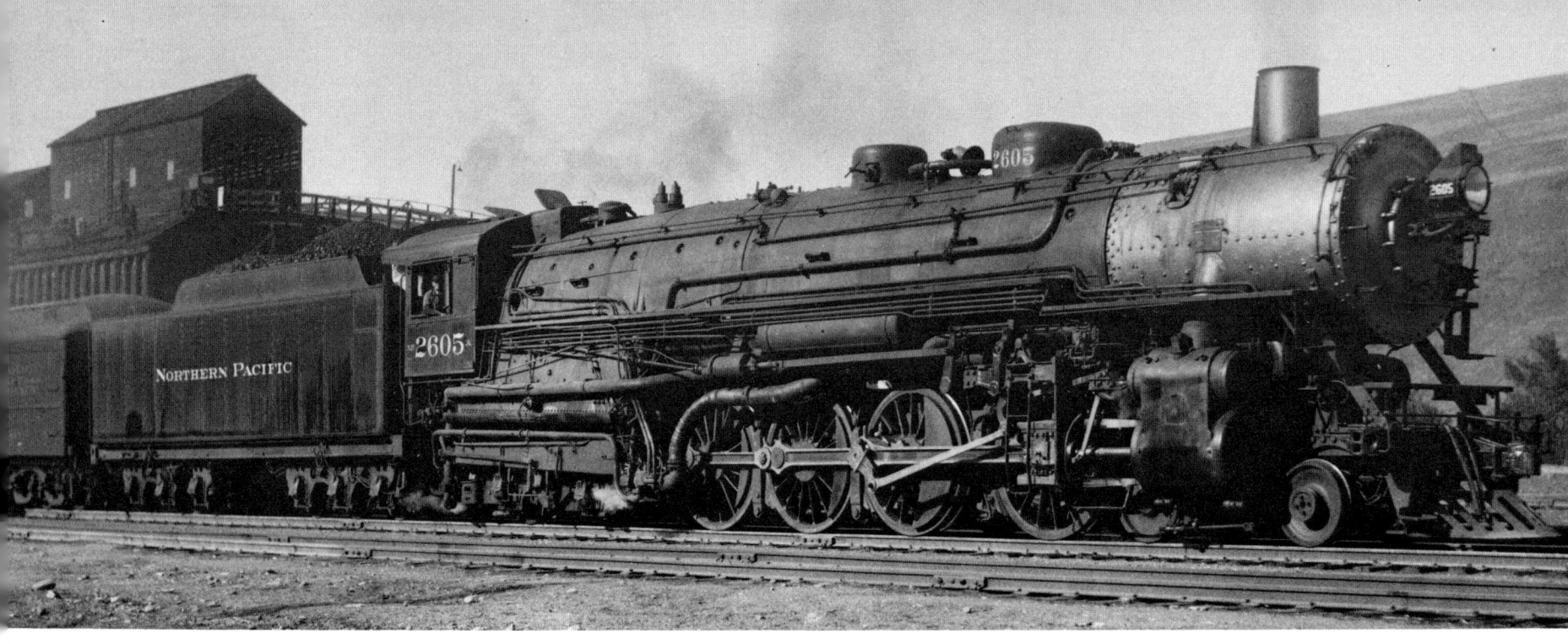

The first 4-8-4's built for a U.S.A. railroad were the 2600-2611, delivered in 1926. Five years later Otto captured the 2605 at Missoula, Montana. In 1939 he found the 2626 in Seattle; it was a unique locomotive, having been built for the Timken Roller Bearing Co. in 1930.

DAVID S. DIGERNESS COLLECTION

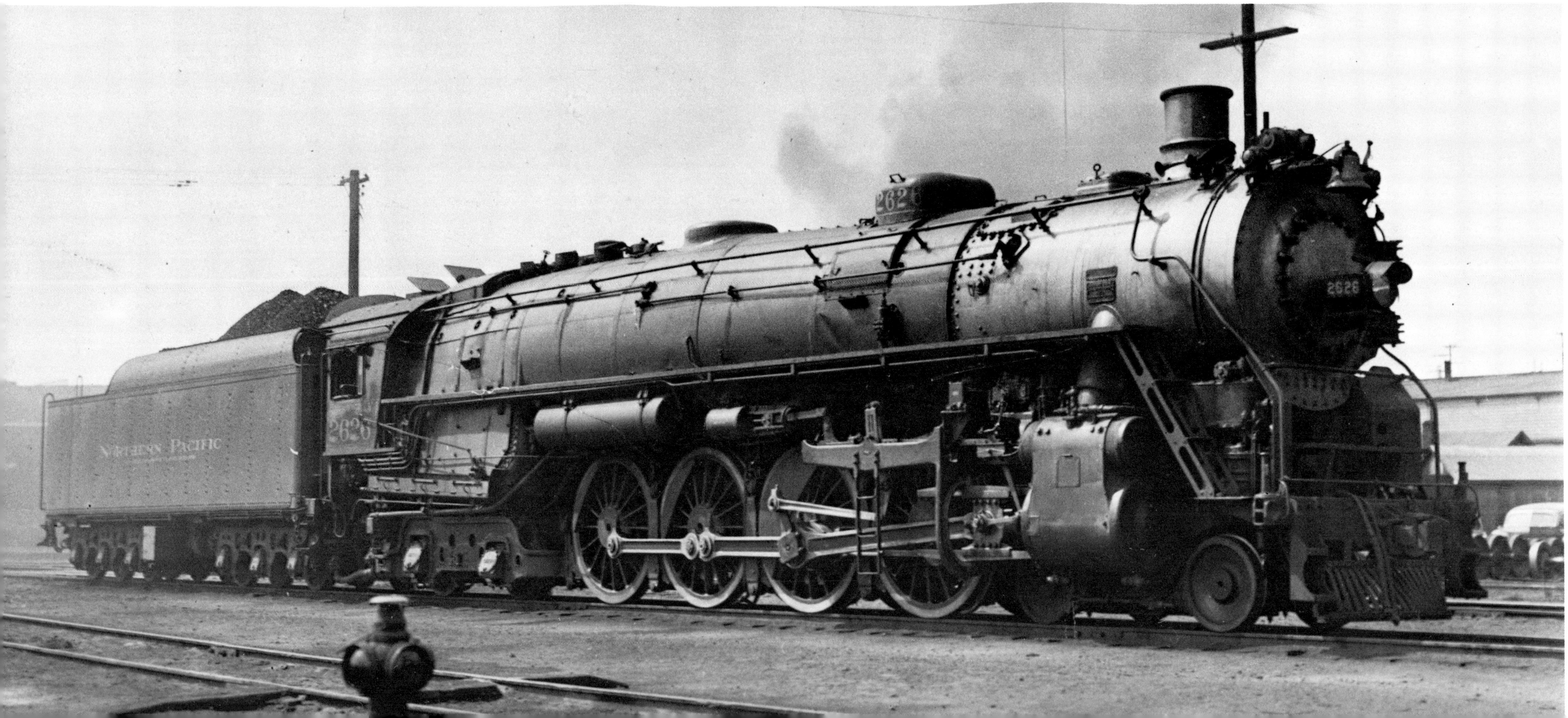

At Ellensburg, Washington, in 1931 Otto found NP 4018, a 1917-model compound 2-8+8-2 preparing to depart westward with a freight train. Note the smoke deflector, which was used in the Snoqualmie Pass tunnel.

DAVID S. DIGERNESS COLLECTION   DAVID S. DIGERNESS COLLECTION

When he visited Livingston, Montana, in 1937 Otto was fortunate to find two of the NP's new 4-6+6-4's, 5100 and 5102, ready to head eastward with freight trains. Built by ALCO immediately after the UP's engines, these monsters exceeded 1 million pounds in weight.

After their delivery the NP's gigantic 2-8+8-4's were assigned to the badlands territory between Bismark, North Dakota, and Glendive, Montana, where Otto caught the 5011 rolling west through Beach, North Dakota with a freight train, in 1931.

The 2588, a 4-8-4 built by Baldwin in 1930, was the last new engine delivered to the GN. Resplendent in green jacket and aluminum smokebox, the engine takes on water at Glacier Park in 1939.

DAVID S. DIGERNESS COLLECTION

DAVID S. DIGERNESS COLLECTION

GREAT NORTHERN

The Great Northern's switchers were ancient pieces of machinery; No. 5 had been built in 1907, the 389 in 1912. During 1931 they were working in Seattle and Spokane, Washington, when Otto photographed them. Note the Belpaire firebox application, typical of GN locomotives.

DAVID S. DIGERNESS COLLECTION

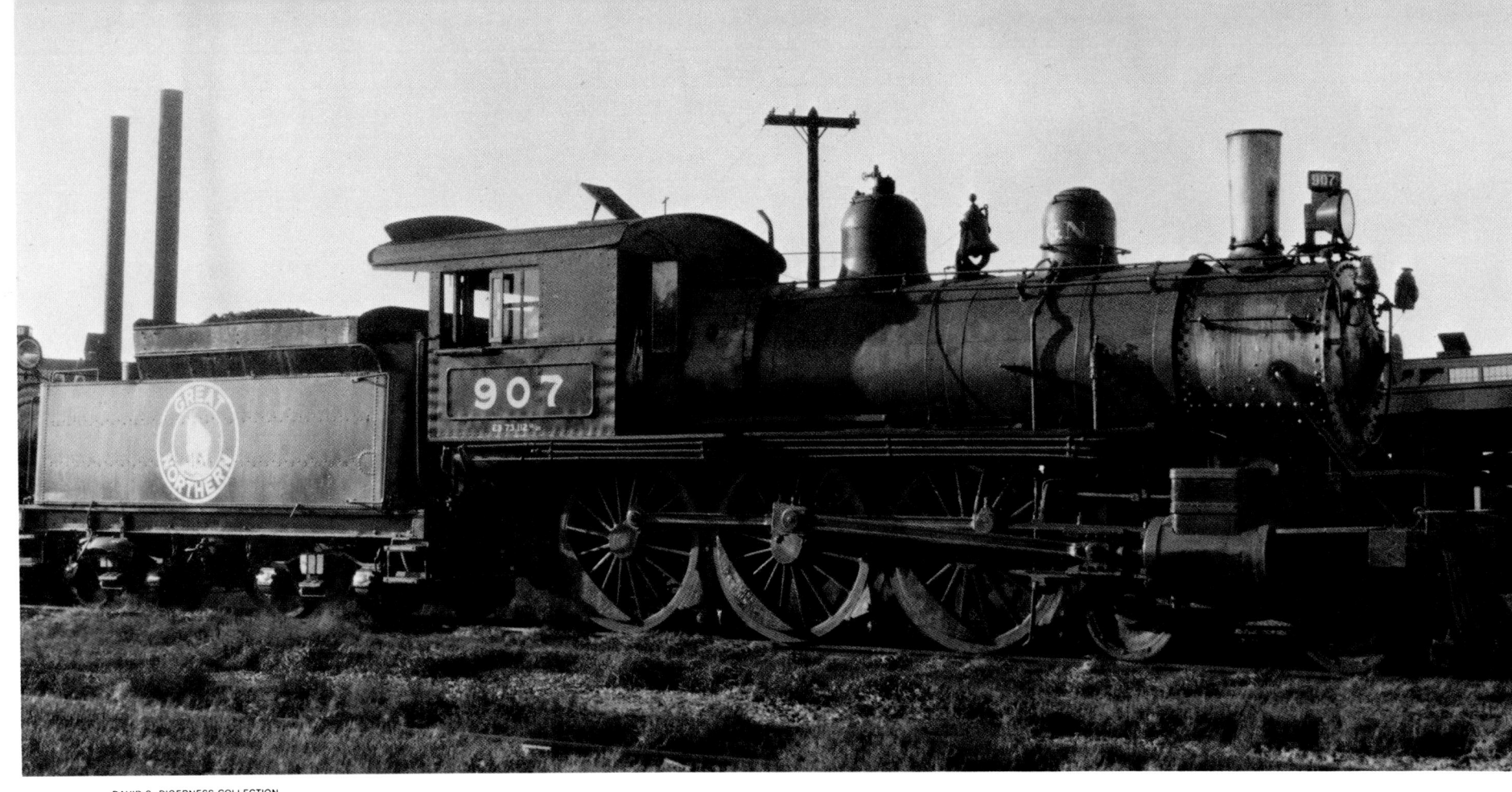

For branch line service, both freight and passenger, the GN used elderly 4-6-0's and 2-6-2's. The 907, built in 1899, ran between Minneapolis and St. Cloud, Minnesota, where this photo was taken in 1931, while the 1524, built in 1906, was operated out of Seattle, Washington.

DAVID S. DIGERNESS COLLECTION

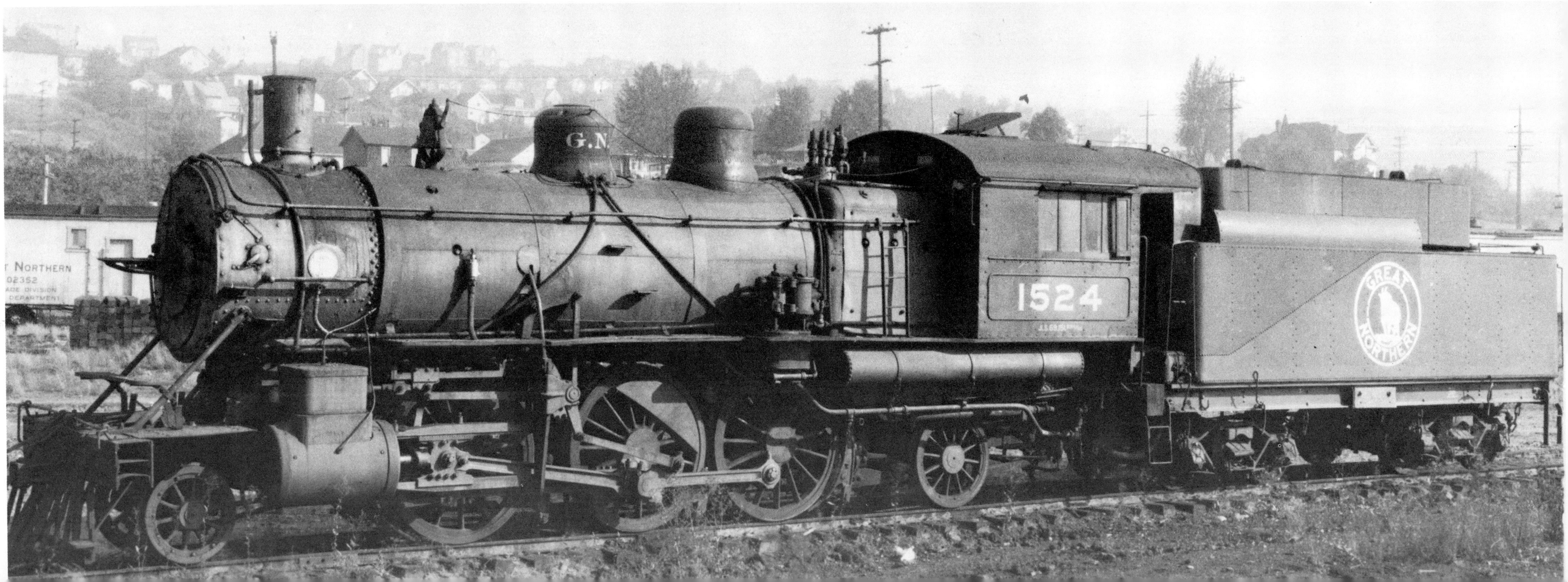

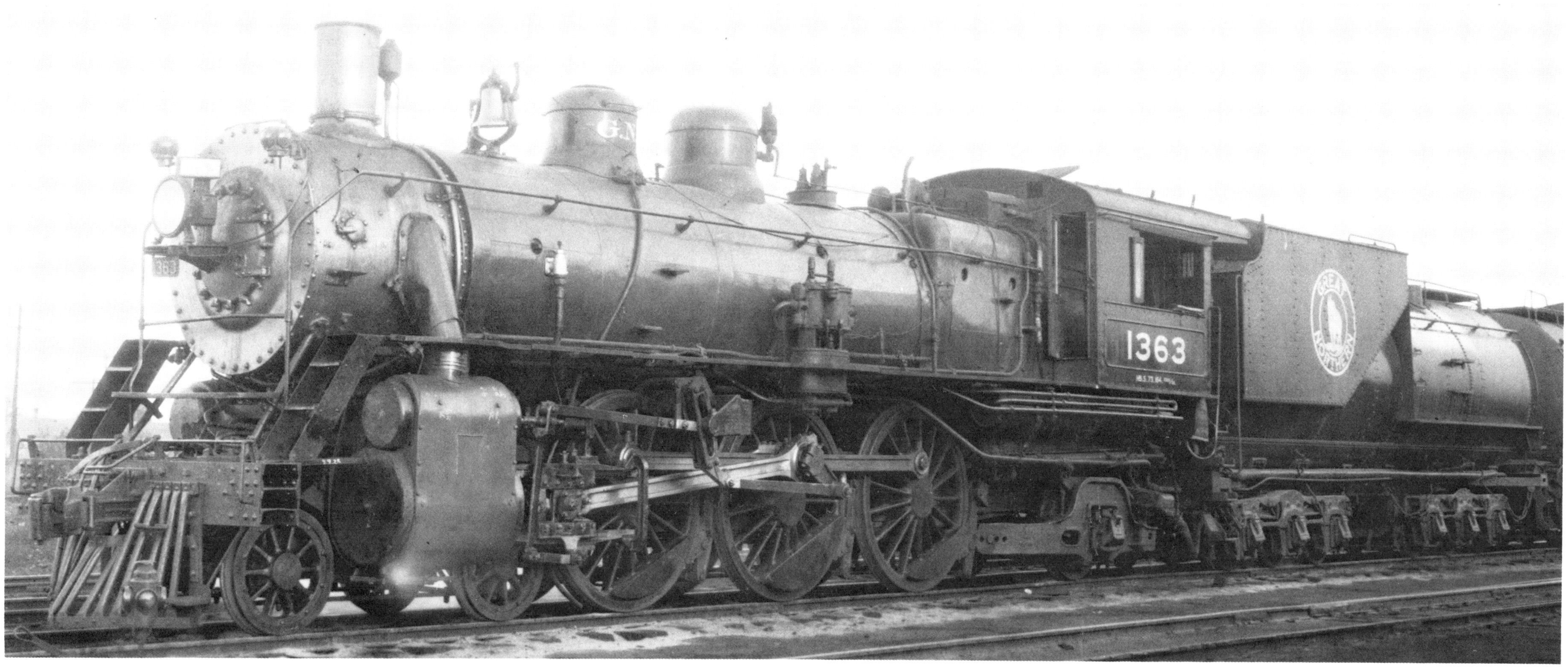

DAVID S. DIGERNESS COLLECTION

DAVID S. DIGERNESS COLLECTION

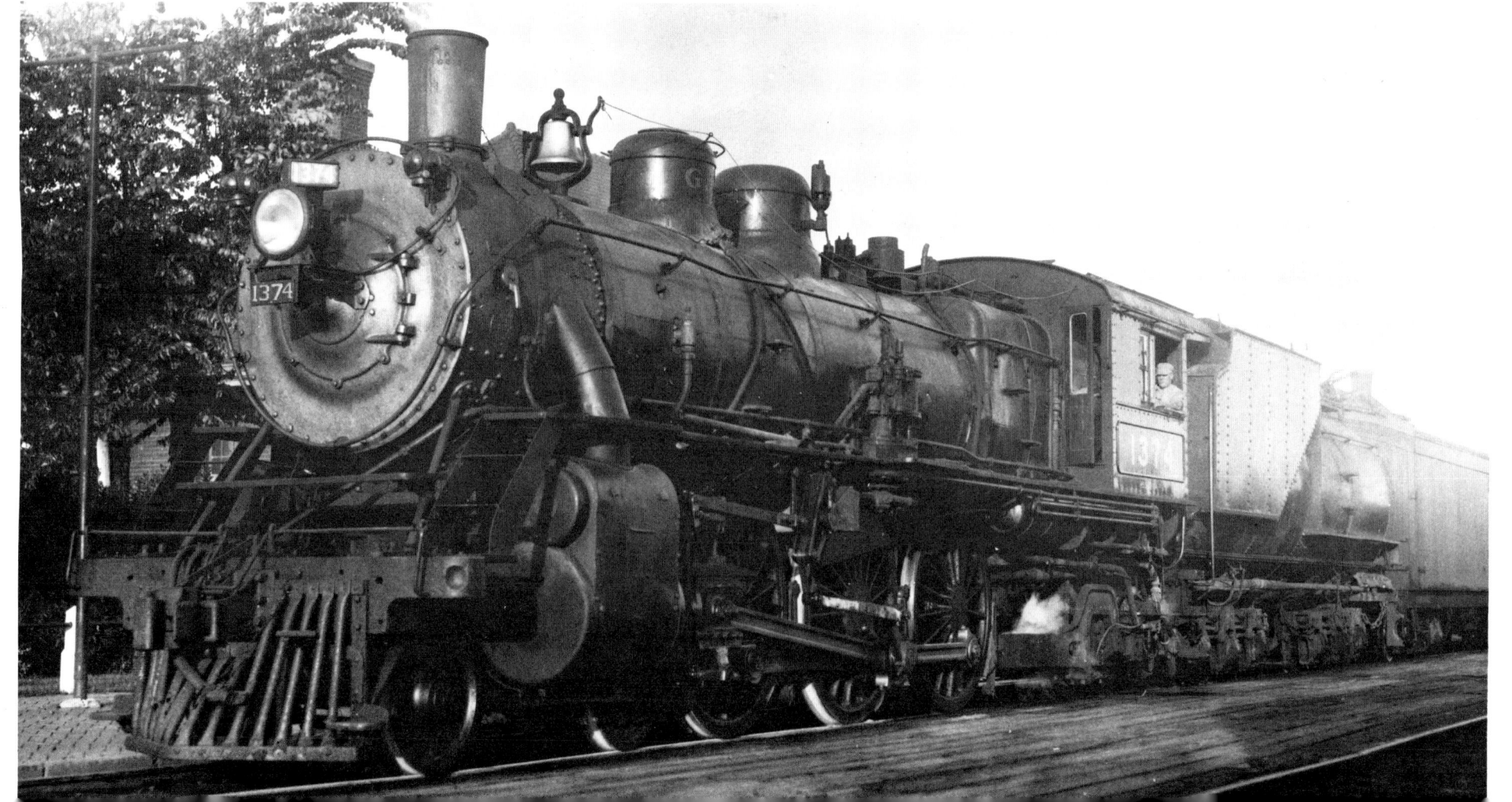

After acquiring 4-8-2's and 4-8-4's, the GN demoted its fleet of 4-6-2's to secondary service on its main lines. The 1363 was at Spokane in 1931, the 1374 at Havre, Montana, in 1938. Both engines had been rebuilt from 1909-model 4-6-0's in 1927.

During 1909 and 1910 the GN received the largest group of 2-6+8-0 Mallets. These were rebuilt to single-expansion in 1926 and 1927, and all but 13 were converted only a couple of years later to 2-8-2's. The 1981, which Otto found at Butte, Montana, in 1931, survived until 1953.

The GN's 25 compound 2-8+8-0's, built by Baldwin in 1912, were rebuilt to single expansion engines between 1925 and 1927. Some, like the 2013, were modified at Great Falls, Montana, in 1934 with three air pumps for iron ore service.

DAVID S. DIGERNESS COLLECTION

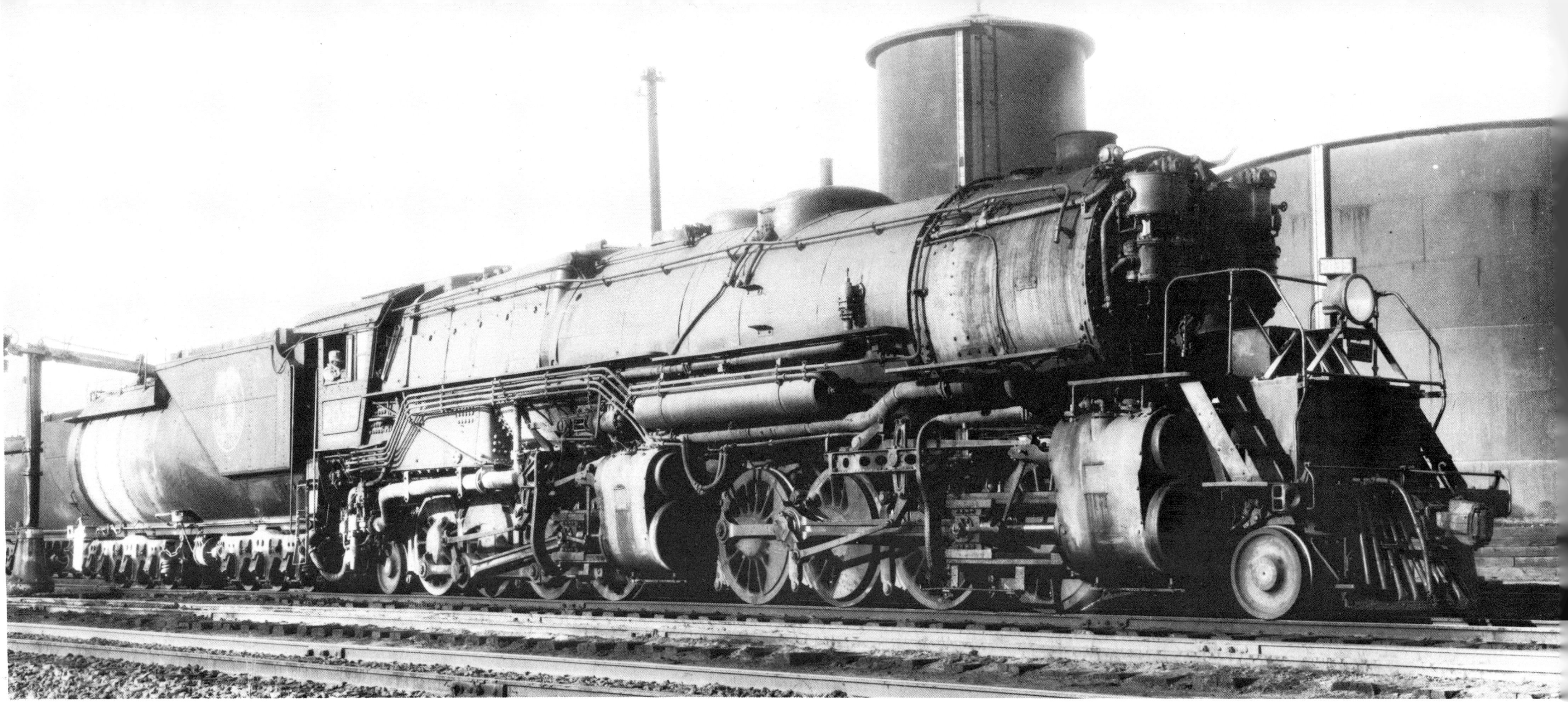

DAVID S. DIGERNESS COLLECTION

DAVID S. DIGERNESS COLLECTION

After receiving its first [four] 2-8+8-2's from Baldwin in 1925, the GN proceeded to build its own, the first one, No. 2035 emerging from the Hillyard Shops in 1927. Eleven years later, Otto photographed it at Spokane, Washington.

The 5309, an EMD NW2-model switcher, was only a year old when Otto took its picture at St. Paul, Minnesota, in 1940.

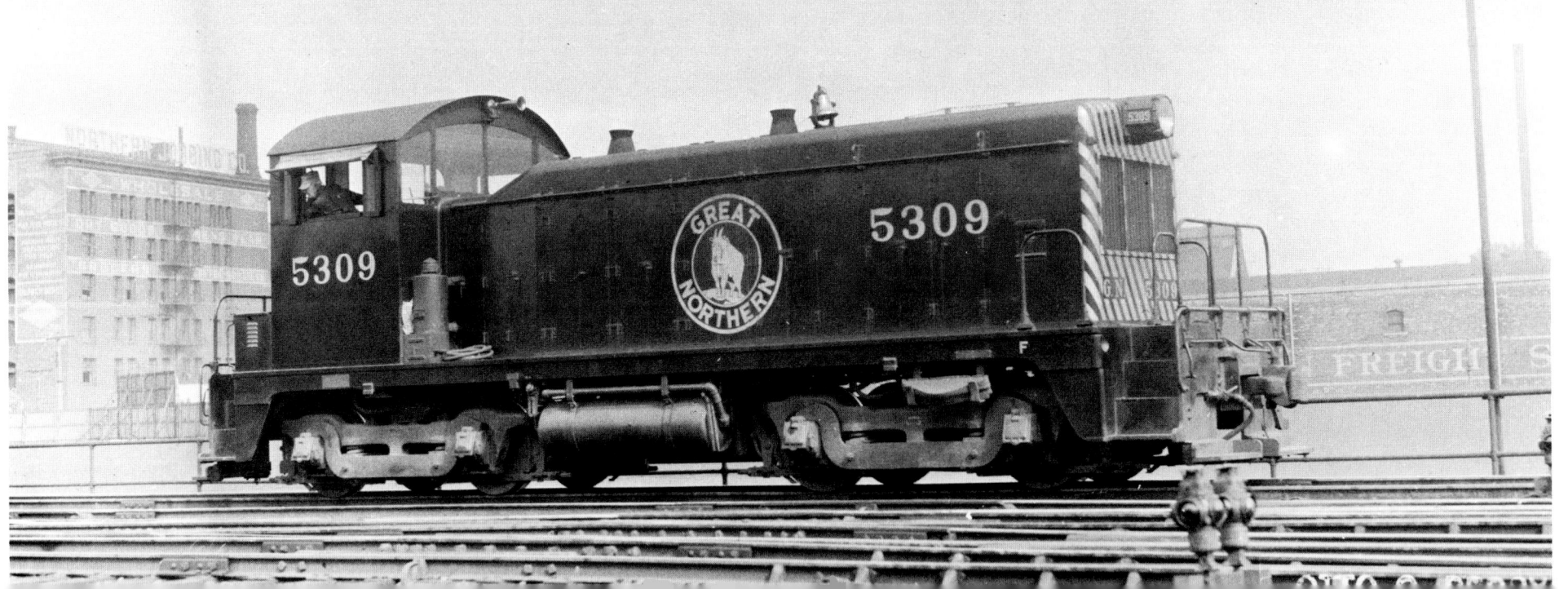

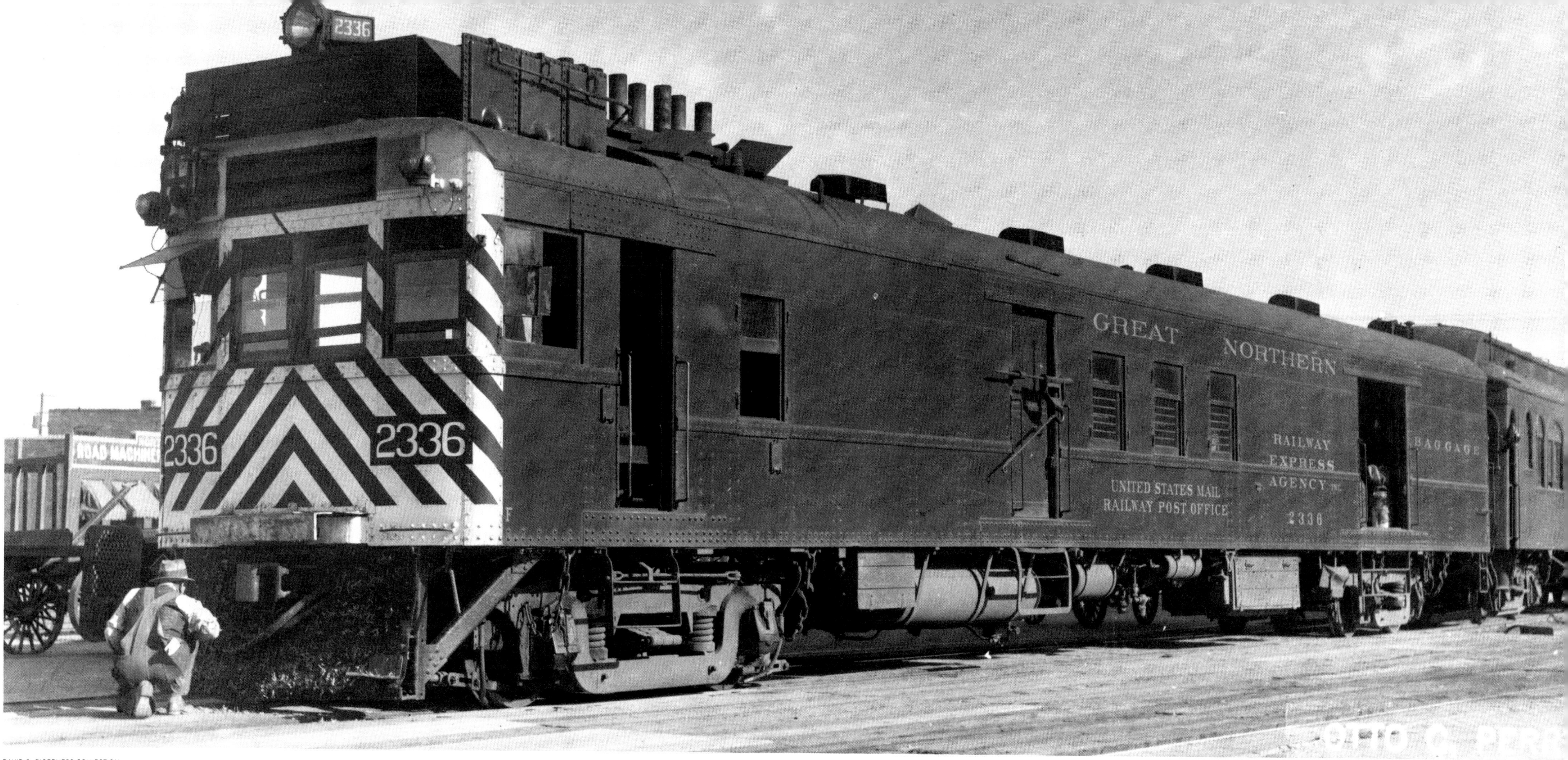

DAVID S. DIGERNESS COLLECTION

DAVID S. DIGERNESS COLLECTION

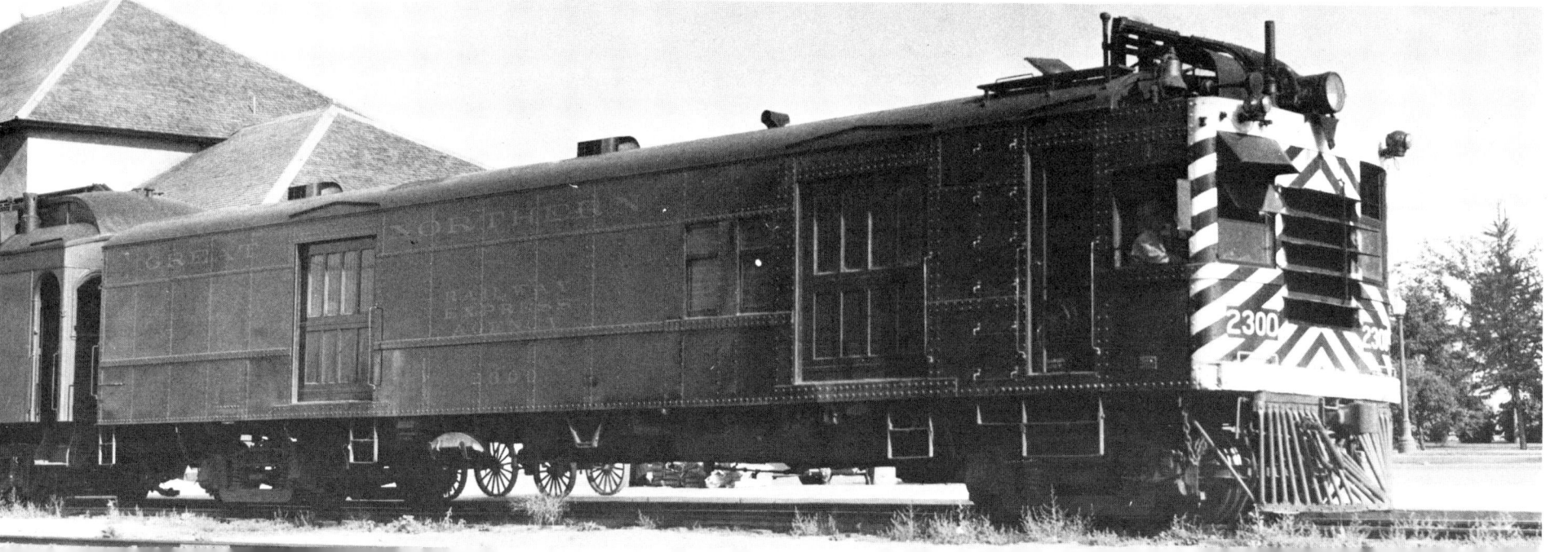

The GN possessed a substantial fleet of motor cars, which replaced light steam engines on lines with little passenger business. The first of these, the 2300, was built in 1926 by St. Louis Car Co. It posed for Otto in 1938 at the Kalispell depot. The 2336, seen at Great Falls, Montana, was one of the last, built by StLCCo. in 1929. The earlier one had a 220-hp engine, the second had 400 hp.

DAVID S. DIGERNESS COLLECTION

DAVID S. DIGERNESS COLLECTION

NORTH WESTERN PACIFIC

All of Otto Perry's photos of the Northwestern Pacific were taken during just three days in October, 1931. At Sausalito, California, the southern terminal, he found two of the railroads ancient 4-4-0s, numbered 10 and 21. The 10's ancestry can be traced to 1888, the 21 back only to 1904. Note that the older engine had been equipped with modern piston-valves.

152

At the time of Otto's visit, No. 103 was the oldest 4-6-0 on the railroad, having been built for the San Francisco & North Pacific in 1901. The 140 was about 10 years younger, and it had been modernized with piston-valves and outside valve-motion.

For switching, the NWP utilized 0-6-0's which had been built by American Locomotive Co. in 1910 and 1912. The 227 was the first of these little engines.

Pride of the SP's passenger power fleet in the 1920 decade were 14 4-6-2's from Baldwin, numbered 2478-2491. Otto photographed the 2487 at San Francisco in 1937, when it was out of service awaiting repairs.

EASTERN U.S. ROADS

On his 1932 trip to the East Coast, Otto spent a day in Conneaut, Ohio, to photograph Nickel Plate railroad locomotives. He posed the crew of the 78, an 0-6-0 switcher, with traditional oilcan and coal scoop. At the coal chutes he found one of the railroad's eight 4-6-4's, Number 173, awaiting the arrival of a mainline passenger train.

The NYNH&H operated 100 4-6-2's like the 1381, which hauled the train which Otto had ridden to Springfield, Massachusetts, in 1923. Many of them were still running 25 years later.

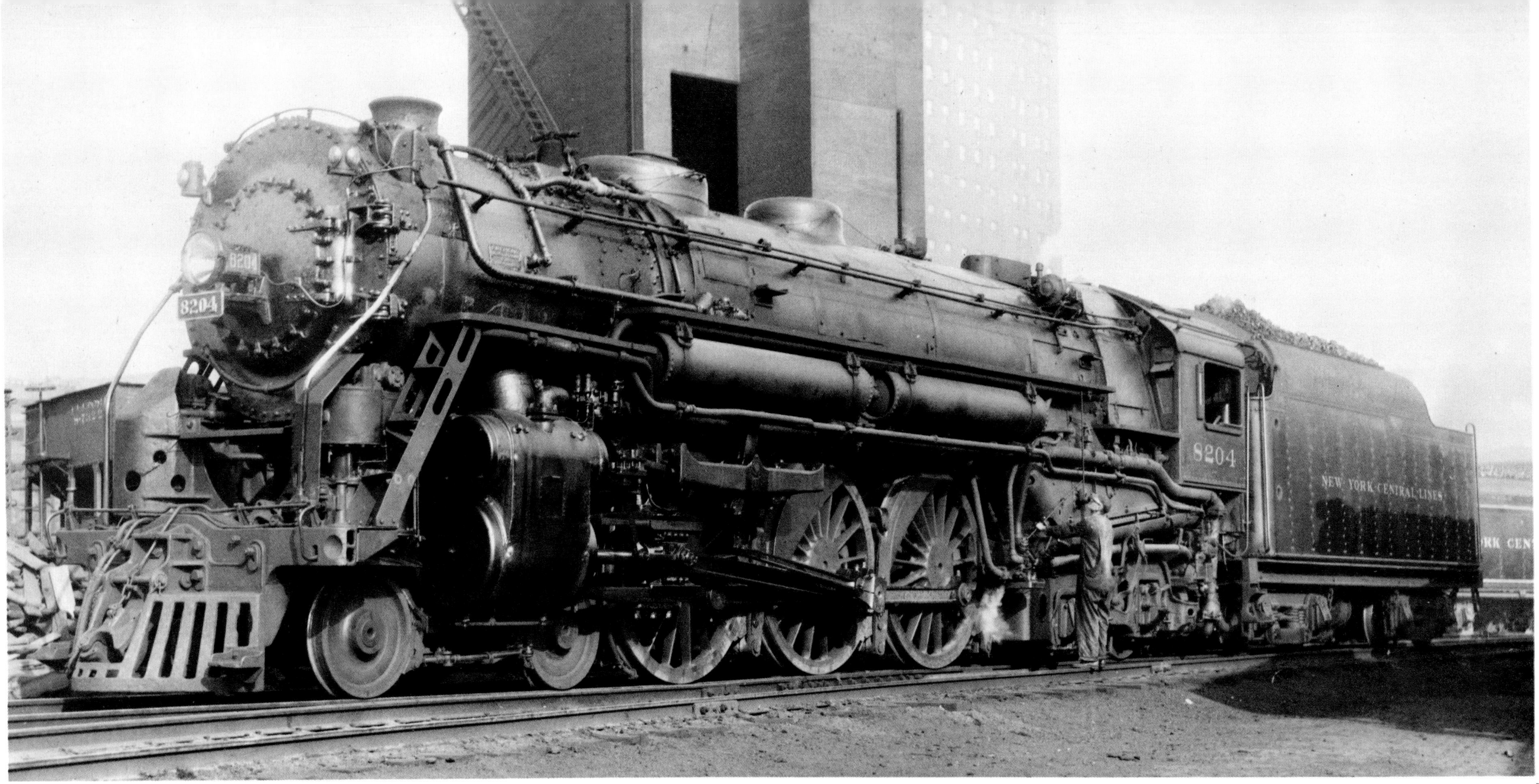

DAVID S. DIGERNESS COLLECTION

DAVID S. DIGERNESS COLLECTION

At Chicago in 1937 Otto found a New York Central 4-6-4 still bearing its Michigan Central number 8204, and with a small tender which had belonged to a Boston & Albany 4-6-4.

Rare indeed was this old 2-8-2, No. 3629, which had been equipped with a modern trailing truck and booster. In 1932 it was working on a local freight at Geneva, Ohio.

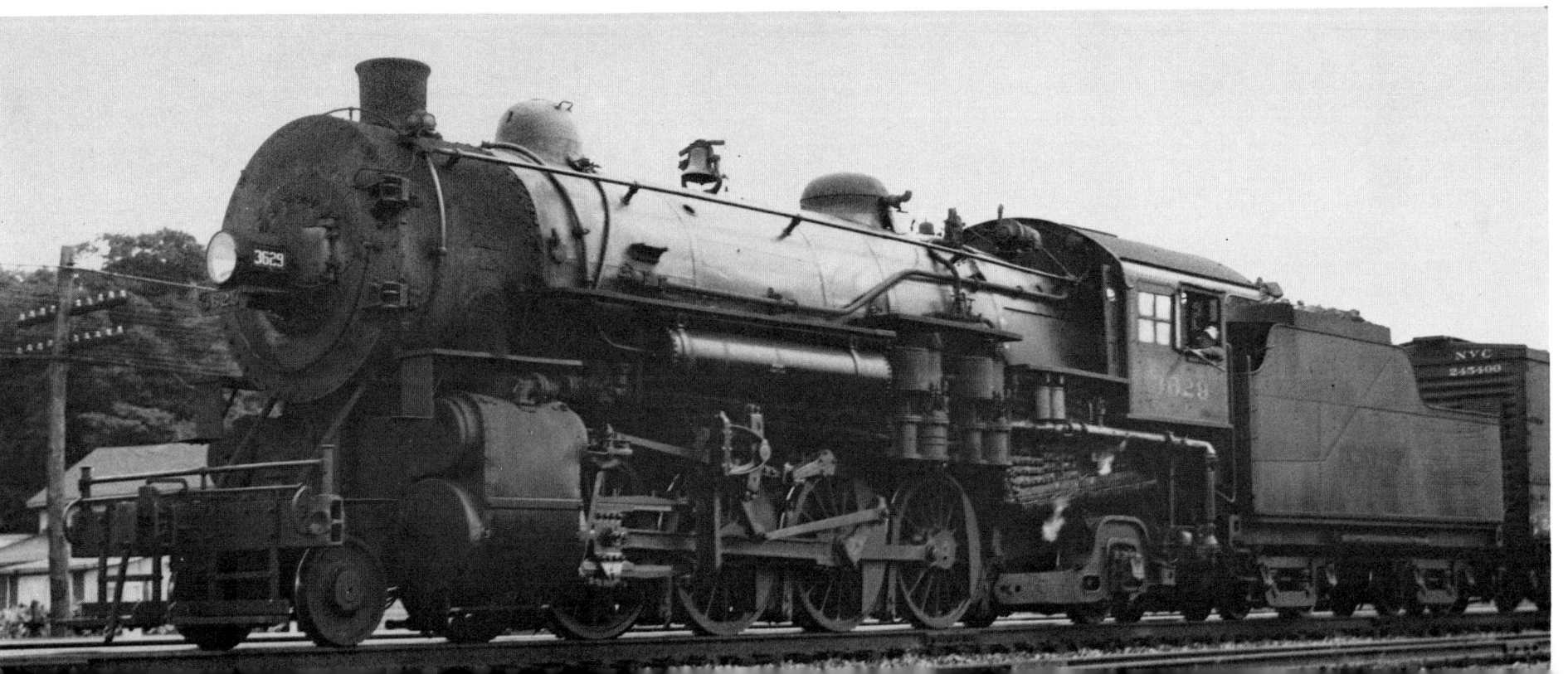

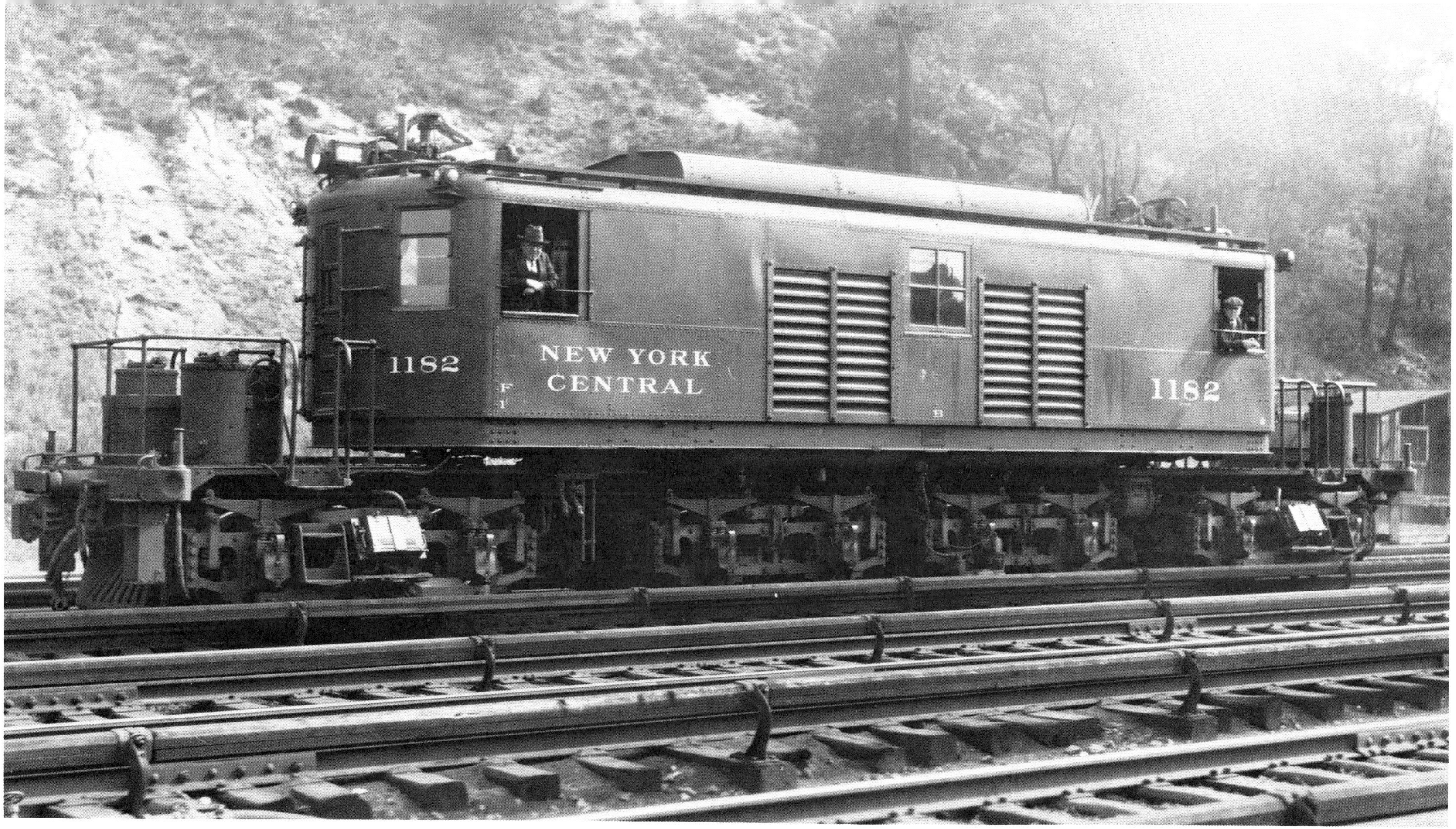

DAVID S. DIGERNESS COLLECTION

DAVID S. DIGERNESS COLLECTION

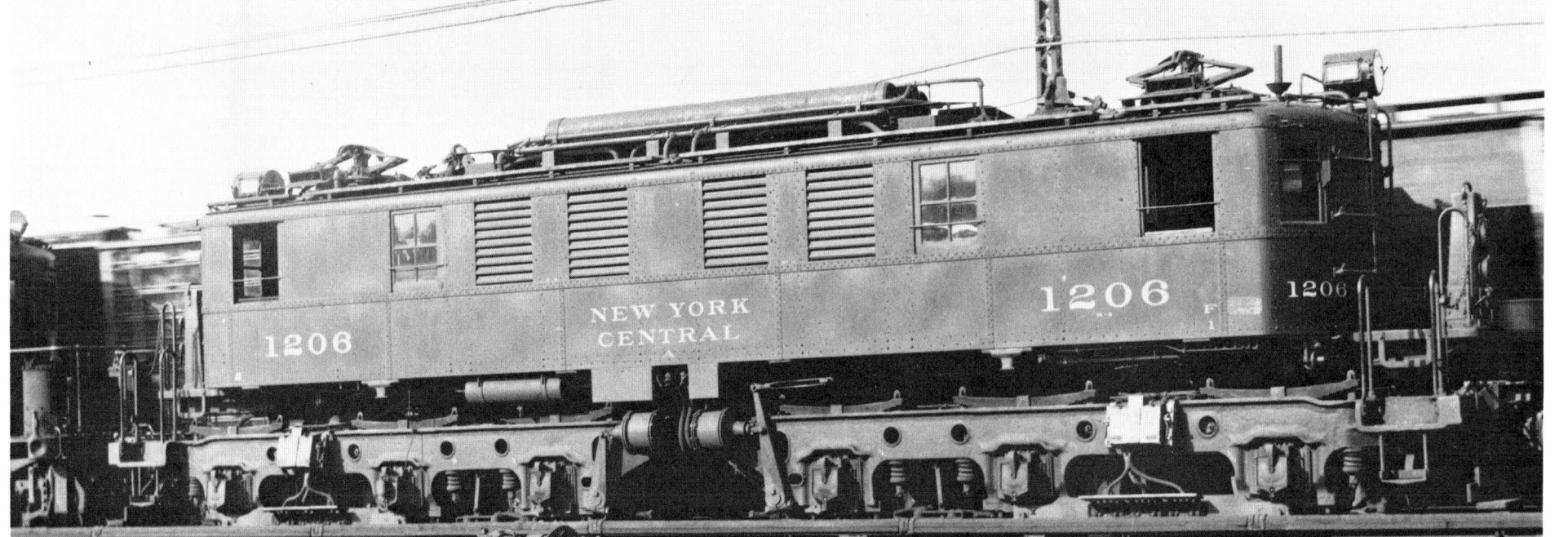

The New York Central's electrified lines connected New York City with a terminal at Harmon, New York. There the C+C freight units, like the 1206, and B-B+B-B passenger units, like the 1182, took over from steam power. These were taken in 1932.

Pride of the NYC's passenger power were stream-styled 4-6-4's Numbers 5445-5454. In 1939 the 5451 was exhibited at the New York World's Fair.

PENNSYLVANIA

The Pennsylvania owned more than 3000 2-8-0's in 10 major classes. The 7924 had been constructed by the railroad's shops in 1899, and was assigned to the western lines, as indicated by the centered headlight. The 8984 was also a product of the PRR's shops in 1912, and it had been rebuilt twice.

DAVID S. DIGERNESS COLLECTION

DAVID S. DIGERNESS COLLECTION

DAVID S. DIGERNESS COLLECTION

DAVID S. DIGERNESS COLLECTION

If the 8711 looks strange, it is because it was one of 12 4-6-2's which had been built by ALCO in 1910 for the TH&V subsidiary of the PRR. Almost as rare was the 7546, of which only 30 were constructed by Baldwin in 1913. Both photos were taken in Chicago in the early 1920s.

DAVID S. DIGERNESS COLLECTION

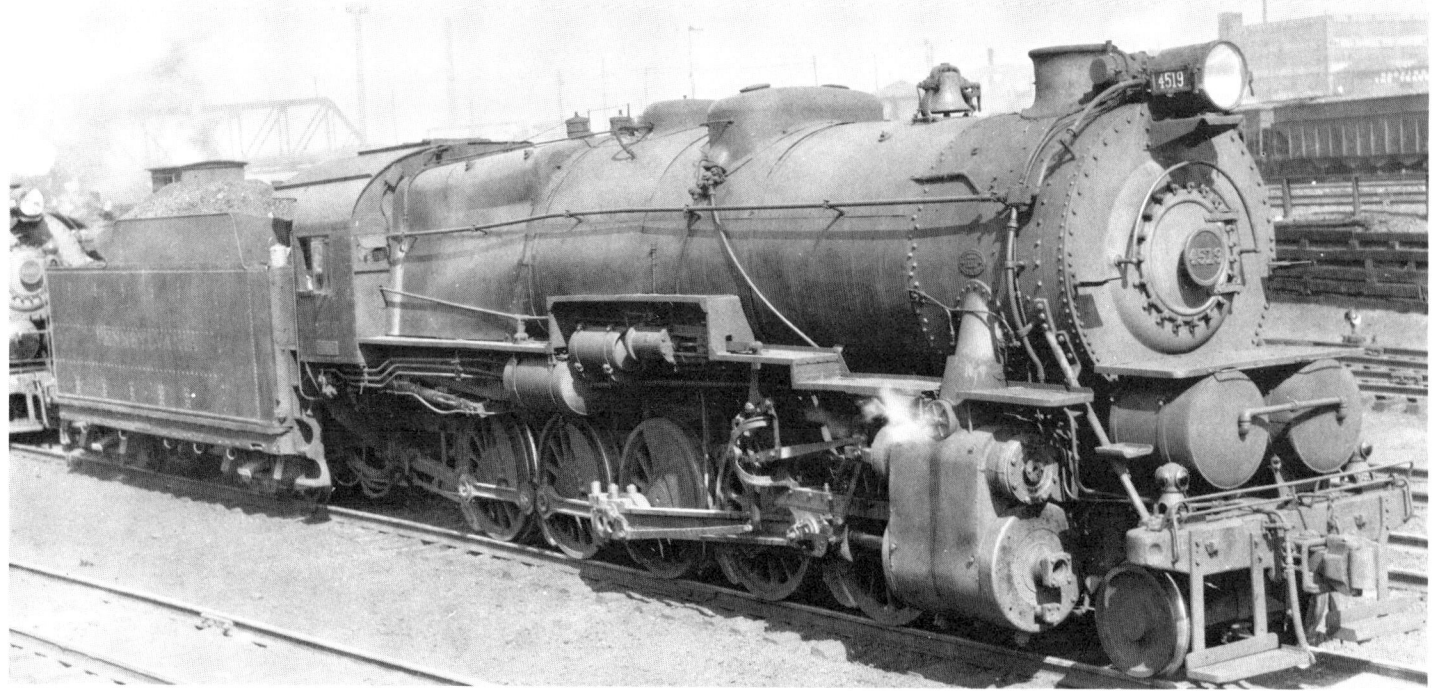

The PRR built and bought 598 2-10-0's between 1916 and 1923. They were found all over the system, and were given three kinds of tenders, 4-4, 6-6, or 8-8. The 4519 was at Cleveland, Ohio, in 1930, and the 4445 was at Chicago a couple of years later.

DAVID S. DIGERNESS COLLECTION

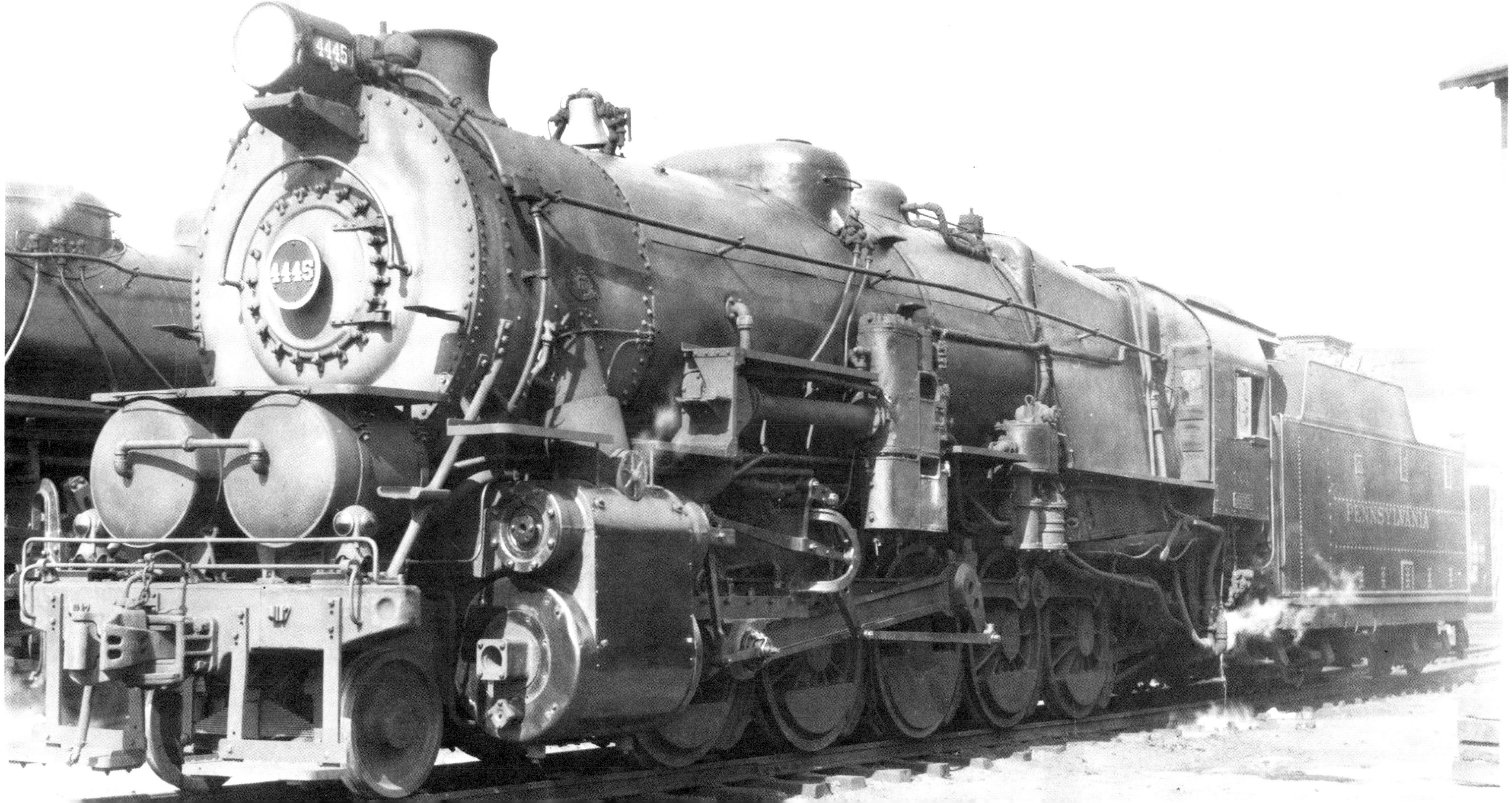

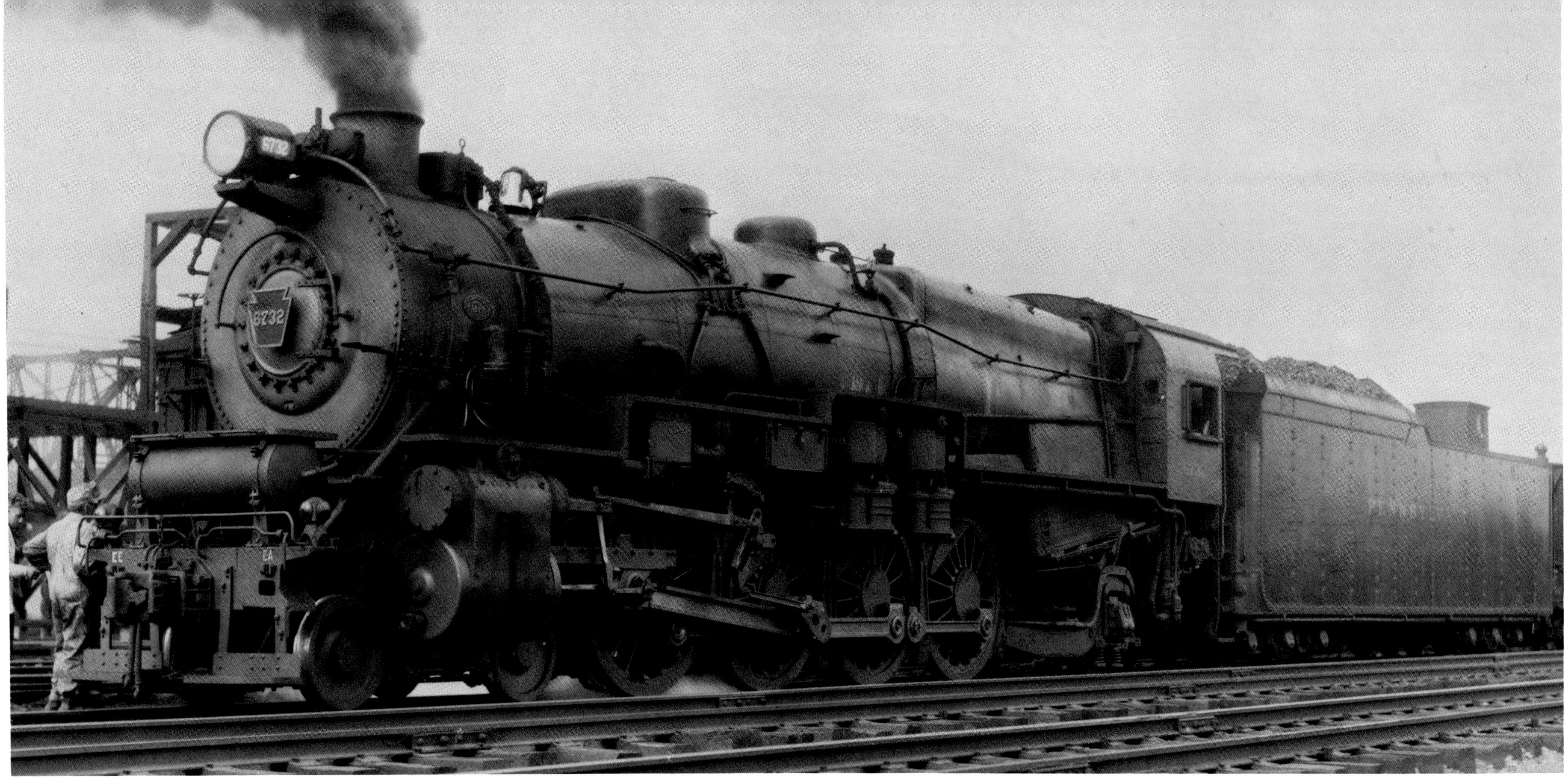

DAVID S. DIGERNESS COLLECTION

DAVID S. DIGERNESS COLLECTION

The Pennsy's mainline freights were hauled by a fleet of 301 monstrous 4-8-2's like the 6732, which Otto photographed as it was ready to leave Buffalo, New York, in 1930, when the engine was brand-new.

Otto visited the railroad convention in Atlantic City, New Jersey, in 1919, and photographed the one-of-a-kind Pennsylvania single-expansion 2-8 + 8-0, No. 3700.

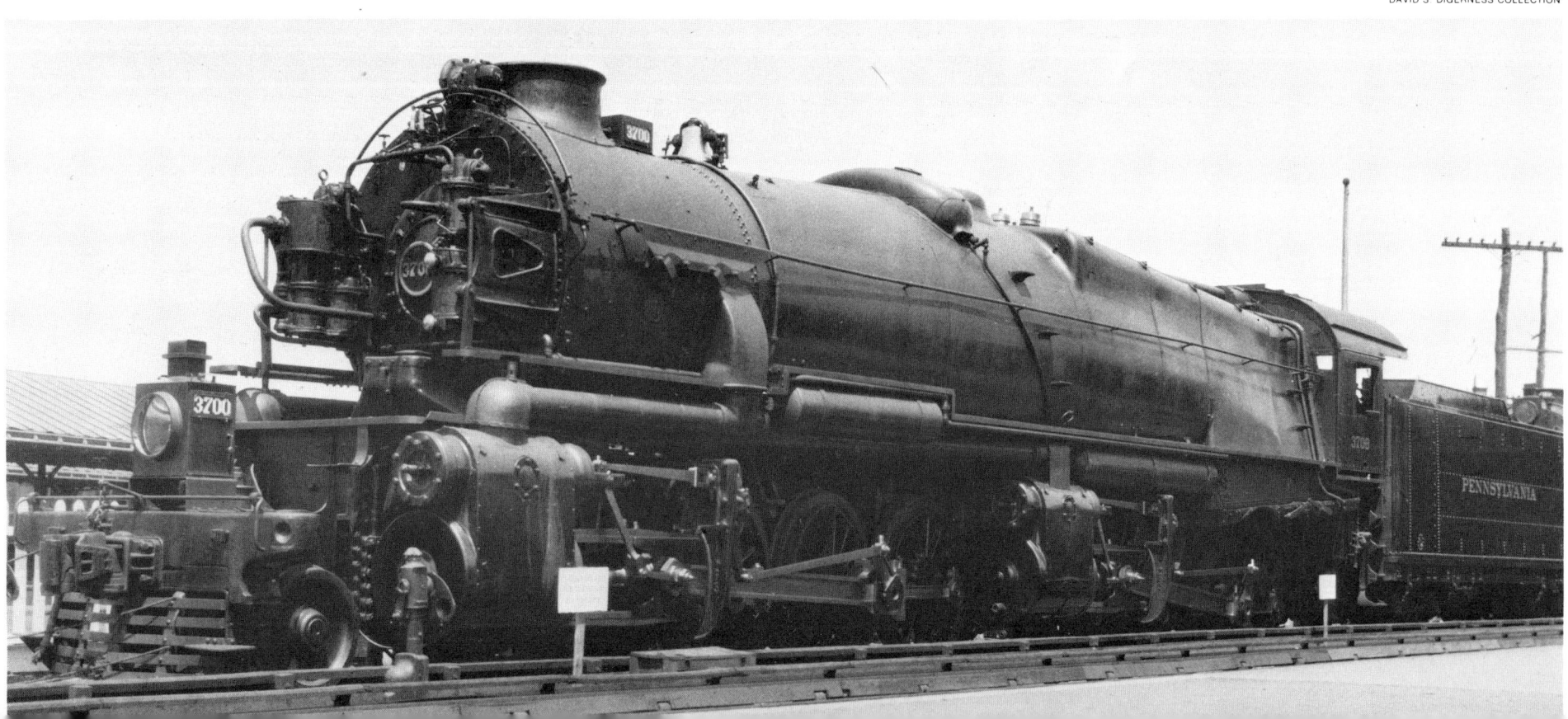

PRR 4750 was only a year old when Otto took its portrait at Washington, D.C. in 1936. This was a 3750-HP 2-C-2 electric locomotive.

DAVID S. DIGERNESS COLLECTION

INDEX

A
Alamosa, 27
Almont, 7
Alpine Tunnel, 97
Argentine, Kan., 128
Argo Tunnel, 80
Atchison, Topeka & Santa Fe
  Locomotives 1—129; 698—131; 778 —132; 827—130; 835—130; 870—133; 885—137; 886—136; 891—136; 2414—129; 2415—129; 2504—134; 2536—134; 3457—135
Atlantic City, N.J., 162

B
Baldwin, 23, 24
Baldwin Branch, D&RGW, 22, 23, 24
Baxter Pass, 100
Beaver Brook, 79
Black Hawk, 82
Boulder, 98, 99
Burnham Shops, 103, 104
Burns Canyon, 55, 56

C
Carbonera, 100
Castleton, 23
Cerro Summit, 2, 25, 26
Chama, 36, 37, 38, 39, 52
Cheyenne, Wyo., 126, 127
Chicago, Burlington & Quincy
  Locomotives 522—119; 4109—123; 5605—121; 6159—120; 6167—120; 7011—119; 9969—5
Chili Line, D&RGW, 28, 29, 30, 31
Chinery Ranch, 21
Cima Summit, 51
Civilian Conservation Corps Special, 54 55, 65, 67, 71, 72, 73
Coke Ovens (RGS), 54
Clear Creek, 77, 78
Colorado & Southern
  Cabooses 1008—93
  History, 75
  Locomotives 5—87; 8—89; 9—90, 93; 10—86; 12—85; 21—83; 22—84, 87; 37—84; 58—89; 59—85; 61—86; 62—83; 64—85; 67—86; 68—81, 89; 69—79, 88, 89, 91, 93; 70—74, 75, 76, 77, 78, 79, 80, 82, 90, 91, 92, 94; 71—82; 72—92; 74—95, 96; 309—118; 350—117; 422—116; 537—92 (from CB&Q) 649—117
  Roundhouse, Denver, 84, 116
  Silica Branch, 88
Colorado Central, 75
Colorado City, 110, 115
Colorado Springs, 112
Colorado Springs and Cripple Creek District Locomotives 1—111; 8—110; 102—112; 103—112
Como, 93
Coxo, 32
Cresco Siding, 34
Crested Butte, 19, 20
Cumbres & Toltec Scenic, 9, 39
Cumbres Pass, 32, 33, 34, 36

D
Dallas Divide, 4, 65, 66, 67, 68, 69, 70, 71, 72
Denver & Rio Grande Western
  Baldwin Branch, 22, 23, 24
  Chili Line, 28, 29, 30, 31
  History, 9
  Locomotives 169—31; 223—24; 227 —52 (RGS); 268—7, 19, 20; 272—10; 278—22, 23; 283—29; 300—10; 319 —47 (RGS); 340—47, 51 (RGS); 345 —25; 361—2, 21, 25, 26; 375—8; 452 —49 (RGS); 453—71, 73 (RGS); 454 —2, 26; 455—66 (RGS); 456—2; 461 —47, 54, 56, 58, 62, 68 (RGS); 464— 69 (RGS); 471—29; 473—28, 29, 30; 34, 35; 476—32; 478—40; 479— 13; 480—17; 481—17, 482—17, 40; 483—17; 484—39; 486—27; 487—38; 488—9, 36; 489—14, 15, 17, 18, 38; 490—14, 36, 39; 491—14; 492—37; 495—10; 496—11; 497—12, 14, 27; 498—12, 14; 499—16, 18; 760—109; 801—107; 804—107; 1136—109; 1701 —103; 1702—104, 106; 1705—102, 105; 1706—105;1709—108; 3404—108
Denver, Boulder & Western, 75, 95, 99
  Locomotives 1—98; 30—98; 31—98; 32—99; 33—99
Denver, South Park & Pacific, 75, 83, 97
Denver Yards, 83, 84, 86, 87, 118, 119, 121, 124, 125
Dolores, 52
"Doodlebugs" (Midland Terminal), 108
Dotsero, 108
Durango, 39, 40, 42

E
Ellensburg, Wash., 141
Embudo, N.M., 28, 29, 30

F
Fall Creek (RGS), 64
Fort Worth & Denver Locomotives 251—122; 308—122; 404—123
Fremont Pass, 95, 96

G
Gallagher, 57, 58, 59
Galloping Goose (See: Rio Grande Southern)

"Mountaineer", 109
"Panoramic", 108
RPO Equipment, 107
"Scenic Limited", 102, 105
"Shavano", 13, 18
Silverton Branch, 8, 41
Silver Vista Car, 21, 41
"Westerner", 106
Denver, Boulder & Western, 75, 95, 99

Garos, 94
Georgetown Loop, 79
Golden, 74, 75, 76
Great Falls, Mont., 149, 151
Great Northern Locomotives 5—145; 389—145; 907—146; 1363—147; 1374 —147; 1524—146; 1981—148; 2013— 149; 2035—150; 2300—151; 2336— 151; 2588—144; 5309—150
Green River, Wyo., 126

H
Hesperus, 47

I
Idaho Springs, 79, 80, 82
Iola, 20

J
Jacks Cabin, 20
"Jukes" Tree, 37

K
Kalispell, Mont., 151
Kindig, Richard, 42, 44

L
La Junta, 135
Lawson, 81
Leadville, 95
Lightner Creek, 43
Livingston, Mont., 142
Lizard Head Pass, 6, 57, 58, 59, 60
Lobato, 35
Lobato Trestle, 34, 36

Lost Canyon, 51

M
Mancos, 49
Manitou Springs, 114
Marshall Pass, 14, 15, 16, 17
Mayday, 48
Meadow Creek Trestle (RGS), 57
Mears Junction, 13, 14
Mears, Otto, 43
Mears Peak, 68, 69
Midland Terminal Locomotives 52— 115; 53—115; 54—113; 61—114; Motor 102—114
Millwood, 50
Missoula, Mont., 140

N
New York Central Locomotives 1182— 157; 1206—157; 3629—156; 5451— 158; 8204—156 (from Michigan Central)
New York, New Haven & Hartford Locomotives 1381—155
New York World's Fair, 158
Nickel Plata Locomotives 78—155; 173 —155
Northern Pacific Locomotives 25—138; 1370—139; 2388—138; 2605—140; 2626—140; 4018—141; 5011—5, 143; 5100—142; 5102—142
Northwestern Pacific Locomotives 10— 152; 12—152; 103—153; 140—153; 227—153

O
Ophir Trestles, 62
Osier, 32
Overland Park, 87

P
Palmilla Siding, 29
Parlin, 18
Pennsylvania Railroad Locomotives 3700—162; 4445—161; 4519—161; 4750—163; 6732—162; 7546—160; 7924—159; 8711—160; 8984—159
Pine Ridge, 45
Placerville, 65
Platte Canyon, 91, 92
Poncha Junction, 13
Poncha Pass, 11, 12
Porter, 44, 46, 49
Pueblo, 129

R
Rico, 54
Ridgway, 73
Rio Grande River, 109
Rio Grande Southern
  Cabooses 402—4, 43, 72
  Galloping Geese, 43; 4—57; 7—6
  History, 43
  Locomotives (See Also: Denver & Rio Grande Western) 20—43; 46, 48, 49, 51, 65, 67; 22—52, 53, 55, 65, 67; 40—4, 60, 61; 41—73; 42—62, 44, 45, 50, 56, 66, 70; 44—54; 74—61
Royal Gorge, 102

S
Salida, 9, 10
Santa Fe Branch, D&RGW (See: Chili Line)
Sapinero Needles, 21
Sargents, 18
Sawpit, 64
Seattle, Wash., 140, 145, 146
Silica Branch, Colorado & Southern, 88
Silverton Branch, D&RGW, 8, 41
Southern Pacific Locomotives 2487—154

T
Tacoma, Wash., 139
Trout Lake, 60, 61

U
Uintah, 75, 100, 101
  Locomotives 50—100, 101; 51—100
Union Pacific Locomotives M-29—5; 2809—126; 2855—124; 2874—127; 2879—125; 3310—124; 9508—126; 9511—127
Ute Pass, 113, 114

V
Villa Grove, 12

W
Wallace, Idaho, 138
Waterton, 89, 90
Webster, 92
Windy Point (RGS), 61
Woodstock Tank, 97

163

ELMORE FREDERICK COLLECTION

FAREWELL